AF269626

A FIELD GUIDE TO THE VERNACULAR BUILDINGS OF THE SAN ANTONIO AREA

Publication of this book was assisted by a generous gift from the Summerlee Foundation.

Texas A&M University Press
College Station

A FIELD GUIDE TO THE VERNACULAR BUILDINGS OF THE SAN ANTONIO AREA

Edited by

Brent R. Fortenberry

This paper meets the requirements of ANSI/NISO Z39.48–1992
(Permanence of Paper).

Binding materials have been chosen for durability.

Manufactured in Canada by Friesens

Library of Congress Cataloging-in-Publication Data

Library of Congress Control Number: 2021934618

ISBN-13 (flexbound): 978-1-62349-911-2

ISBN-13 (ebook): 978-1-62349-912-9

Contents

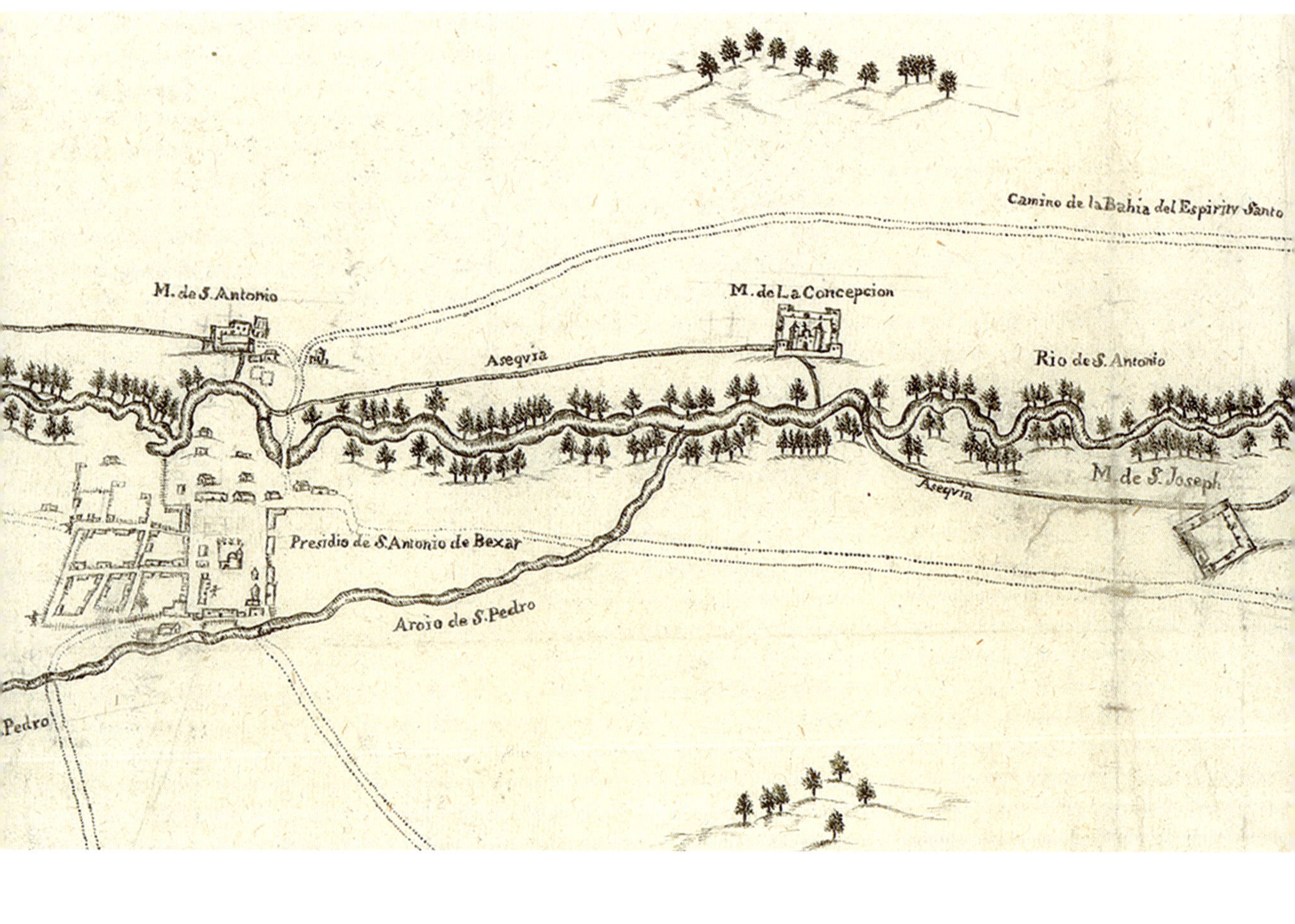

Camino de la Bahia del Espiritu Santo
M. de S. Antonio
M. de La Concepcion
Rio de S. Antonio
Asequia
Asequia
M. de S. Joseph
Presidio de S. Antonio de Bexar
Aroio de S. Pedro
Pedro

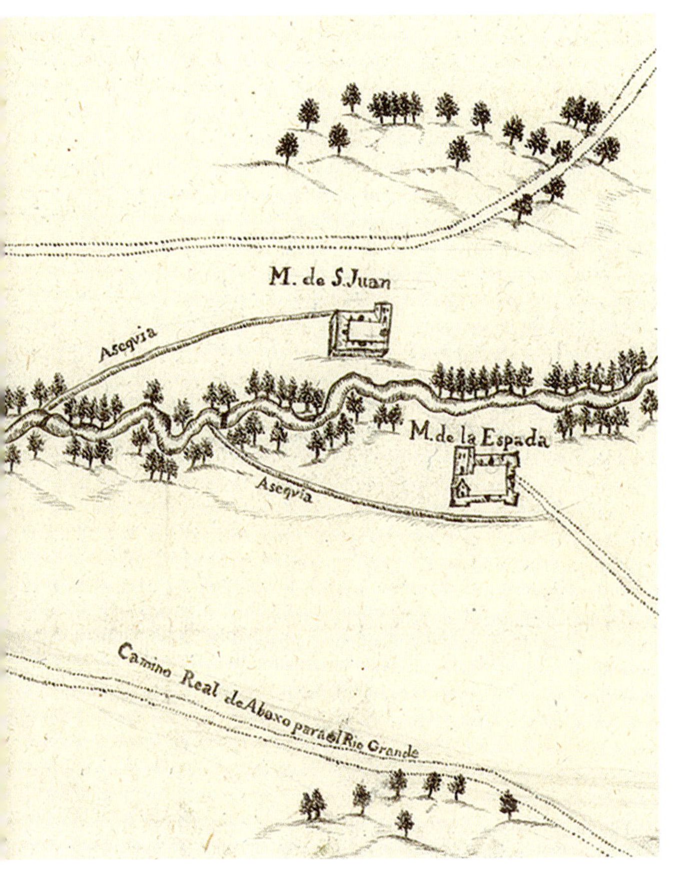

A FIELD GUIDE TO THE VERNACULAR BUILDINGS OF THE SAN ANTONIO AREA

Experiencing the Complex Character of San Antonio and South Central Texas through Their Vernacular Buildings and Cultural Landscapes

Kenneth Hafertepe

When the Vernacular Architecture Forum (VAF) decided to hold its annual meeting in San Antonio, it set off a flurry of new research into the ordinary buildings and cultural landscapes of Texas. The key values of the organization are laid out on every page of this book: a commitment to the meticulous documentation of floor plans, systems of framing and other construction techniques, and careful tracking of the evolution of buildings and places over decades and even centuries. The emphasis on ordinary buildings means that a tiny country church is as important a cultural document as an urban cathedral and that a neighborhood of shotgun houses contains as much Texas history as an elegant suburban enclave. Further, it is the firm belief of the contributing authors that the story of different cultural groups is not simply one of adaptation and assimilation to an increasingly dominant "mainstream" culture but a dynamic interplay of cultural perspectives that has played out over many decades—and continues to be in play.

Building culture is a product of place and experience, and Texas boasts a fascinating mix of people, materials, and architectural ideas. For the Spaniards coming from the south, Texas was part of the northern end of empire and a bulwark against French expansion beyond the Mississippi River valley. For Anglo-Americans and Germans coming from the east a century later, the border was not a barrier but a zone of cultural mixing. In Texas the mixing included materials, building methods, and ideas, which were then iterated in place. The study of this creolized mixing of materials, architectural forms, and building methods provides insight into the wider fashioning of identities of Texans over the last four centuries of occupation. San Antonio sits at the confluence of these architectural streams.[1]

Frederick Law Olmsted was struck by the creolized city when he visited in 1854. He noted in *A Journey through Texas*, published in 1857, that "we have no city, except, perhaps, New Orleans, that can vie, in point of the picturesque interest that attaches to odd and antiquated foreignness, with San Antonio." He noted that in spite of its seemingly isolated location the city possessed a "jumble of races, costumes, languages and buildings." Olmsted estimated that the town was one-third Hispanic, one-third Anglo, and one-third German. And he foresaw that the "rattling life" of the American immigrants would infuse the town with a new sort of energy.[2] As he wrote, the Anglo and German populations were on the increase and the Hispanic population on the decline. However, those of Spanish descent never ceased to live in San Antonio and were reinforced by immigrants from Mexico fleeing the revolutionary turmoil of the early twentieth century. Thus, the process of creolization, in effect since the mid-nineteenth century, continues to this day.

Founded in 1718 as part of the Spanish Empire, San Antonio was tied to dreams of harvesting native souls for the Catholic Church and mining untold amounts of gold and silver for the Crown.[3] The oldest surviving buildings in San Antonio are the five missions, along with the heavily restored Comandancia of the presidio (now mistakenly referred to as the Spanish Governor's Palace) and the apse of what is now San Fernando Cathedral.[4] These are easily the most "Spanish" buildings in the city, although it could be argued that they reflect a generic Spanish Colonial mentality or that of the northern cities of Querétaro and Zacatecas, where the Franciscan missionaries came from. San José was administered by the College of Zacatecas from the beginning, while the others were under the College of Querétaro; after 1773, all the missions were under Zacatecas (fig. 1.1).

For the first fifty-five years of San Antonio's existence, the capital of Texas was at the tiny outpost of Los Adaes, which was there to assert the presence of New Spain against New France. After England defeated France in the Seven Years' War, France was forced to cede Louisiana to

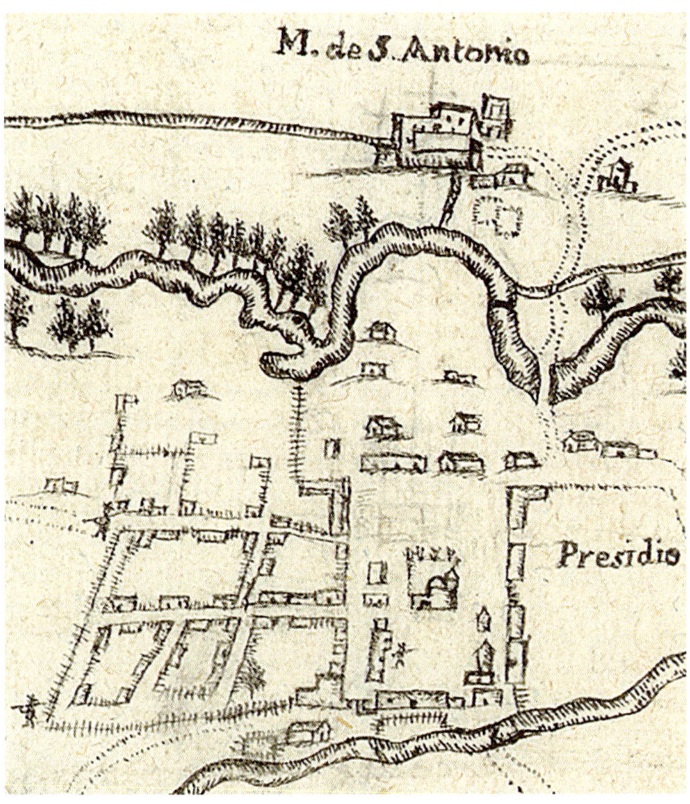

Figure 1.1. *Mapa del Presidio de San Antonio de Bexar* (detail), by Luis Antonio Menchaca, March 1764. Courtesy of the John Carter Brown Library, Brown University, Providence, RI.

Spain. Thus, an outpost near the border was unnecessary, and the capital was moved to San Antonio in 1773. Four years later the population of San Antonio was 2,060, which included 709 Native Americans living in the missions. The Casa Real, or government house, was built on the east side of Plaza Mayor, opposite the church of San Fernando, and was completed by 1779.

Perhaps the most unusual feature of San Antonio is that it had three eighteenth-century plazas: Plaza Mayor, now known as Main Plaza; Plaza de Armas, now Military Plaza; and Alamo Plaza, all of which have survived into the twenty-first century in one form or another. Alamo Plaza was essentially the central gathering place of the mission, while Military Plaza was the site of the quarters of the troops of the presidio and the home of their *comandante*. Main Plaza, laid out after the arrival of settlers from the Canary Islands in 1731, followed the Laws of the Indies, which governed Spanish settlements in the New World. The plaza had an open space, with the Casa Real on the east and the parish church of San Fernando on the west. In characteristic Spanish fashion, a *campo*

santo, or burying ground, was place directly in the front of the church. Though the great open space remains, the Casa Real was demolished in the nineteenth century, and only the apse of the parish church was incorporated in the much larger and more grand Cathedral of San Fernando, built 1868–73 (fig. 1.2).

An emphasis on the founding date for each mission has caused considerable confusion about the dating of the mission churches. San Antonio de Valero, better known as the Alamo, was founded in 1718 but at a site on the other side of the river and closer to the springs of the San Antonio River. The church building at the current site was begun in 1744. San José was founded in 1720, but the present church was built between 1768 and 1783. The other three missions were moved to San Antonio in 1731, but the present churches all date a decade or more after that.

San Antonio de Valero is now represented by the mission church and the remains of the *convento* in which the padres lived, but the compound was originally enclosed by rooms for native converts and a wide variety of shops (figs. 1.3 and 1.4). The roof of the church failed in 1756 while construction was still under way, and the building was still roofless when

Figure 1.2. Cathedral of San Fernando from Plaza de Armas, ca. 1875. Courtesy of Library of Congress.

the mission was secularized in 1793. Apparently the design called for the principal facade to have twin towers, but these were never built. The current curvilinear parapet dates only to 1850, and there was no record of the original design from which to work.[5]

Figures 1.3 and 1.4. Ruins of the Alamo. Drawings by Edward Everett, 1847. Courtesy of Amon Carter Museum of American Art, Fort Worth.

Figure 1.5. Mission San José. Photo by Kenneth Hafertepe.

Mission San José was sited at its present location only in 1739 or 1740 (fig. 1.5). There was an adobe church by 1744, and a stone church was completed by 1758, which seems to have experienced some sort of structural failure, as the cornerstone for the present building was laid in 1768. The nave had a vaulted ceiling and a dome over the crossing. The stone walls were plastered and given a geometrical paint treatment; the principal facade is embellished with statuary and other ornament in a fashion characteristic of the late Baroque. Father Juan Agustín Morfi, who visited the mission in January 1778, wrote that "it is, in truth, the first mission in America, not in point of time but in point of beauty, plan, and strength, so that there is a not a presidio along the entire frontier that can compare with it."[6]

The church of Mission Nuestra Señora de la Purísima Concepción was under construction by 1745 and completed in 1755 (fig. 1.6). Like those of San José, the stone walls of Mission Concepción were plastered and painted. The craftsmen who worked on the building had previously been engaged on San Antonio de Valero, and the two towers echoed what is presumed to have been the intended scheme for Valero, though the carved ornament around the entrance lacked the Baroque energy of Valero and San José. Though the church may have been lacking in ornament, it was

Figure 1.6. Interior of Mission Concepción. Photo by Kenneth Hafertepe.

sound in structure and is the only one of the five missions to still have its original roof.[7]

The church buildings of the two outer missions, San Juan Capistrano and San Francisco de la Espada, are much smaller in scale and thus provide a sense of what the other missions would have looked like in their earlier days. A stone church was completed at Capistrano by 1756—presumably the present church—and work on a larger one was begun around 1777. However, Father José Antonio López noted in 1785 that there was neither the money nor the Indians necessary to complete the structure. The latter is a telling indication of who actually did most of the heavy lifting in the construction of the missions. The 1756 church was distinguished again by painted plaster walls but also by a belfry, or *campanario*, above the main entrance.[8]

Espada was the southernmost mission and had a small stone church by 1756. A larger church was built between 1762 and 1777 but had to be torn down because of structural failures. While the large church was standing, the old church became the sacristy but reverted to being the main building when the newer one was taken down. Espada, like Capistrano, had a *campanario* but stood out for the unusual design of its portal. Debate has continued into the twenty-first century about whether the curious pattern reflects the original design or confusion among the stonemasons.[9]

The process of secularization—the transition from a mission to a regular parish—started in 1793 but was not completed until 1824. San Antonio de Valero was secularized first, on the rationale that there were currently no neophytes as the mission had no prospective converts within a 150-mile radius. That there were still native residents at the others meant that they could still be considered missions. (Most of the residents were of mixed race, with one Indian parent and one Spanish parent.) Concepción was placed administratively under San José, and Capistrano under Espada. These four missions were formally and finally secularized in 1824 under the new Republic of Mexico.

In the 1810s San Antonio took part in the bloody struggle to free Mexico from Spanish rule and to create the Republic of Mexico. However, the dual forces of increasingly authoritarian rule from Mexico City and the influx of immigrants from the United States—some but by no means all slaveholders—led to a second revolution, this one against Mexico in a quest for Texas independence. In the aftermath the Hispanic population continued to live there but found discrimination from new settlers who could not differentiate between authoritarian armies and local Tejanos (as native Mexicans were known) who had grown accustomed to a great deal of self-rule. Perhaps because of two violent revolutions in a very short period of time, or perhaps because of disdain of old things by new arrivals, virtually no buildings survive from the end of the missionary period to the admission of Texas into the United States.

By contrast, much remains from the fifteen years between the admission of Texas into the Union in 1845 and secession in a vain attempt to preserve the peculiar institution of slavery in 1861. This period saw a large immigration from various German states and other parts of Europe. This balancing of three cultures provided a significant impulse toward creolization.

Native Mexicans retained traditional materials and familiar floor plans in their buildings while erecting a more formal, somewhat Anglicized face toward the street. Theodore E. Giraud, who visited San Antonio in 1846 when his father was named French consul, wrote that "their houses, built more for defence than convenience, are generally long, low buildings, of only one story in height, with dirt floors, and few openings besides the doors, with flat roofs parapeted—this parapet being pierced by a large number of openings, to allow the water to run off by the long gurgoils or spouts that project all around the wall."[10]

There had been a long-standing hierarchy of materials used in construction in San Antonio. At the top was a small number of houses built of stone; more common were houses built of adobe (unfortunately, few survive today). Poorer people lived in jacales, which were woven around a framework of saplings. The Yturri-Edmunds complex is an extraordinarily rare survival of the use of adobe. Sometimes dated to the 1830s, it is more likely to date to the 1850s, which indicates that adobe was not completely abandoned after Texas became a state. Whether built of stone or adobe, homes were generally covered with stucco. This was essential for the adobe structures, as rainfall could melt away the adobe. Olmsted noted that, in 1854 at least, buildings were "washed blue and yellow."[11]

In terms of floor plan, Tejanos maintained the tradition of connected rooms that also opened onto the street. The notion of a central passage was alien to them, unless one counted *zaguanes*, passages for carriages, horses, and pedestrians that led from the street into an interior plaza. The large *portón* of Casa de Veramendi (1781–83), essentially large paneled gates with a smaller door for pedestrians, survives and is in the collection of the Alamo. The Yturri-Edmunds house was expanded from two rooms by adding another front room and three smaller back rooms. Casa Navarro, the home of José Antonio Navarro, also had two front rooms and was expanded to the rear. Almost all Tejano houses were one story; a rare exception was the house of the parish priest, Pedro Fuentes y Fernández, built in 1780, since demolished.

Pitched or hipped roofs were not part of the Tejano tradition; the norm in eighteenth- and early nineteenth-century San Antonio was the flat roof. Olmsted made note of the "flat roofs down upon their single story."[12] The only surviving building with a flat roof is the Comandancia (the Spanish Governor's Palace), which had a flat roof from 1749 to the 1870s, then a pitched roof, which was removed when the building was restored and enlarged in 1930. Casa Navarro had a pitched roof over the front rooms and another perpendicular to the street over the rear ell. On Tejano houses, such roofs were a marker of a creolized form. Some Hispanic houses were remodeled by Anglo settlers, such as Sam and Mary Maverick (from South Carolina and Alabama, respectively), and this included a new hipped roof.

Front porches were also a novelty; those at the Yturri-Edmunds house and Casa Navarro made the homes look more Anglo-Southern, in spite of the two or three front doors. In the case of Navarro, this may have been a conscious calculation, as he was a community leader who later served as a state senator in Austin.

No chimneys or fireplaces survive from San Antonio before 1850. The Tejano tradition was to use braziers, which could be moved from room to room or heat a specific part of a room. This probably relates to the warm climate in Texas. All fireplaces at the missions and the Spanish Governor's Palace date to the restorations and reconstructions of the 1930s, when architect Harvey P. Smith apparently could not believe that Texans could live without a fireplace. Many of these were corner fireplaces, which reflect architect Smith's interest in the Santa Fe style. The two earliest surviving chimneys are at the Yturri-Edmunds house and Casa Navarro. Both were centered in partition walls so that they could heat two rooms. Again, Anglos remodeling Tejano houses were likely to add a fireplace or two.

A great many American immigrants had no interest in adopting local customs. Olmsted noted American houses mixed with Mexican and German houses along Commerce Street between Alamo Plaza and Main Plaza: "The American dwellings stand back, with galleries and jalousies and a garden picket-fence against the walk, or rise, next door, in three-story brick to respectable city fronts."[13] Though he identified brick as an Anglo innovation, at this early date it was rarely used. Anglos tended to build with stone or wood, though this was to change in the latter decades of the nineteenth century.

Perhaps the most imposing house built before the Civil War was that of Irish-born merchant James Vance, built in 1853–55, now demolished. It was two stories on a raised basement, with two-story galleries front and back. A central passage with an elegant staircase ran down the middle, providing (or denying) access to four rooms on each floor. Other families from the east opted for houses without a central passage. Sam and Mary Maverick, tiring of their Hispanic house on Main Plaza, built a house at the northwest corner of Alamo Plaza with three rooms on each floor and a two-story side gallery that contained the only stairway. Sam, a native of the Pendleton District of South Carolina, spent much time in Charleston, and the house on Alamo Plaza certainly reflected his familiarity with the Charleston "single house."[14] In 1856 Major Jeremiah Dashiell, the paymaster of Fort San Antonio, built a one-story house above a raised basement in La Villita. There were two front rooms and no central passage; to the rear, facing the river, was an open galerie enclosed by small rooms on each side. Dashiell was a native of Maryland who practiced medicine in Louisville, Kentucky, and lived in New Orleans before being posted to Texas, which may explain his use of a typical Creole floor plan.[15]

Each of these houses was built by a different German stonemason. The Vance house was built by Johann Fries, who also built the upper part of the Alamo facade, including the famous curvilinear parapet when the US Army put a wooden roof on the building. The Maverick house was built by Joseph and Frank Schmitt, German-immigrant stonemasons, who also built the home of John James on Commerce Street and may have built the stone walls of the house of James's father-in-law, Joseph H. Polley, in Sutherland Springs. And the Dashiell house, which still stands in La Villita, was by John H. Kampmann, who after the Civil War became a leading contractor and also opened the earliest door, sash, and blind factory.

Compared to the landscapes of Northeast Texas and the area first settled by Austin's Colony along the Brazos and Colorado Rivers, San Antonio and environs had relatively few enslaved workers, which affected patterns of work and housing. In 1850 Bexar County had only 238 enslaved workers. By 1860 that number had more than doubled to 593; the typical slave owner had 3 people working for him in slavery. Of the 181 slave owners, 141 provided a separate slave house. For 115 owners this was only one slave house, while 15 provided two houses and 1 provided three houses. Virtually nothing of this landscape of urban slavery survives. Best documented are the two houses, long gone, of Sam and Mary Maverick. In both their early house on the northeast corner of Main Plaza and their 1850 house on the northwest corner of Alamo Plaza, they provided two houses for their slaves. In the latter house female slaves lived above a kitchen/laundry building, while male slaves lived in a house north of the main house. In 1850 six of their slaves were living in town, and ten years later all eighteen were.[16]

Among the German immigrants to Texas were skilled stonemasons, carpenters, and cabinetmakers who could create buildings and spaces that might remind their fellow immigrants of home but who also could build in a fashion acceptable to Anglo clients. Comparatively few houses for

Germans from before 1860 remain in San Antonio. One of the most impressive was the Gustav Blersch house in the King William neighborhood, built circa 1859. The architect was Gustav Freisleben and the contractor was J. H. Kampmann, but the house is closely related to the James R. Sweet house north of town, built by Kampmann in 1854. Both houses were one story on a high basement, with a shallow central passage and one large room to each side. In neither house did the passage have a staircase; it was on the back gallery of the Sweet house and on the back wall of the Blersch house. The John Ball house, built at 120 King William Street not long after the Civil War, has German tendencies with two front rooms and two front doors rather than a central passage. The most Anglo-Southern feature of the house is the front porch.[17]

In the 1850s groups of European immigrants stepped up to improve the quality of education for the youth of San Antonio. The Catholic Church opened St. Mary's School for young men and the Ursuline Academy for young women. Francois Giraud, a native of Charleston whose parents had been born in France, oversaw their construction. The church of St. Mary, which served the Irish community in the city, was designed by Giraud and built by Joseph and Frank Schmitt. Frank Schmitt later built the second building at the Ursuline Academy (1854) as well as a dormitory (1865–66).[18]

Meanwhile, Germans across town, mostly members of the Casino Club, decided to open the German-English School. This started with two one-story structures facing each other; a two-story rock building was added after the Civil War. The Ursuline Academy made it clear that students of all denominations were welcome, but all were expected to attend Divine Worship. By contrast, the charter of the German-English School made it clear that "no religious or sectarian tenets would be taught in the school."[19] While the schools had sharply different views of the role of religion in education, both embraced a multilingual education. The German-English School taught classes in English, German, and Spanish, while the Ursuline Academy offered classes in English, Spanish, German, and French, a clear indication of the multicultural nature of the city.

The Hill Country had the densest concentration of German residents and German buildings (fig. 1.7). Although Germans in the Hill Country were—at least initially—living together with little interaction with Anglo-Texans or Tejanos, the preferred temporary house in the Hill Country was a one-room log house. By the 1840s the skills necessary to join logs into walls had died out in Germany. In Texas German immigrants had to

Figure 1.7. Seth Eastman, *Dutch Church at Fredericksburg*, January 24, 1849. Courtesy of McNay Art Museum, San Antonio.

hire Anglo carpenters and/or their enslaved African American craftsmen. However, German immigrants seem to have been dismayed by the draftiness of American log houses and by the perpetual maintenance required to keep chinking in place. Within ten years the Germans devised their own version of a log house, with logs alternating with rows of mortared rocks. Such a house was less drafty and low maintenance.[20]

An early example is the Goldbeck-Faltin house in Comfort; a slightly later example is the first room of the Sauer log house at the Sauer-Beckmann Living History Farm. Both houses have V-shaped notches at the corners, which led Terry G. Jordan to hypothesize that the builders learned the technique from Upland Southerners. The subsequent additions to both of these houses abandoned log technology. Three rooms were added to the Goldbeck-Faltin house, all using traditional German *fachwerk*, a system of construction in which heavy wooden beams create a framework that is then infilled with some other material that was less expensive than wood, or at least more easily available. The first was a lean-to addition, which was infilled with adobe, an intriguing bit of creolization; the two additional rooms were also *fachwerk* but infilled with stone. Three rooms were added to the Sauer house, all with solid rock walls.[21]

In Fredericksburg most houses built after 1855 were either *fachwerk* or rock. The infill was usually rock, though the Klingelhoefer house still has its infill of adobe bricks, and the Peter Walter house once had such an infill. Additions to *fachwerk* houses were typically made of rock. It is unclear whether the *fachwerk* was originally exposed, but once an addition was made using a different material, the entire house would be stuccoed to give it a unified appearance.[22]

Fachwerk houses might start with one room, as at the Krieger house; two front rooms, as at the Walter house; or even three front rooms, as at the Kammlah house. Yet another option was two front rooms separated by an open passage, as at the Klingelhoefer house. Rock houses could be either one front room with a lean-to room in back or two front rooms. In the latter case, there could be two front doors, as at the Kiehne house, or just one door into the *stube* (parlor), as at the John Peter Tatsch house. Most early houses were one story, although houses with a large front room and lean-to back room often had a half story above the front room. The only early two-story house was the Kiehne house, which began with two rock rooms on the first and second floors. Rock houses might have an internal staircase on one of the side walls; after the Civil War, staircases on the front wall of the back room became more typical.[23]

German Texans were far less likely than Anglo Texans to own slaves. In 1860 there were only 33 slaves in Fredericksburg and surrounding Gillespie County, and almost all of these were owned by Anglos, notably the Doss and Riley families. German settlers in Seguin and Guadalupe County meant there was a smaller percentage of enslaved workers in that area. In 1850 there were 331 slaves in the county, though that number increased to 480 by 1860. In 1850 Joseph H. Polley, who was preparing to build his plantation house known as Whitehall, owned 10 slaves, while Joshua Young, who would soon build the house known as Sebastopol in Seguin, owned 21 slaves. The log kitchen at Whitehall is an extraordinarily rare survival of a space where an enslaved cook worked.

Gonzales County was much closer to a typical plantation economy. In 1850 some 168 enslaved workers lived in the town of Gonzales, while 252 lived on plantations along Peach Creek. Although log houses are sometimes seen as a badge of poverty, log-house owner Horace Eggleston of Gonzales was a merchant who also owned 5 slaves. At Peach Creek Charles Braches owned 10 slaves, which was typical for the twenty-four slave owners who owned 252 slaves. Ten years later Braches owned 15 slaves who lived in three houses, and his stepson Joel D. McClure owned another 7 slaves who lived in one house. Though the main McClure-Braches house survives, none of the outbuildings do. Between 1850 and 1860 the number of slaves in Gonzales County increased from 601 to 2,838.

German settlers and craftsmen also settled in towns to the east of San Antonio, especially Seguin. The Zorn family—originally from Alsace, on the border between Germany and France—eventually bought Sebastopol, the impressive Greek Revival house made of limecrete. However, Joseph Zorn, born in Illinois to immigrant parents, lived in the one-room *fachwerk* house known today as Los Nogales. The infill was adobe—rock houses were relatively rare in Seguin. Though a small house, it still had double doors and two sash windows in front and a casement window on the south side, an indication that the owners were by no means destitute.

In Gonzales and Guadalupe Counties log houses could be found in both town and country. The Eggleston house in Gonzales is an example of the former. Horace Eggleston was a native of New York and a merchant, and in Gonzales he lived in a log house that was separate from his store. It had two rooms and a dogtrot, an open passage that was the log equivalent of a central passage. The logs were hewn, which gave them a more regular appearance; they were joined at the corners by half-dovetail notches, which were the most commonly used notches in Texas. His prosperity was marked particularly by the four sash windows on the front facade, which provided ample light, though they also weakened the front walls.

The log house now in Seguin was originally on a farm five miles south of town, built for Peter and Bridget Campbell, immigrants from Ireland. It had only one front window in each room. Like those in the Eggleston house, the logs were hewn, but on the Campbell house the logs were joined with a double notch, which was extremely rare in Texas and, indeed, in the United States. Terry Jordan knew of only four examples in the state, two of which were in D'Hanis in Medina County, settled by Alsatians and Germans.

The area to the east of San Antonio is Blackland Prairie, which is suitable for raising cotton as well as livestock and made the terrain suitable as well for the use of slave labor. This was the case at the McClure-Braches house east of Gonzales. The land was granted to Bart McClure, a native of Kentucky, in 1831. He died a decade later, and within a year his widow, Sarah, married Charles Braches, an immigrant from Germany. The Braches house is built with a wood frame on rock piers. It has a central passage but also a number of Creole features, including a two-story inset front porch and a petite galerie (what the English call a loggia) flanked by cabinets on the rear. Nothing in their upbringing in Germany or living in Texas would have predicted that they would build such a house.

Whitehall, the Polley mansion south of Seguin, was quite different, even though it, too, was a plantation based on slave labor. Whitehall is a two-story stone house with a central passage and four rooms each on the first and second floors. Joseph Polley was from Upstate New York, and the doors and windows were originally shipped from New York to Texas. The Polley mansion is the only surviving plantation house in Texas with stone walls: a few other were brick, many more were built with a wooden frame, and a large number of big houses, perhaps a majority, were built of logs. The Polley mansion is thus atypical but no less remarkable. Behind the house is a log kitchen and quarter, which is an even rarer survival from antebellum times.[24]

Another remarkable house in Seguin is the suburban villa known as Sebastopol, which was built in the 1850s of limecrete. Joshua W. Young, a native of South Carolina, built the house for his widowed sister, Catherine LeGette, around 1856–57. The house, one principal story on a raised basement, was built on a site that sloped down to the rear. As a result, the ceiling heights in basement rooms varied from low in the front to moderate in the middle and high in the rear. The back range of rooms included a large dining room, a kitchen, and another room; above were a parlor, around which a porch wrapped on three sides, and three bedrooms.[25]

The years after the Civil War were boom times for San Antonio. The population was only 8,325 in 1860 but rose to 20,550 in 1880 and 53,321 in 1900. The Galveston, Harrisburg and San Antonio Railway reached town in 1877, and new residents, new materials, and new ideas came with it. The railroad facilitated a number of businesses: the Pioneer Flour Mills, Alamo Iron Works, the Steves lumber mill, the Lone Star Brewery, and the Frank Teich marble yard, which produced gravestones in marble or granite and, after 1890, more than its fair share of Confederate monuments. An agricultural census of Bexar County in 1887 found 26,061 (Anglo-)Americans, 7,688 Mexicans, 6,146 Germans, 3,395 African Americans, and 1,022 Irish, with lesser numbers of English, French, Poles, Italians, Spaniards, Hebrews, Russians, Swedes, Danes, Chinese, and Norwegians. Clearly San Antonio and Bexar County remained unusually diverse.

Even before the Civil War San Antonio had been the central military post in Texas, which grew after the war. Fort San Antonio, which had occupied the grounds of the Alamo after statehood, moved to a new complex on the north side of town, pointedly rechristened Fort Sam Houston for the governor who had been removed from office after refusing to take an oath of loyalty to the Confederacy. Designed by the English émigré architect Alfred Giles, work began in 1876 and the first phase of construction concluded in 1878. Fort Sam Houston was the headquarters for the series of US Army forts that drove Native Americans farther and farther west and finally onto reservations. The city's association with the US military only deepened in the twentieth century with the creation of Randolph and Lackland Air Force Bases and Kelly Field.

The most notable suburban development of the Victorian era was the King William neighborhood, built on land that had once been farmland for Mission San Antonio de Valero. While one might expect Germans living in town to carefully conserve Old-World traditions, many of those in King William were early adopters of the latest architectural styles from the East Coast, at least more so than their Anglo neighbors. The house of Anton and Paulita Wulff aspired to be an Italian villa in the style of architect Samuel Sloan, while the house of Edward and Johanna Steves managed to compress a number of Second Empire features into a sober and symmetrical structure. German Texans were very reluctant to have a central passage with a staircase; apparently they thought that such passages were a waste of space, especially in a small house, and that space could be better used by making the other rooms larger. Edward and Johanna may have been nudged in the direction of a central passage by their architect, Alfred Giles.[26]

Giles took full advantage of the railroad extending into the Hill Country to pursue additional clients as well as to found his own ranch, Hillingdon. In Comfort, Giles designed a store with residence above for the merchant August Faltin, worked on the Ingenhuett Hotel, and designed a number of other buildings for the Ingenhuett family, including the house of Paul Ingenhuett. From Comfort Giles could take the stagecoach to Fredericksburg, where he designed a new Gillespie County Courthouse (1881–82) and a house for William and Lina Bierschwale (1888–89). The specifications for the latter, one of the earliest houses with an asymmetrical floor plan in the Hill Country, called for stonework of a quality similar to that of the officers' quarters at Fort Sam Houston.[27]

The decades after the Civil War led to a new generation of public buildings in San Antonio. Francois Giraud designed a new Church of San Fernando. The original nave and bell tower were demolished, and the new church built forward on top of the old *campo santo*. The new facade with its twin towers spoke of the Gothic Revival—Giraud is said to have studied in France—but was done in distinctive Texas limestone. Within a year of its completion, the Diocese of Texas was formed, and San Fernando was designated as the cathedral.[28]

Between 1889 and 1891 a new city hall was built in the middle of what had been Plaza de Armas, just to the west of the cathedral. The architect was Otto Kramer, a native of Bavaria who immigrated to the United States and practiced in New York City and elsewhere before moving to Texas in 1888. Originally the building was more picturesque, with a central dome and towers, but those were removed in 1927 to make way for a fourth floor decorated with a few rows of red tiles in a halfhearted Spanish Colonial style.[29]

Finally, a large new Bexar County Courthouse was built on the south side of Main Plaza between 1892 and 1897. The red sandstone building was an essay in the Richardsonian Romanesque, but with an exotic ovoid dome thrown in for good measure. The architect was J. Riely Gordon, a native of Virginia, who was a prolific designer of Texas courthouses in the 1880s and 1890s. The contractor was Otto P. Kroeger, a native of Prussia whose family immigrated to American around 1872. Gordon and Kroeger also worked together on the Gonzales County Courthouse.[30]

Historic preservation in Texas began in San Antonio around the turn of the century, with the debate about whether or not to preserve the *convento* of Mission San Antonio de Valero, by that time better known as

Figure 1.8. Adina De Zavala in front of Spanish Governor's Palace. Photo in *San Antonio Light*, November 22, 1926. Courtesy of Institute of Texan Cultures, University of Texas at San Antonio, No. L-0696-A.

the Alamo. Leading the charge for preservation was Adina De Zavala, granddaughter of Lorenzo De Zavala, the first vice president of the Republic of Texas, and an early member of the Daughters of the Republic of Texas (DRT). She recruited another member of the DRT, Clara Driscoll of Corpus Christi, to work on the project with her, having noted that Driscoll was quite wealthy and might be able to fund a large part of the restoration on her own. The two, however, had a falling out and became bitter enemies. De Zavala left the DRT but went on to advocate for the restoration of what she claimed was the Spanish Governor's Palace (fig. 1.8) and the so-called Cos house in La Villita.[31]

Though few Hispanics immigrated to San Antonio between 1836 and 1910, the Mexican Revolution, which began in 1910, led to a new influx of people from Mexico, which resulted in a rebalancing of the population toward the Hispanic. These new Texans tended to live in their own neighborhood on the Westside, which survives to this day. The community centered around the Catholic parish church. After World War I the Vatican discouraged parishes focused on a single ethnic group, and the church was designed by Leo M. J. Dielmann, a San Antonio native and son of German immigrants, who designed Catholic churches across Texas, including those in San Antonio, Seguin, and Fredericksburg.

Most houses on the Westside were small; some were in the form of shotgun houses. Economic opportunities for these immigrants were limited. One source of income was the shelling of pecans, a task largely performed by Hispanic women. However, the abysmally low pay for these workers led to labor unrest and a three-month strike early in 1938. Ironically, in northern suburbs such as Alamo Heights and Olmos Park, the Spanish Colonial Revival became a popular option in the age of the period house. Perhaps best known is the McNay-Atkinson mansion, now the McNay Art Museum, designed by the local firm of Ayres & Ayres.

Preservation took on a new urgency in the 1930s, partly because the 1936 centennial of the Texas Revolution was fast approaching and partly because President Franklin D. Roosevelt was willing to spend freely on Texas to keep the state in the Democratic coalition. The New Deal paid for a museum building for the Alamo (now the gift shop); a museum for Trail Drivers, Settlers, and Texas Rangers in Brackenridge Park (now part of the Witte Museum); and much work at Mission San José, including the reconstruction of the roof and dome. The largesse extended to the east and west: the New Deal paid for the Gonzales Memorial Museum in Gonzales and for a reconstruction of the Vereins-Kirche, the communal

Figure 1.9. Writers' Program of the Work Projects Administration in the State of Texas, *Old Villita* (San Antonio: The City of San Antonio 1939) cover. Courtesy of Texas Collection, Baylor University.

church in Fredericksburg. In addition, Texas was documented by the Historic American Buildings Survey, the Index of American Design, and the Federal Writers' Project, which produced a state guide and interviewed many former slaves. Many of these projects were compensation for the fact that Dallas was hosting the Centennial Exposition, even though the city had not existed in 1836.

One of Roosevelt's most ardent supporters was Maury Maverick, who represented San Antonio in Congress from 1934 to 1938. He was primaried in 1938 and lost his seat in Congress, but he was elected mayor of San Antonio the next year and immediately began lobbying the president for funds to restore the little community just south of downtown known as La Villita (fig. 1.9). Maverick also urged Roosevelt to support a project that would simultaneously prevent flooding in downtown San Antonio and create an attractive district of shops designed by Robert H. H. Hugman. Maverick was successful on both fronts, and the River Walk was born. Alas, as a commercial development it was a resounding flop, as few locals could be persuaded to do their shopping at river level. After World War II, restaurants began to open along the river, but not until HemisFair in 1968 did the River Walk began to attract visitors.[32]

The Conservation Society of San Antonio, founded in 1924 in an unsuccessful attempt to save the Market House of 1859, has been an integral player in the preservation movement. In 1952 a granddaughter of Edward and Johanna Steves donated their house on King William Street to the society, and in 1954 it was opened as a historic house museum. The King William neighborhood became the first National Register Historic District in Texas in 1972. Preservation in the area was spearheaded by Walter Nold Mathis, who purchased the old Norton-Polk house in 1967, restoring it and making it his final home. In 2004 he bequeathed the house, known as Villa Finale, to the National Trust for Historic Preservation.

Today San Antonio has embraced its Hispanic heritage even more fully, with the successful nomination of the five missions as a UNESCO World Heritage site. Laser-light shows have been developed that can show the original treatment of painted plaster at Mission Concepción and Mission San José without damaging the historic fabric. The River Walk, now seen as a historic gem and a tourist magnet, has been expanded to the north, known as the Museum Reach, and to the south, known as the Mission Reach. At the same time there are struggles over preservation of the Westside and fierce wrangling over the fate of Alamo Plaza, which is to be closed to vehicular traffic in an attempt to create a rough approximation of what existed in 1836. These controversies show that certain key questions remain unresolved: What does it mean to be a San Antonian, and what does it mean to be a Texan?

Notes

1. On creolization in Louisiana, see Jay D. Edwards, "The Origins of Creole Architecture," *Winterthur Portfolio* 29, no. 2/3 (1994): 155–89. On the struggle to preserve traditional Norwegian building practices on the Texas frontier, see Kenneth A. Breisch and David Moore, "The Norwegian Rock Houses of Bosque County, Texas: Some Observations on a Nineteenth-Century Vernacular Building Type," in *Perspectives in Vernacular Architecture II*, ed. Camille Wells (Columbia: University of Missouri Press, 1986), 64–71.

2. Frederick Law Olmsted, *A Journey through Texas; or, A Saddle-Trip on the Southwestern Frontier* (1857; repr., Austin: University of Texas Press, 1978), 150–51.

3. On early San Antonio, see Gerald E. Poyo and Gilberto M. Hinojosa, eds., *Tejano Origins in Eighteenth-Century San Antonio* (Austin: University of Texas Press for the University of Texas Institute of Texan Cultures at San Antonio, 1991); Jesus F. de la Teja, *San Antonio de Béxar: A Community on New Spain's Northern Frontier* (Albuquerque: University of New Mexico Press, 1995); and Jesús F. de la Teja, ed., *Tejano Leadership in Mexican and Revolutionary Texas* (College Station: Texas A&M University Press, 2010).

4. On the missions, see Jacinto Quirarte, *The Art and Architecture of the Texas Missions* (Austin: University of Texas Press, 2002). On the Spanish Governor's Palace, see Kenneth Hafertepe, "The Romantic Rhetoric of the Spanish Governor's Palace, San Antonio, Texas," *Southwestern Historical Quarterly* 107, no. 2 (2003): 239–77; and Kenneth Hafertepe, "Restoration, Reconstruction, or Romance? The Case of the Spanish Governor's Palace in Hispanic-Era San Antonio, Texas," *Journal of the Society of Architectural Historians* 67, no. 3 (2008): 412–33. On the Church of San Fernando, see Adán Benevides, "Sacred Space, Profane Reality: The Politics of Building a Church in Eighteenth-Century Texas," *Southwestern Historical Quarterly* 107, no. 1 (2003): 1–30.

5. Quirarte, *Art and Architecture of the Texas Missions*, 43–64.

6. Quirarte, 66.

7. Quirarte, 103–30.

8. Quirarte, 131–48.

9. Quirarte, 149–75.

10. Theodore E. Giraud, "Missions of Texas," *United States Catholic Magazine*, April 1847, 219.

11. Olmsted, *A Journey through Texas*, 149–50.

12. Olmsted, 150.

13. Olmsted, 150.

14. Kenneth Hafertepe, "The Texas Homes of Sam and Mary Maverick," *Southwestern Historical Quarterly* 109, no. 1 (2005): 1–29.

15. Maggie Valentine, *John H. Kampmann, Master Builder: San Antonio's German Influence in the 19th Century* (New York: Beaufort Books, 2014), 47–51.

16. On the impact that slavery had on the houses and landscapes of San Antonio, see Kenneth Hafertepe, "Urban Sites of Slavery in Antebellum Texas," in *Slavery in the City: Architecture and Landscapes of Urban Slavery in North America*, ed. Clifton Ellis and Rebecca Ginsburg (Charlottesville: University of Virginia Press, 2017), 106–22, especially 108–11.

17. On the King William neighborhood, see Mary V. Burkholder, *The King William Area: A History and Guide to the Houses* (San Antonio: King William Association, 1973); for specific houses, see Kenneth Hafertepe, *The Material Culture of German Texans* (College Station: Texas A&M University Press, 2016), 141–48, 172–86. On the Blersch house, see Valentine, *John H. Kampmann*, 51–53; and Hafertepe, *Material Culture of German Texans*, 145–46.

18. Maria Watson Pfeiffer, *School by the River: Ursuline Academy to Southwest School of Art & Craft, 1851–2001* (San Antonio: Maverick, 2001).

19. *Daily Ledger and Texan* (San Antonio) July 18, 1860, 2.

20. Hafertepe, *Material Culture of German Texans*, 44–73.

21. Hafertepe, 61–63, 68–71.

22. Hafertepe, 98–100.

23. Hafertepe, 118–28.

24. On the house, see Melinda Creech, "The Material Culture of the Polley Mansion, Whitehall: Vernacular Architecture, Decorative Arts, and Domestic Arts" (master's thesis, Baylor University, 2018); on the kitchen, see John Michael Vlach, *Back of the Big House: The Architecture of Plantation Slavery* (Chapel Hill: University of North Carolina Press, 1993), 50, and John Michael Vlach, "Slave Quarters as Bi-cultural Expression," in *Black and White: Cultural Interaction in the Antebellum South*, ed. Ted Ownby (Jackson: University Press of Mississippi, 1993), 89.

25. Sandra R. Sauer, Art Black, and Cynthia Brandimarte, *Sebastopol: Sebastopol State Historic Park (41GU9): Seguin, Texas: Archeological Excavations, 1978–1988*, Reports of Investigations no. 111 (Austin: Texas Parks and Wildlife Department, 1998).

26. Hafertepe, *Material Culture of German Texans*, 171–86.

27. Mary Carolyn Hollers Jutson, *Alfred Giles: An English Architect in Texas and Mexico* (San Antonio: Trinity University Press, 1972).

28. Richard Cleary, "Texas Gothic, French Accent: The Architecture of the Roman Catholic Church in Antebellum Texas," *Journal of the Society of Architectural Historians* 66, no. 1 (2007): 60–83.

29. Willard B. Robinson, *Texas Public Buildings of the Nineteenth Century* (Austin: University of Texas Press, 1974), 192–93; Willard B. Robinson, *The People's Architecture: Texas Courthouses, Jails and Municipal Buildings* (Austin: Texas State Historical Association, 1983), 143.

30. Chris Meister, *James Riely Gordon: His Courthouses and Other Public Architecture* (Lubbock: Texas Tech University Press, 2011), 54–75, 283–84.

31. Lewis F. Fisher, *Saving San Antonio: The Precarious Preservation of a Heritage* (Lubbock: Texas Tech University Press, 1996).

32. Lewis F. Fisher, *American Venice: The Story of San Antonio's River* (San Antonio: Trinity University Press, 2015).

Materials and Methods of Everyday Building in Central Texas

Brent R. Fortenberry

Building culture is a product of place and experience, where notions of architectural needs meet the constraints of location. Texas' vernacular landscapes are ones of creolized building forms. Central Texas boasts an unrivaled mixing of people, materials, and architectural ideas. This chapter, which highlights some of the building methods and materials distinctive to San Antonio and its environs, is designed to guide readers and the viewers of buildings as they traverse Central Texas' vernacular landscapes.

Texas was once considered the "frontier" or the "borderlands" for immigrant communities: the English and Germans coming from the north and west, and the Spanish from the south and west. These populations moved into the areas around San Antonio, displacing existing indigenous communities with their own building cultures. We thus cannot conceive of Texas' architectural patrimony as anything other than mixtures, a confluence of materials, methods, and ideas iterated in place. Perhaps then we should view buildings as conversations about how people viewed themselves, what kinds of spaces they sought to inhabit, and how they wanted to position themselves to others.

The diversity of building is heavily influenced by the varied geology and flora of Central Texas. San Antonio sits at the nexus of three major geologic zones: the South Texas Plain, comprising sands and mud; the Blackland Prairie, consisting of chalks and marls; and the Edwards Plateau, comprising limestone bedrock.

These varying subsoil and bedrock compositions influenced the everyday building materials employed by Texas builders.[1]

Four subregions of surface vegetation also influenced the kinds of timber used in building construction. Mesquite dominated the areas directly east and south of San Antonio, while pockets of oak mixed with mesquite dominated the Hill Country. Historically, timber from the pine forests of East Texas, as well as imported cypress from points east, particularly Mississippi and Louisiana, were used for building. Cypress also notably grows along the Guadalupe and Pedernales Rivers in the Hill Country.

Gordon Echols's *Early Texas Architecture* identified five settlement regions of Texas, each with idiosyncratic building forms (fig. 2.1). But rather than view these as invisible borders that articulate isolated building traditions, this field guide demonstrates that ideas about building are in constant exchange.[2] San Antonio neatly sits at the intersection of three of these regions: Central Texas, with early log construction later supplanted by timber framing and brick masonry; the Hill Country, with similar early log construction that gives way to *fachwerk*—a heavily German-influenced

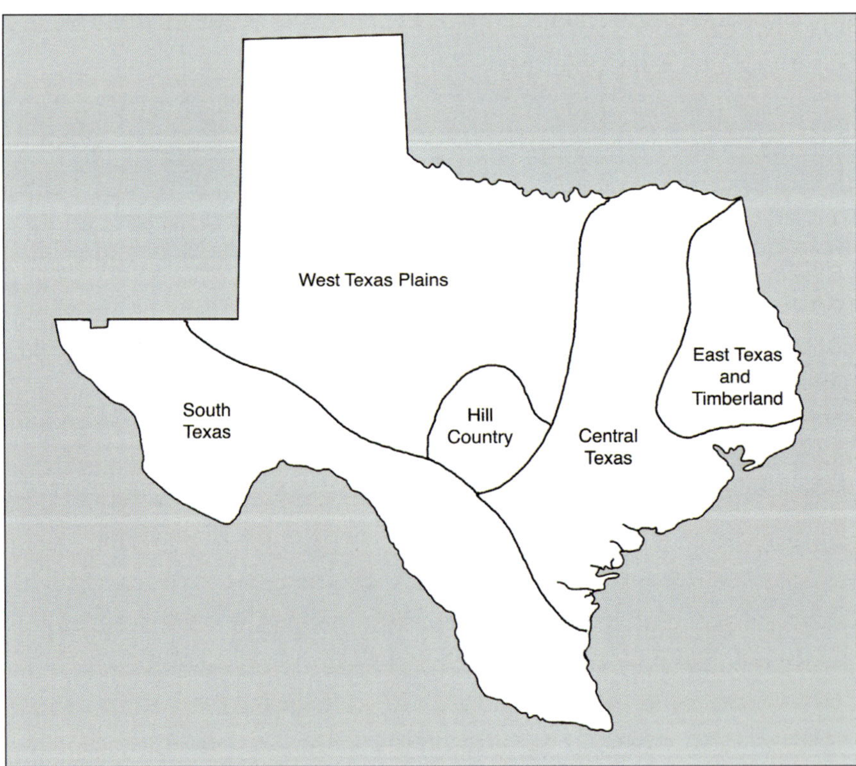

Figure 2.1. Architectural regions of Texas. Image by Brent R. Fortenberry after Gordon Echols, *Early Texas Architecture* (Fort Worth: TCU Press, 2000).

exposed timber framing—and the rock house, an exposed stone construction; and South Texas, with adobe and stone construction. The San Antonio region can thus be understood as a central component of a wider process of creolization that fused indigenous and colonial knowledge of building traditions with local materials and architectural needs.

But the complexities of building materials and form cannot be viewed simply within the framework of the European metropole and colonial periphery. In the eastern towns of Seguin and Gonzales we see the influence of other North American building traditions and how these influenced the everyday buildings of Texas. The introduction of limecrete shares cultural influences from the tabby architecture of the Lowcountry of South Carolina and Georgia. Similar in form, the Gulf Coast plan of rear galleries and upper loggia flanked by cabinet rooms can be seen at the Charles and Sarah Braches house outside Gonzales, an arrangement often associated with Creole architecture in southern Louisiana. But this form is deeply anglicized by the builders along the Mississippi and also, as the Braches house demonstrates, by those in Central Texas.[3] These hybridized building forms, with influence from differing spatial and temporal scales, even more deeply articulate Central Texas architecture not on the periphery but at the confluence of larger building patterns in North and Central America.

This chapter begins with two of the earliest local building methods, adobe and log construction, before moving to later technologies, including *fachwerk* and rock construction for German settlement areas, notably in Fredericksburg and the King William neighborhood of San Antonio, and timber framing for the Anglo-influenced areas to the east of the city. It concludes with a discussion of limecrete technology found in Seguin. While not comprehensive, it sets the stage for following chapters by taking a wide-angle view on the larger building patterns in the region.

Adobe Construction

Spanish colonial builders deployed creolized architectural forms, mixing European designs with the materials of North and Central American colonial contexts and local indigenous building knowledge. While southeastern Spanish building typically used tabby or local coquina stone construction, in the Southwest Spanish colonial building techniques, particularly adobe, rapidly replaced indigenous building technologies. In adobe construction, a binder such as straw or a similar aggregate is added to unburned clay, which is sun-dried before being employed for construction.[4] In North

America, a limewash or thin stucco coat is typically applied to the exterior to create a protective barrier between the clay and exterior elements. Adobe placed design constraints on Spanish builders—these buildings typically have flat roofs and vigas, exposed heavy transverse tie beams—and generally dictated a rectangular form.[5] Texas adobe construction was often limited to one or two stories, unlike examples in New Mexico, and primarily consisted of non-mission construction. Unsurprisingly, adobe building often presents as a compact room arrangement with thick walls. At the Yturri-Edmunds house (see chapter 5), the walls are one foot, seven inches thick, with room dimensions that do not exceed eighteen feet wide and sixteen feet deep. At Casa Navarro, the adobe walls range from one foot to one foot, four inches thick.[6] A room size and plan composition can also be seen at the much-altered and restored Governor's Palace.

Outstanding surviving examples of adobe brick dot San Antonio, most notably small portions of Casa Navarro, now a Texas State Historic Site, which consists of three adobe structures, the earliest a jacal, dates to 1832, with later additions by 1854.[7] Other examples in San Antonio include the north wall at Mission Valero (the Alamo) and the Urrutia-Menchaca-Perez house (also known as the Spanish Governor's Palace).[8] Adobe also survives beyond the core of Spanish colonial settlement, such as Los Nogales in Seguin, a simple one-room adobe structure with a full cellar (see chapter 8).

Gerald J. Mulvey and K. Allison Mulvey's recent study of the chemical composition of adobe provides insight into its historic recipe. Brick at the Casa Navarro site consists of 40.5 percent sand and limestone chips, 23 percent fines, 14.3 percent clay, and 22 percent lime powder mixed with clay. Their analysis also demonstrates the wide variety in size and weight of surviving adobe construction in San Antonio, generally getting smaller and lighter through time. Adobe as a creolized building material illustrates the hybrid nature of everyday construction on the northern edge of the Spanish colonial landscape.

On the Edge: Log Construction

Texas log building was heavily influenced by Anglo-American arrivals to the region by the first quarter of the nineteenth century.[9] Across the greater San Antonio region, log construction was the earliest building solution for Anglo immigrants but was also used by German-immigrant communities, though fewer such structures survive. Terry Jordan's seminal work,

Texas Log Building: A Folk Architecture, is the authority on log construction in Texas and argues that log construction should be considered Texas' core vernacular building tradition. He identifies specific dates of log buildings in Natchitoches, Louisiana, on the Texas border, as early as 1795. Farther west, the earliest examples in Texas were on the south side of the Red River, but log construction was also introduced by immigrants associated with Stephen F. Austin between 1821 and 1824. By the third quarter of the nineteenth century, log building "became the dominant pioneer building method" in Texas.[10] Jordan surveyed the extent of log building within the eastern and central regions of Texas, with fewer examples farther west and north.[11] Across Texas, oak was the material of choice for log builders.[12] Logs were generally hewn and set into place. Log building in Central Texas took two primary forms: the single room and the dogtrot, an open central passage. The single room is the most common plan associated with outbuildings, such as the surviving quarter at Polley Plantation and the earliest phase of construction at the Sauer-Beckmann house. Jordan also identifies four types of multiroom plans in Texas: the basic double room with a single end chimney, the central hall with end chimneys, the central chimney, and the dogtrot.[13] The dogtrot was an environmental adaptation for the Texas heat, providing a central channel for air to flow through the building.[14] This book describes several surviving dogtrot log buildings, most notably the circa 1850 Joseph Campbell house in Seguin. Although the front and rear porches have been replaced, the general form remains.[15]

The foundations of log buildings in Texas vary from cut stone to timber piers, or they are simply set on the ground surface. Integrity of these foundations on many log buildings is suspect. Because many log and other historic buildings are moved in Texas, the foundation elements often do not survive.[16] In the eastern part of the state, the raised floors of log buildings were often left open, primarily for ventilation. From surviving examples in Greater San Antonio, we can see the diversity of foundation approaches: at Polley Plantation the single-room cabin was historically raised on stone piers, which were replaced by a concrete pad after 1936.[17] At the Sauer-Beckmann house in Stonewall, the original log core was built directly on a finely cut rock pad that extends beyond the footprint of the building to also serve as the floor surface for the front porch. The foundations of surviving log examples from Seguin and Gonzales are less certain as these were moved from their original construction location.[18]

Corner notching is the most distinctive feature of log buildings and often the aspect that researchers map and dissect to understand how a regional tradition changes over time. Terry Jordan has identified the half-dovetail, square, V, and saddle notches as the most common notching technology in Texas.[19] Jordan's exhaustive survey found that half-dovetail corner joints were used in 187 of 537 buildings, or 35 percent. Saddle notching, a cheaper alternative to the more intricate V and dovetail notching, was used most often in outbuildings.[20] In our

Figure 2.2. Saddle notching at Sauer-Beckmann log building. Photo by Brent R. Fortenberry.

Figure 2.3. Chinking at Sauer-Beckmann log building. Photo by Brent R. Fortenberry.

survey of buildings in this book, the Eggleston log building (ca. 1854) utilized half-dovetail connections, while at Polley Plantation, builders took advantage of V notching. Farther west at Sauer-Beckmann is an example of saddle notching (fig. 2.2).

Chinking, or the fill used in gaps between horizontal logs, varies widely in Central Texas, with gaps ranging from four to eight inches wide. Chinking material (or lack thereof) comes in various forms, and its composition varies by region. At Polley Plantation, despite the existing boards being replacements, we can see horizontal boards on the interior surface of the structure. At Sauer-Beckmann, builders used a combination of limestone and clay infill, a product of the heavy limestone bedrock of the Hill Country (fig. 2.3).[21] The chinking solutions for the Gonzales and Seguin buildings are less certain, but historical references indicate that mud and daub was used for infill in a slave quarter in the area around Seguin.[22]

While many of the earliest chimneys attached to log construction were made of "mudcat" or "stick and mud," later log buildings sometimes attached stone chimney stacks for more durable construction, as in the Polley Plantation. This was not necessarily unusual given the use of sandstone in the main plantation house to the west of the quarter. Elsewhere, evidence for original chimneys is unclear after the building move, and at Sauer-Beckmann the evidence for the early chimney does not survive later additions.

Many log buildings were razed and replaced as new building materials and techniques became available, illustrated by the Sauer-Beckmann Living History Farm (see chapter 7). The earliest building was a single-room log cabin with saddle notching. A rock structure with splayed sash windows and plastered interior walls was added to the log core. Later, a rear structure with exposed rock walls was added to create a four-room, double-pile plan. As building technology evolved, to the east, a later Victorian structure exhibited the dogtrot form and balloon framing with industrially produced architectural details.

Hill Country Materials: *Fachwerk* and Limestone

The architecture of the Hill Country is influenced by the geology and geography of the area north and west of San Antonio. Heavily settled by German immigrants in the mid-nineteenth century, the region boasts two major building traditions: *Fachwerk* and the rock house.

Fachwerk

Fachwerk is a form of wood framing that relies on standing-timber joinery with various forms of infill. *Fachwerk* appears throughout areas of North America settled by German immigrants, including Pennsylvania and Wisconsin.[23] In Central Texas, *fachwerk* is most closely associated with the German-immigrant communities of Fredericksburg and surrounding settlements.[24] As is common in vernacular building, materials at hand often prove the most useful for construction. While the framing grammar of *fachwerk* remains the same across North America, the infill is more closely related to place, with surviving examples of brick, stone, or even wattle and daub.[25] For German Texans, limestone rubble was the material of choice because of the ubiquity of stone in the Hill Country; however, in New Braunfels (to the east) brick infill was often used.[26] Ken Hafertepe, the leading authority on Hill Country architecture, maintains that *fachwerk* buildings in Fredericksburg peaked in the 1850s and then had a period of revival in the 1870s (fig. 2.4).[27]

Fachwerk was often finished with an exterior and interior coat of plaster and limewash; however, the framing and infill are now exposed at the Heinrich and Auguste Kammlah house in Fredericksburg (see chapter 7), giving scholars unique insight into the building tradition. The earliest examples of *fachwerk* construction in Fredericksburg show hand-hewn framing members, with later revival examples taking advantage of indus-

Figure 2.4. Exposed *fachwerk* from rural Gillespie County. Photo by Brent R. Fortenberry.

trial mill production, which allowed for slimmer framing elements. This can be seen in the Speier's house, with timber elements as thin as two inches wide.[28]

The Kammlah house, whose construction began between 1853 and 1854, can serve as a bridge to understand the *fachwerk* and rock building traditions of the Hill Country. These two building materials should not be understood in evolutionary terms but rather as products of changing tastes and the changing availability of materials. Originally the core rect-

Figure 2.5. Dovetail joint at Krieger-Henke-Staudt house, Fredericksburg. Photo by Brent R. Fortenberry.

angular structure had three rooms with wooden partitions. The partitions were eventually removed to create a single space for the Kammlah store. The back left room was added by 1858, and by 1865 a rear room was added along with the large kitchen wing, perpendicularly projecting from the core. The *fachwerk* core was originally plastered, but by 1890, the plaster was proving troublesome to maintain and was replaced by clapboard siding.[29]

Various framing approaches were used in Fredericksburg *fachwerk* houses. The Kammlah house used mortise-and-tenon joints almost exclusively, while at the Krieger-Henke-Staudt house, early mortise-and-tenon joints using full dovetail laps were used to reconnect horizontal braces (fig. 2.5).[30]

The Rock House

While the original core of the Kammlah house comprised *fachwerk*, the later additions used limestone-rock construction prepared in various ways. Construction of the rock house, as it has become affectionately known, took place during 1845–95; such houses were generally no taller than one and a half stories and had a saltbox form.[31] These buildings are

Figure 2.6. Outbuilding at the Guenther complex south of Fredericksburg.
Photo by Brent R. Fortenberry.

found in both urban and rural areas across the Hill Country: for example, the John Peter and Marie Tatsch house in the Hill Country (see chapter 7); the Anton Friedrich Wulff house in the King William District in San Antonio (see chapter 5); and outbuildings such as the barn, smokehouse, and store at the Carl Hilmar Guenther complex southwest of Fredericksburg (fig. 2.6).

The earliest documented rock house is the Kiehne house dating from 1850.[32] Roughly cut limestone was more durable and sturdy than *fachwerk*

Figure 2.7. Exposed rock surface on west side of Heinrich and Auguste Kammlah house second kitchen. Photo by Brent R. Fortenberry.

and had the advantage of not requiring much timber (principally for the roof framing). The quality of stone preparation varies from roughly cut limestone to meticulously cut stone blocks. We can see the evolution of this preparation at the Kammlah house. The second-phase kitchen has roughly hewn stones in various shapes and sizes. Contrast this seemingly haphazard size and mortaring of stone to the more well-defined courses at the rear of the building, its latest iteration from the latter decades of the nineteenth century (figs. 2.7 and 2.8). A similar pattern can be seen on Bowie Street in Fredericksburg. The roughly cut Hill Country limestone of the earlier John Peter and Maria Elizabeth Tatsch house (ca. 1858–59) varies widely in size and quality, with little elaboration. Indeed, the added kitchen with an asymmetrical chimney-stack profile epitomizes the vernacular description (lacking precise symmetry in form) of early

Figure 2.8. Rock outbuilding at Kammlah house. Photo by Brent R. Fortenberry.

rock houses in the region. The later William and Lina Bierschwale house (ca. 1888–89) has more regular and finely cut limestone; the building is further elaborated by fashionable quoins on the forward-projecting wing, with projecting sills and jack arches over the windows. Ultimately, these two Bowie Street examples demonstrate the evolution of rock house construction and style as Hill Country builders embraced Victorian building details and plans,[33] which is indicative of the wider adoption of more varied building details and plans in the Hill Country's built environment at the turn of the twentieth century (see chapter 7).

Anglo Influences on Timber Framing

While *fachwerk* is a wholly German-influenced framing method, Anglo-influenced timber framing pervaded the areas east of San Antonio during the nineteenth century. While few examples survive in totality, the Braches house (ca. 1853) near Gonzales (see chapter 8) boasts a near-intact Anglo timber-framing example that demonstrates the transitional state of timber framing in Texas at midcentury.[34] This single-pile house, now devoid of its external chimney stacks, has classic Anglo box framing. Heavier posts frame the fenestration with studs in between at regular intervals. At Braches, the principal wall framing is sash-sawn; however, the walls are covered with split lath and plaster. This mixed-timber preparation shows the growing influence of industrial mills in the region (figs. 2.9 and 2.10). The second-period common rafter roof is made of timbers cut by a circular saw. The rafters are butted and nailed to the false boards and at the ridge. The roughly hewn struts are perhaps original, just renailed to the second-period rafters; they do not retain evidence for lath, inferring that the attic space might never have been inhabited. The roof at Polley Plantation was contemporary with the first-period roof system of the Braches house and likely mirrors its now lost first-period construction. The common rafters there are sash-sawn, as at Braches; the later replacements are circular-sawn. In both cases a ridge board is used for connections at the ridge. Unlike at the Braches house, the joists are set directly into the sandstone walls at the Polley main house. More study is needed to understand the trajectory of *fachwerk* and Anglo-influenced timber framing in Texas. Deeper analysis and recording more surviving examples could lead to insight into the creolization process of framing construction in the region (see chapter 8).

Figure 2.9. Exposed framing on the upper north room at the Charles and Sarah Braches house. Photo by Brent R. Fortenberry.

Figure 2.10. Lath detail at Braches house. Photo by Brent R. Fortenberry.

Limecrete in Seguin

While Hill Country *fachwerk* was a creolized form of Old-World German building traditions, in Seguin the use of limecrete, a mid-nineteenth-century precursor to concrete, illustrates a building tradition that draws from the geology of Guadalupe County and influences from coastal traditional building in South Carolina, Georgia, and Texas. Seguin was so well known for its limecrete construction that in 1854, the *Texas Mercury* proclaimed the town the "Mother of Concrete Cities" (see chapter 8). Frederick Law Olmsted even wrote about the material on his tour of Texas: "A number of buildings in Seguin are made of concrete—thick walls of gravel and lime, raised a foot at a time, between boards, which holds the mass in place until it is solidified. As the materials are dug from the cellar, it is a very cheap mode of construction, is neat in appearance, and is said to be as durable, while protected by a good roof, as stone or brick. One man may erect a house in this way, calling mechanics only to roof and finish."[35]

Limecrete in its basic form is a type of concrete that predates the widespread adoption of Portland cement in North America at the end of the nineteenth and early twentieth centuries. As Sarah Beth Hunter argues in the only major study of the building material to date, limecrete buildings are easily identified by their "thick walls and pebbled surfaces."[36] In surviving examples, limecrete walls are one foot, three inches thick and covered by exterior stucco or interior plaster.[37] Historically, limecrete walls were covered by stucco to protect the load-bearing surface; however, the lack of regular stucco replacement and improper conservation treatment in the twentieth and twenty-first centuries has meant that these once ubiquitous buildings are now in regular decay. By the twentieth century, Seguin boasted more than ninety limecrete buildings. Today, however, only twenty survive.

Most of the oral and secondary histories credit John E. Park with introducing limecrete in Seguin, but its development is complicated. Park was instrumental in commissioning some of the earliest limecrete buildings in Seguin and, not surprisingly, was a great proponent of its technology. Born in the central Georgia town of Eatonton, he might have been exposed to the tabby construction methods of the South Carolina and Georgia Lowcountry. Tabby construction is likely the closest construction cousin of limecrete. A building material prevalent in the coastal regions of South Carolina and Georgia, tabby was used to construct a wide array of structures from the seventeenth century onward.[38] Tabby's distinctive rough texture derives from a mix of sand, lime, oystershell, and water. The tabby mixture was poured into forms and allowed to harden over several days. Tabby construction in Texas, known as shellcrete, was also present on the coast. A few such buildings survive, with notable examples near El Copano and the Fulton mansion near Rockport. Limecrete and tabby walls are formed in a similar manner. But unlike tabby construction, in which oystershell is burned to create quicklime, limecrete uses locally mined gravel as the aggregate.[39] Limecrete was thus a technique influenced by a wider array of vernacular building techniques in North America and more widely known within English-speaking building knowledge networks.[40]

In 1873, Park, still living in Seguin, was granted a patent for the "Improvement in the Manufacture of Cement," proclaiming that his new recipe advanced the uses of hydraulic cement. It includes "any forms of lime, with thirty to forty percent of clay (alumina and silica), five to ten of fine sand (Silex), and five percent soda (carbonate, muriate, or caustic) or potash."[41]

Hunter's scientific analysis of limecrete demonstrates the divergence between limecrete and Park's recipe. The limecrete used in Seguin buildings is not Park's formula with cement binder. The buildings were constructed using local limestone, not that from San Marcos quarries to the north as prescribed in Park's patent.[42] The molecular analysis pointing to the local mining of lime and gravel makes sense within the context of vernacular building practices in Texas and North America, an argument further substantiated by Hunter's discovery of property-specific pits during her fieldwork. It seems that Seguin builders valued the convenience of their local geologic deposits for their vernacular limecrete construction.[43] Thus, limecrete construction was a contributor to Park's patented formula, not a commercialization of the technique; he was aiming to capitalize and more widely spread the construction technique for his own economic benefit.[44]

Two of the more robust buildings in Seguin are constructed with limecrete technology—Sebastopol and the Magnolia Hotel. At the Magnolia Hotel, the use of limecrete was a part of a secondary building phase after the demolition of an earlier log structure sometime after 1874. The limecrete section sits to the south of the now elaborated building, which is three rooms wide and one room deep (chapter 8). The walls are ten inches thick on the front and rear walls and one foot thick on the left and right standing walls. A single chimney stack with a double flue services both primary spaces in the building. At Sebastopol, the walls are more generally uniform in thickness—roughly one foot, one inch. It is not surprising that limecrete was never full adopted beyond the catchment area of Seguin because access to industrially produced timber and brick became much easier at the end of the nineteenth century. The material components and production of limecrete were likely too specific to the area for widespread adoption.

The chapters and building discussions that follow provide the first synthetic examination of everyday buildings in this part of the state and will undoubtedly be a departure point for more detailed and wider studies of Texas' vernacular landscapes.

Notes

1. United States Geological Survey, "Texas Geology," *Pocket Texas Geology*, accessed September 1, 2019, https://txpub.usgs.gov/txgeology/.

2. Gordon Echols, *Early Texas Architecture* (Fort Worth: TCU Press, 2000), 4–5.

3. Wyolah Plantation in Church Hill, Mississippi, north of Natchez, is an outstanding example of this rear exterior arrangement outside Louisiana. See Brent R. Fortenberry, *Architectural Investigations at Wyolah Plantation, Church Hill MS* (College Station: Texas A&M University, 2019).

4. Kathleen Deagan, "Southeastern Spanish," in *America's Architectural Roots: Ethnic Groups That Built America*, ed. Dell Upton (New York: John Wiley and Sons, 1986), 86–91; and Joe S. Graham, "Southwestern Hispanics," in Upton, *America's Architectural Roots*, 92.

5. Graham, "Southwestern Hispanics," 92. Beyond adobe material, Joe Graham identifies other major building elements introduced by Spaniards that include the Roman arch, corbels, wood and stone carving for decoration, dome and vaulted ceilings and roofs (see chapter 4), hooded and bell-shaped fireplaces, and zambullo doors made of hand-split lumber and a pintle hinge.

6. Gerald J. Mulvey and K. Allison Mulvey, "Adobe Brick in San Antonio, Texas," *Journal of the Life and Culture of San Antonio* (2017), https://www.uiw.edu/sanantonio/adobebrick.html.

7. See T. Irwin Sessions, *San Antonio's Historic Architecture* (San Antonio: Arcadia Publishing, 2016), for a discussion of the history of Casa Navarro within the context of San Antonio's historic built environment.

8. See Kenneth Hafertepe, "Restoration, Reconstruction, or Romance? The Case of the Spanish Governor's Palace in Hispanic-Era San Antonio, Texas," *Journal of the Society of Architectural Historians* 67, no. 3 (2008): 412–33; and Kenneth Hafertepe, "The Romantic Rhetoric of the Spanish Governor's Palace, San Antonio, Texas," *Southwestern Historical Quarterly* 107, no. 2 (2003): 238–77.

9. For a wider overview of log construction from regional and national perspectives, see Alison K. Hoagland, *The Log Cabin: An American Icon* (Charlottesville: University of Virginia Press, 2018); Terry G. Jordan, "Alpine, Alemannic, and American Log Architecture," *Annals of the Association of American Geographers* 70, no. 2 (1980): 154–80; Matti Kaups, "Log Architecture in America: European Antecedents in a Finnish Context," *Journal of Cultural Geography* 2, no. 1

(1981): 131–53; Wilbur Zelinsky, "The Log House in Georgia," *Geographical Review* 43, no. 2 (1953): 173–93; Charles F. Gritzner, "Log Housing in New Mexico," *Pioneer America Society Transactions: PAST* 3, no. 2 (1971): 54–62; Rexford Newcomb, "The Architecture of Old Kentucky," *Register of Kentucky State Historical Society* 31, no. 96 (1933): 185–200; and William C. Wonders, "Log Dwellings in Canadian Folk Architecture," *Annals of the Association of American Geographers* 69, no. 2 (1979): 187–207.

10. Terry G. Jordan, *Texas Log Buildings: A Folk Architecture* (Austin: University of Texas Press, 1982), 24.

11. Jordan, 28.

12. Jordan's research found that oak made up the largest share of log material (more than 50 percent), and whole pine was second (25 percent). See Jordan, 76.

13. Jordan, 114–15.

14. Jordan, 120.

15. Echols, *Early Texas Architecture*, 58.

16. Jordan, *Texas Log Buildings*, 32–33. Often, surviving Texas buildings are moved from their original locations to centralized town squares as a part of heritage parks. The log buildings in Seguin and Gonzales and historic structures in Fredericksburg in the Pioneer Museum are examples of this Texas phenomenon.

17. One might expect that the addition of the concrete pad took place when the quarter had a metal stirrup installed to prevent the stone chimney stack from falling away from the building.

18. The Campbell-Hoermann log building was moved from its original location outside Seguin to its current location on Live Oak Street in 1979 as a part of the development of the Seguin Conservation Society.

19. Jordan, *Texas Log Buildings*, 50. Jordan goes on to identify five lesser, or what he calls minor, types of notching that appear in a minority of buildings: a full-dovetail, semi-ilinate, double, half, and half-notch false-corner timbering.

20. Jordan, 51.

21. While Sauer-Beckmann shows little evidence, other surviving log buildings in the Hill Country have hewn stones mortared in place. Jordan, 46–47.

22. Jordan, 43.

23. For an overview of the timber-framing tradition in Europe and its development on the East Coast of North America and Wisconsin, see Mezentsev Sergey Dmitrievich, "Social and Cultural Background of the Emergence and Development of Fachwerk Architecture," *Vestnik MGSU* 10, no. 8 (2015): 7–17; William H. Tishler, "Fachwerk Construction in the German Settlements of Wisconsin," *Winterthur Portfolio* 21, no. 4 (1986): 275–92; and Richard W. E. Perrin, "German Timber Farmhouses in Wisconsin: Terminal Examples of a Thousand-Year Building Tradition," *Wisconsin Magazine of History* 44, no. 3 (1961): 199–202.

24. For a wider overview of German vernacular buildings in Fredericksburg and Texas, see Kenneth Hafertepe, *The Material Culture of German Texans* (College Station: Texas A&M University Press, 2016); Kenneth Hafertepe, *A Guide to the Historic Buildings of Fredericksburg and Gillespie County* (College Station: Texas A&M University Press, 2015); Terry G. Jordan and Terry G. Jordan-Bychkov, *German Seed in Texas Soil: Immigrant Farmers in Nineteenth-Century Texas* (Austin: University of Texas Press, 1966); Ethel Hander Geue, *New Homes in a New Land: German Immigration to Texas, 1847–1861* (Baltimore: Genealogical Publishing, 1982); and Hubert G. H. Wilhelm, "German Settlement and Folk Building Practices in the Hill Country of Texas," *Pioneer America Society Transactions: PAST* 3, no. 2 (1971): 15–24.

25. Hafertepe, *Material Culture of German Texans*, 74.

26. Hafertepe, 88–95.

27. Hafertepe, *Guide to the Historic Buildings of Fredericksburg and Gillespie County*, 5.

28. See Hafertepe, 149–50.

29. Hafertepe, *Material Culture of German Texans*, 103.

30. For a full discussion of the Krieger-Henke-Staudt house, see chapter 7 and Hafertepe, *Material Culture of German Texans*, 96–98.

31. Hafertepe, *Material Culture of German Texans*, 111.

32. Hafertepe, 118.

33. For a detailed history of each of these buildings, see chapter 7. For the wider shift from unelaborated rock houses to those with Victorian details, see Hafertepe, *Material Culture of German Texans*, 111–206.

34. The styles of more highly finished buildings in Central Texas show the architectural influence of trends from the Eastern Seaboard and Gulf Coast. For example, Greek Revival architecture is introduced to Texas by 1838, but unlike in the eastern United States, Greek Revival remains a relevant architectural style through the 1870s.

35. Frederick Law Olmsted, *A Journey through Texas; or, A Saddle-Trip on the Southwestern Frontier; with a Statistical Appendix* (1857; repr., Austin: Bison Books, 2004).

36. Sarah Beth Hunter, "Nineteenth Century Concrete in Seguin, Texas: Construction Materials and Techniques" (master's thesis, University of Texas, Austin, 2014), 4.

37. Hunter, 5.

38. Tabby had likely been used in St. Augustine, Florida, by Spaniards and by native groups on the coast prior to its adoption by English colonial builders.

39. Lauren B. Sickels-Taves, "Understanding Historic Tabby Structures: Their History, Preservation, and Repair," *APT Bulletin* 28 (2–3): 22–29.

40. Sarah Beth Hunter has also identified Orson Fowler and Joseph Goodrich as contemporary proponents of the "gravel wall" building technology, though both were based in the Northeast. Together, the trio indicate a move toward concrete-based building technology in North America during the late nineteenth century.

41. Hunter, "Nineteenth Century Concrete in Seguin, Texas," 11.

42. Hunter, 40–41.

43. Hunter, 8.

44. John E. Park, "Improvement in the Manufacture of Cement," US Patent 138,924, filed April 6, 1871, and issued May 13, 1873.

Vernacular Buildings of San Antonio's Core, La Villita, and the River Walk

Kenneth Hafertepe, Lewis S. Fisher, and Lewis F. Fisher

Comandancia, Presidio of San Antonio de Béxar
(aka Spanish Governor's Palace)
Military Plaza
1749, restored and enlarged 1929–30

The presidio was founded in 1722, roughly one mile west of the earliest mission, San Antonio de Valero, now known as the Alamo (fig. 3.1). The function of the presidio was to protect Indians being Christianized from other, more hostile Indians. In 1726 forty-five soldiers and their commandant lived in the presidio, and another nine guarded the missions. Forty years later, in 1763, seven soldiers, a sergeant, and a captain lived at the presidio, while another fifteen guarded the missions. When San Antonio de Béxar became the capital of Texas in 1772, the garrison increased to eighty men, though twenty of them were stationed on Cibolo Creek between San Antonio and the mission at Goliad. The presidio continued in operation until Texas revolutionary forces defeated General Martín Perfecto de Cos in December 1835. Though briefly back in operation after the fall of the Alamo in March 1836, the garrison surrendered on June 4, 1836.

Although the captain had previously been living in an adobe house, the four front rooms of this building were erected in 1749 to serve as the residence and office of Toribio de Urrutia, captain of Spanish troops in the province of Coahuila y Tejas. Urrutia lived

Figure 3.1. Comandancia, Presidio of San Antonio de Béxar (Spanish Governor's Palace), Plaza de Armas, 1749, restored and enlarged 1929–30. Photo by Kenneth Hafertepe.

here from 1749 until his death in 1763. He was succeeded as captain of the presidio by his nephew, Luis Antonio de Menchaca. While not commanding the presidio, Menchaca was founding a ranching empire; by 1779, he was the wealthiest man in Texas.

His son, José Menchaca, also pursued a military career, joining the presidio in 1771, becoming its lieutenant in 1775, and serving as its commander for nine months in 1780. José Menchaca sold the house in 1804 to Ignacio Perez. During the Mexican Revolution, the troops stationed in San Antonio favored separation from Spain, while the officers remained Royalists; Perez, too, was a Royalist and served as interim governor from July 1816 to March 1817. The house remained in the Perez family for 124 years—during which time it served as a pawn shop, feed store, grocery store, tin shops, and bar.

In 1915 local teacher and preservationist Adina De Zavala recognized that the front rooms dated from the eighteenth century and declared that they were the remains of the Spanish Governor's Palace. Santa Fe, New Mexico, had recently restored its governor's house as a museum, calling it the Palace of the Governors; De Zavala believed that San Antonio should also preserve its Spanish heritage to attract tourists. Moreover, American architects were beginning to appreciate the beauties of the Spanish Colonial style. One of the best examples of the Spanish Colonial Revival can be seen at the Marion Koogler McNay house, now the McNay Art Museum, in the northern part of the city. Ultimately, De Zavala's insistence that the Comandancia was actually the palace, though not literally true, led to its preservation and restoration (fig. 3.2).

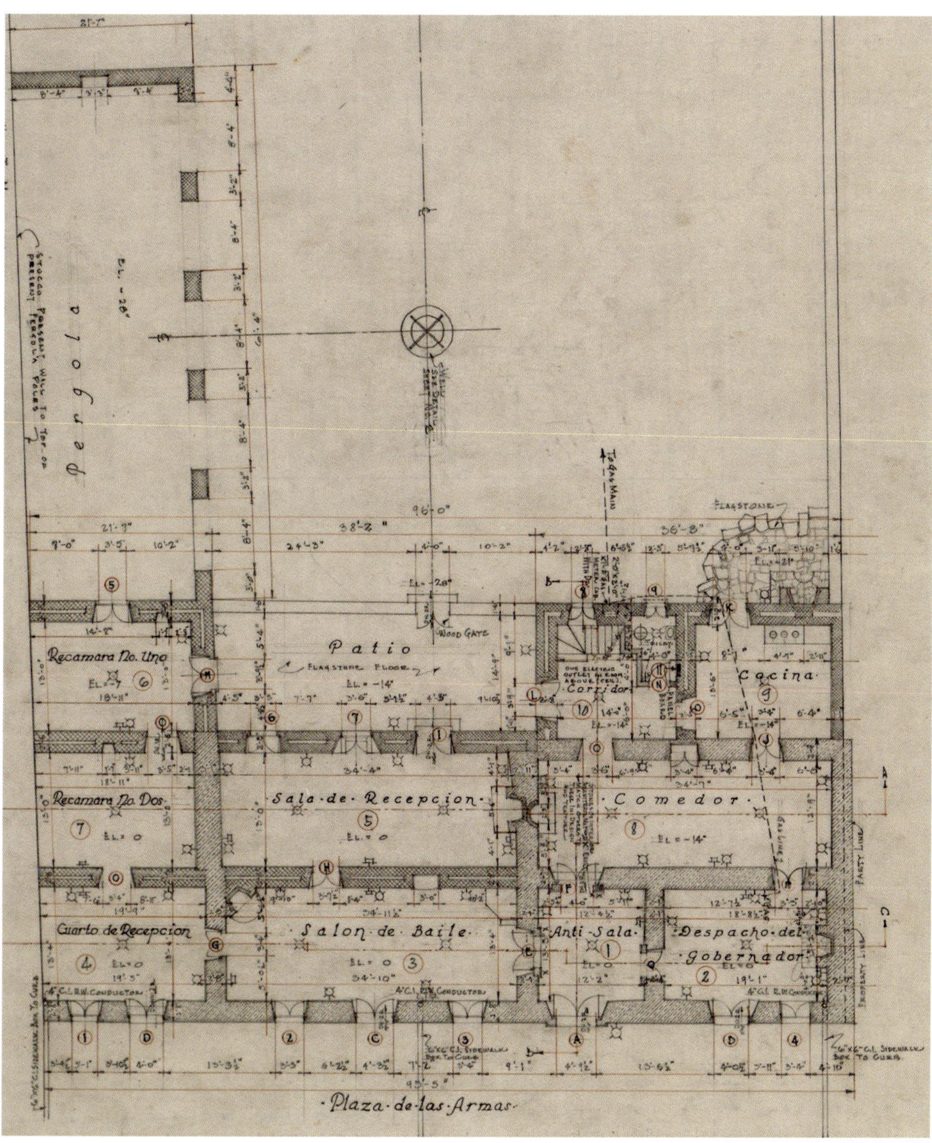

Figure 3.2. Reconstruction of the Spanish Governor's Palace—floor plan showing entire plot. Drawing by Harvey P. Smith. Courtesy of the Alexander Architecture Archive, the University of Texas at Austin.

Figure 3.3. Sala of the Comandancia. Photo by Kenneth Hafertepe.

The building was purchased by the City of San Antonio in 1928 and restored in 1929–30 under the auspices of the San Antonio Conservation Society and other interested groups. The restoration architect, Harvey P. Smith, went on to supervise restoration work at Mission San José and most of the other San Antonio missions. The building had been so altered over the years that the original state of the rear rooms could not be positively determined; the dining room, kitchen, rear *sala* (salon or parlor), bedchambers, and patio were all added based on the presumption that a Spanish governor would expect to have such rooms. The giant vigas that support the roof are actually old telephone poles and in their form alludes more to the Santa Fe style than to any documented Texas examples (fig. 3.3).

Though many rooms have been added to create a more romantic and luxurious atmosphere, the front rooms of this building are largely original and are among the oldest and best preserved in the state of Texas. These rooms were the residence of presidio commanders and of one of the wealthiest men in Spanish Texas. It was among the first historic preservation projects in Texas and one of the earliest history museums in the state.[1]

Casa Navarro
228 South Laredo Street
Circa 1855

Along with Lorenzo De Zavala and Juan Nepomuceno Seguín, José Antonio Navarro was one of the three most prominent Hispanic founding fathers of the Republic of Texas and the only one whose house has survived into the twenty-first century (fig. 3.4). The son of Don Angel Navarro and María Josefa Ruiz, he was also linked to the Veramendi family by his aunt, María Josefa Navarro, who married Don Juan Martín de Veramendi, a prominent second-generation merchant. His wife was Margarita de la Garza, whose family house was in the block across Soledad Street from the Veramendi house. Navarro served at the independence convention of 1836, and he also served in the Congress of the Republic of Texas and in the convention that wrote the constitution of the new state of Texas. From 1846 to 1849 he represented Bexar County in the first three years of the state legislature.

José Antonio and Margarita lived on their ranch but also wanted to have a house in town. At the time of the 1850 US census they were living

Figure 3.4. Casa Navarro, ca. 1855. Photo by Kenneth Hafertepe.

on their ranch in Guadalupe County, known as the San Geronimo Ranch, north of Seguin, and Navarro identified himself as a farmer. Navarro had owned numerous town lots in San Antonio for many years, including his father's old house at West Commerce and Flores Streets. Bexar County tax records show the sale of five lots but a sharp increase in the value of the remaining four lots between 1854 and 1855, the years in which the Navarros built their new house. Confirmation of this can be found in a letter from George Wilkins Kendall to Thomas Falconer in October 1856: "Our old and esteemed friend, Antonio Navarro, spends most of his time in San Antonio, in a new and very tidy house he has constructed. His affairs prosper, he is perfectly happy under the new or American rule, and I can assure you looks just as young as when you last saw him in Mexico."

In 1860 the census taker found him living on another of his ranches, the Atascosa Ranch. However, his twenty-two-year-old daughter, Josefa, was living in San Antonio with her husband, Dan Tobin, and their three children, even though they claimed no real estate or other property; this suggests that they were living in her father's house. In 1870 José Antonio, age seventy-five, was living with them, and he was still the only family member claiming to own property, to the tune of twenty-two thousand dollars, a substantial sum. Clearly Don José built the house as a town house for himself but also allowed his daughter and son-in-law to live there.

The house was on Laredo Street on the western edge of town. The lot backed up to San Pedro Creek, so the household had a relatively predictable source of water. A porch stretched across the front; it had a pitched roof sloping to the front and back. The porch and roof made the Navarro house look like the house of a well-to-do Anglo family, but the patterns of doors and windows said something very different. The sequence window-door-window-door-window announced that there were two rooms, that there was no central passage, and that one of the rooms was larger than the other. This pattern could also be found in some German Texan houses, and it is entirely possible that Navarro hired a German contractor; however, Don Pancho Ruiz, a relative of the Navarro family, had listed his occupation in 1850 as contractor, and it would not be surprising if Navarro turned to him. The fact that the rooms were unequally sized suggests that the larger south room was a *sala*, at least in the mind of José Antonio, and that the smaller north room was a *recamara* (bedchamber). The house also included a free-standing kitchen and a two-story building at the corner of Laredo and Nueva.

In his will of December 1870 Navarro referred to the two-story building as "the rooms on the corner"; it was marked as a dwelling on the 1892 and 1896 Sanborn Fire Insurance Maps and as a store in 1912. Casa Navarro was acquired by the San Antonio Conservation Society in 1959, opened as a historic house museum in 1964, donated to the Texas Parks and Wildlife Commission in 1975, and transferred to the Texas Historical Commission in 2008.[2]

Ursuline Academy (now Southwest School of Art)
300 Augusta Street
1848–51, 1854, 1866, 1867–68, 1872, 1880

Because the Roman Catholic Church could not appoint priests or bishops who were Anglo-Texan or Hispanic Texan without infuriating one important constituency or another, the church decided to send French clerics. The first bishop of Texas was Jean Marie Odin, a native of France who was able to persuade the Congress of the Republic of Texas to return the property of the San Antonio missions to the church and to allow the church to

Figure 3.5. Ursuline Convent, 1878. From Homer Thrall, *Pictorial History of Texas* (San Antonio: n.p., 1878). Courtesy of the Texas Collection, Baylor University.

flourish. This resulted in the founding of St. Mary's School for young men and the Ursuline Academy for young women (fig. 3.5).

Both schools were sited along the San Antonio River but were several blocks apart on opposite sides of the river. The school for young men was immediately to the east of St. Mary's Church, which quickly emerged as the home of Irish Texan Catholics and all others who wished to worship in English. Hispanic Texans, known as Tejanos, continued to worship at San Fernando on Main Plaza, while German Texan Catholics worshipped at St. Joseph's Church, just south of Alamo Plaza and northeast of La Villita, which was the home of many Germans.

The design of St. Mary's Church, St. Mary's School, and the Ursuline Academy for young women have all been attributed to Francois Giraud. A native of Charleston, South Carolina, Giraud and his brother, Theodore, came to Texas with their parents (both natives of France) when their father was appointed French consul. Theodore designed St. Mary's Cathedral in Galveston and then moved to New Orleans, while his brother stayed in San Antonio and eventually rebuilt and remodeled the Church of San Fernando in a Gothic Revival style, which was soon to become the second cathedral in Texas.

The first building for the Ursuline Academy, built between 1848 and 1851, had a foundation of local limestone and wood from the pine forests in Bastrop, northeast of San Antonio and east of Austin. However, a shortage of stone (possibly caused by anti-Catholic sentiment) led to the use of pisé de terre. Jules Poinsard, a native of Paris who offered his services to San Antonians in a wide variety of areas, including contracting, masonry, carpentry, cabinetmaking, printing, gardening, and sculpture, advertised that walls constructed of pisé de terre would cost $1.75 per perch. The building was said to be ready for occupancy in the summer of 1851, though when the Ursuline sisters arrived from New Orleans, they found that much remained to be done before the school could open.

After the opening in November 1851, the school grew quickly, and by 1854 there was a need for a second building. The sisters did not invite Jules Poinsard back and instead hired Frank Schmitt, a native of Germany who often worked with his brother Joseph. This second building, adjoining the original building on the east side, had a small chapel, a kitchen, more classrooms on the first floor, and more dormitory space above. The first building had galleries on the south and north, and the new building also had galleries. Its hipped roof gave it something of the appearance of buildings in Louisiana.

During the Civil War, little changed. By the end of 1865, however, the school was expanding once again. Apparently the Ursulines had been satisfied with the work of Frank Schmitt, who was brought back to erect a two-story stone dormitory to the north of the first building that would engage with Schmitt's earlier dormitory. Not long after this, a large chapel was built on the west side of the complex. The L shape of the interior seems odd today, but as built, the north wing was reserved for the Ursuline sisters, while the space on the west was for visitors. The chapel has also been attributed to Francois Giraud, who was then embarking on his largest project, the dramatic enlargement of the Church of San Fernando. In 1872 and 1880, smaller buildings were erected by the Irish immigrant John Campbell and by Henry Pauly, a second-generation German Texan stonemason.

With the construction of the chapel and dormitory the core of the academy was completed, though other rock buildings and a house for the priests were added before the end of the century. In 1910 a new three-story building was erected on the newly extended Navarro Street. This became the new face of the school for decades. In 1954 the Ursuline Order decided to move to north San Antonio as soon as they could sell the property on the river. This proved to be more difficult than imagined. Most plans for the old site featured the demolition of the old buildings and construction of a luxury hotel or a luxury apartment complex.

Finally, in 1965 the San Antonio Conservation Society purchased part of the property, and a developer, the other. A 1967 five-alarm fire destroyed the 1910 academy building. In the 1970s the Conservation Society acquired most of the property and gradually sold it to the Southwest Craft Center (SCC), now known as the Southwest School of Art. Architect O'Neil Ford, a longtime advocate of preservation of the complex, advised the SCC on the restoration efforts, and after his death in 1982 his firm, Ford, Powell, and Carson, continued to work on the complex. In 1981, the eastern part of the property, which included the 1873 kitchen, laundry room, and music room, was restored to become a private club known as Club Giraud.[3]

San Fernando Cathedral
Main Plaza
1868–73 (incorporating the remains of the 1755 church)

The site of the Church of San Fernando was determined in 1731 when Main Plaza was laid out. The cornerstone for a permanent church was laid in 1738, but there is scant evidence as to whether it was ever completed. Ten years later a master stonemason, Gerónimo de Ibarra, was brought from San Luis Potosí, along with stonecutter Felipe de Santiago. Apparently the previous work was demolished and a larger structure planned. They completed the church in 1755 (figs. 3.6 and 3.7). The church was set back from the plaza to allow for a walled *campo santo*, which served both as a burial ground and as a space for outdoor rituals. The principal door was on the right side of the facade; from the left side rose the single tower. The nave had three buttresses on each side. There were no windows on the side walls, but above the sanctuary was a dome.

Although the church was damaged by flood, fire, and neglect, it continued to stand after the Civil War. In 1868 the diocese (which then had its seat in Galveston) decided to dramatically enlarge and rebuild the structure. The design was from Francois P. Giraud, a native of Charleston, South Carolina, whose parents had immigrated from Bordeaux, France. Francois journeyed to France and studied at the Ecole Centrale des Arts et Manufactures, receiving his degree in 1841. His younger brother, Theodore, was also an architect and designed St. Mary's Cathedral in Galveston (1847–48) as well as a number of Catholic churches in New Orleans, where he settled. Francois Giraud was a civil engineer and architect involved in the design and construction of the Ursuline Convent and School and St. Mary's Church, the parish for the Irish Catholics of San Antonio. He also served as mayor of San Antonio from 1872 to 1875.

Figure 3.6. San Fernando Cathedral, 1893. From Adolph Witteman, *San Antonio Illustrated: In Photo-gravure from Recent Negatives* (New York: Albertype, 1893). Courtesy of the Texas Collection, Baylor University.

Figure 3.7. San Fernando Cathedral, ca. 1936. Photo by Historic American Buildings Survey, Library of Congress.

The nave and principal facade were demolished, leaving only the domed sanctuary of the old church. The new building extended all the way to the plaza, incorporating the space formerly occupied by the *campo santo*. The facade was now consistently Gothic, with twin towers facing the plaza and lancet windows alternating with engaged buttresses on the north and south sides. Inside, octagonal limestone columns rose to support Gothic arches, which divided the nave from the side aisles. Though the columns might raise the expectation that the ceiling would be vaulted, it was always wood framed and shingled. To the west was a barrel vault that made the transition to the domed altar area. In 1872, when the new church was almost finished, the dome collapsed and had to be rebuilt. The church was completed in 1873, although the south tower was not finished until 1902. In 1874 a second diocese was created, and the church was made a cathedral.

Major restoration and remodeling were undertaken in 2003, which cost some fifteen million dollars. This included stabilization of the foundation and restoration of the church and also pushed a movable main altar forward into the nave. At this time a Cathedral Center was built to the south of the cathedral, which contained a museum, gift shop, small cafeteria, and other spaces. In 2011 a new archbishop, Gustavo Garcia-Siller, created a new and fixed main altar closer to the sanctuary.

Two of the oldest artifacts in the cathedral are the pulpit and the baptismal font, both of which are much older than the 1868 building. The pulpit may well be original to the 1755 church, while the baptismal font is said to have been moved from Mission San José. Some remnants of the Victorian-era paint treatment are visible on the south side of the sanctuary.

Richard Cleary has noted that in the antebellum era the Catholic Church decided to use French priests rather than Anglo or Hispanic priests. The church hierarchy was happy to extend this preference for things French to the choice of architects Theodore and Francois Giraud. Cleary has also noted the irony that building over the old church of San Fernando with a French Gothic church ended up obscuring the heritage and the continuing presence of Hispanics in San Antonio and Texas.[4]

San Antonio City Hall
100 Military Plaza
1888–91

In May 1888 a competition was held for a design for a new San Antonio
City Hall (fig. 3.8). At that time the location of the building had not been
decided, but ten architectural firms submitted an entry, perhaps because
the winning design would earn the architect $500, with $250 and $100 for
the second- and third-place entries. The competitors included the firm of
Alfred Giles, James Wahrenberger & Albert Beckmann and the up-and-
coming architect J. Riely Gordon. However, the first prize was awarded to
a relative newcomer, Otto Kramer.

Kramer immigrated to the United States and lived in New York City,
where he was listed in the US census as a thirty-five-year-old architect,
born in Bavaria, whose wife and eight-year-old son were both natives of
Prussia, which suggests that the family immigrated sometime after 1872.
Kramer and family later moved to Cincinnati and St. Louis before moving to Texas.

Figure 3.8. San Antonio City Hall, pre-1927. Courtesy of the Ernest Wilhelm Raba
Collection, Conservation Society of San Antonio.

In June 1888 it was announced that the City Hall would be built on Military Plaza, just west of Main Plaza. The decision was delayed by the question of whether the Laws of the Indies, the basis for the layout of the two plazas in 1731, were still in effect. Mayor Bryan Callaghan apparently solved the problem by marking out the site himself, even though a large public building would obliterate the character of the eighteenth-century Plaza de Armas, not to mention the modern Military Plaza where Hispanic women sold spicy tamales and other Tex-Mex treats to locals and visitors alike. William Corner, who wrote the first guidebook to the city in 1890, enthused that "its location is the best possible one."

The cornerstone was laid on September 16, 1889, and the building was completed in 1891. William Corner, writing while the building was nearing completion, illustrated his book with an architect's perspective view. He characterized the building as "Renaissance," further commenting that "the effect of the four white façades of native lime-stone relieved by pink granite columns is very fine." The *Galveston Daily News*—the paper of record in nineteenth-century Texas—reported that the building would be 80 × 120 feet and would cover 10,000 square feet (in what used to be a plaza). There were to be three stories above a basement, which would house thirty-three rooms on the three main floors, exclusive of halls, closets, and such. In the center was a rotunda—actually octagonal in shape—that rose 125 feet to its apex with a wooden interior frame and an iron-clad roof. The two towers on the north had mansard roofs, while the two on the south had conical roofs. Within the stone walls were partition walls made of brick. In a text that probably echoed the comments of the architect, the *Galveston Daily News* stated that "the building will embrace every requisite apartment to a first-class modern city hall, and will be provided with every comfort and convenience." The *News* further suggested that "the style is modern and original, and when finished the building will be very handsome and withstand any criticism." The phrase "modern and original" probably translated into "Victorian and eclectic."

Kramer went on to compete for the Aransas County Courthouse in Rockport as well as the Bexar County Courthouse in San Antonio but lost both competitions to J. Riely Gordon. He did design the stables for the Pearl Brewery in San Antonio and the Church of the Assumption of the Blessed Virgin Mary in Praha, east of San Antonio, which has been hailed in modern times not as much for its architecture as for its painted decoration. He died in 1896 in his fiftieth year, cutting short the promise of his earlier commissions.

The San Antonio City Hall is still extant but somewhat defaced by a 1927 enlargement designed by Adams & Adams. The footprint did not change—that is, there was no further intrusion into Military Plaza—but a fourth floor was added. This required the removal of the roofs above the towers at each corner. They were replaced with a rather halfhearted nod to the Spanish Colonial Revival, which was less than persuasive.[5]

Bexar County Courthouse
100 Dolorosa Street
1891–97

In 1872, Bexar County purchased the old Masonic Hall to use as the county courthouse. This was a three-story rock building on Soledad Street, just north of Main Plaza and backing up to the San Antonio River. A two-story rock addition at the rear of the building that housed court records was less than a hundred feet from the riverbank, which raised concerns about the potential for flooding. In 1883 the county hired Alfred Giles to remodel and enlarge the building. Among the additions was a new facade: twin towers at the front corners were surmounted by French roofs (mansard roofs) covered in slate. Less than a decade later, the commissioners had given up hope that the building would suffice.

After discussion of a building that would house both city and county governments, the city decided to build a new city hall on Military Plaza. As that building was nearing completion, Bexar County decided to hold a competition for a new courthouse that would cost around three hundred thousand dollars. The winning proposal—as determined by the county commissioners—would receive a prize of one thousand dollars, and the runner-up would receive five hundred dollars. By May 11, 1891, the county had received entries from twenty-six competitors, including architects from Atlanta, Birmingham, Chicago, Columbus (Ohio), Denver, Kansas City, Louisville, Omaha, and St. Louis, as well as entries from Austin, Dallas, San Antonio, and Waco. One of the Kansas City entrants was the well-known firm of Van Brunt & Howe, but the prizes went to San Antonio architects: first prize to Gordon & Laub and second prize to James Wahrenberger. After receiving seven bids from contractors, the Commissioners Court awarded the first phase of the contract to

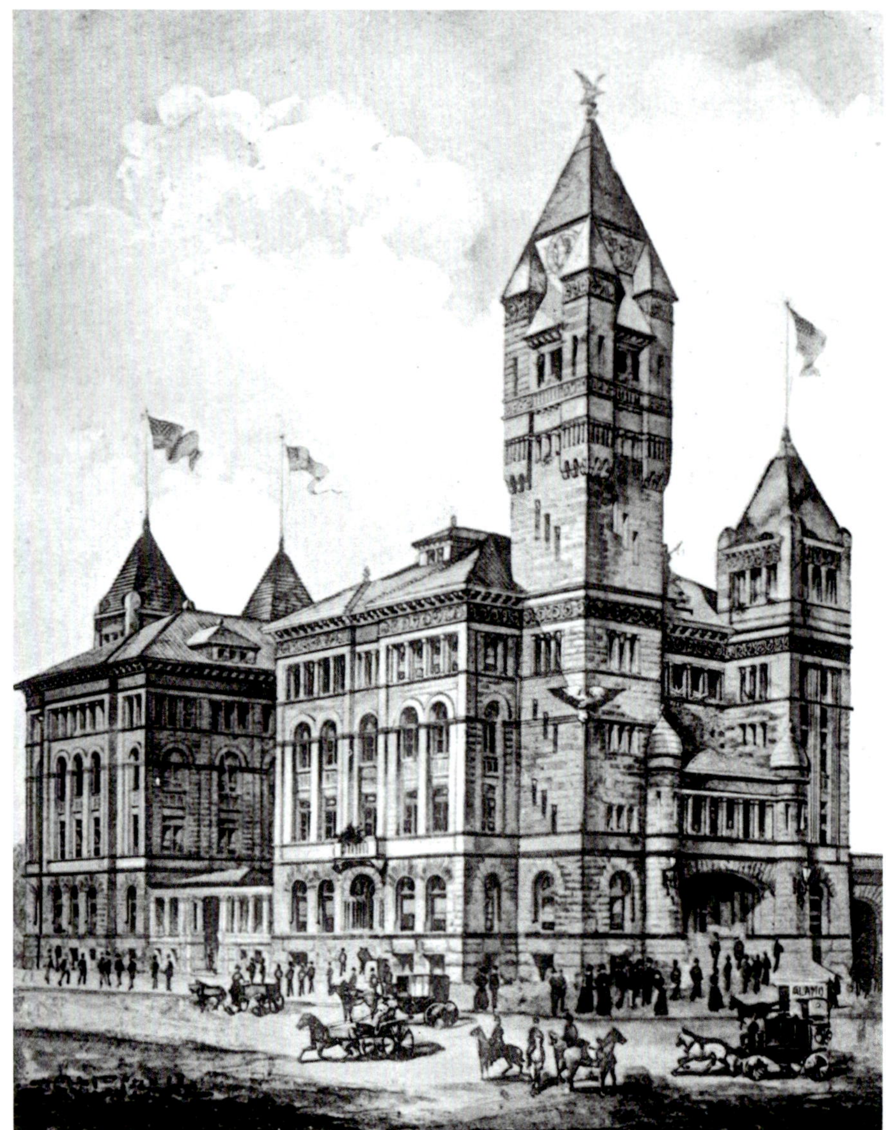

Figure 3.9. Bexar County Courthouse, 1893. Image from A. Wittemann, *San Antonio Illustrated* (New York: Albertype Co., 1893). Courtesy of the Texas Collection, Baylor University.

George Dugan of Kansas City, who promptly formed a partnership with Otto P. Kroeger, an unsuccessful bidder who actually lived and worked in San Antonio.

Gordon & Laub consisted of J. Riely Gordon and D. Ernest Laub. Gordon was born in Winchester, Virginia, in 1863, the son of a civil engineer with the US Army who first came to Texas in 1850 as part of the commission that formally determined the boundary between the United States and

Figure 3.10. Bexar County Courthouse, 1968. Photo by Dewey G. Mears for the Historic American Buildings Survey, Library of Congress.

Mexico. In 1874 the family moved to San Antonio, where the senior Gordon worked as a civil engineer. His son Riely attended public schools, then started working in the offices of local architects, first William K. Dobson and then Jasper N. Preston and Son. Gordon was practicing on his own (and with partners) by 1885. Two years later he was named superintendent on the new Federal Courthouse and Post Office to be built at the north end of Alamo Plaza. This job probably brought him into contact with Ditlev Ernest Laub, who had emigrated from Denmark in 1881. Before the San Antonio competition Gordon had designed courthouses for Aransas County in Rockport and Fayette County in La Grange.

The original Gordon & Laub plan (fig. 3.9) was to use limestone or sandstone as the principal material for the walls—either from the quarries at Brackenridge Park in town or from Muldoon in southwestern Fayette County, about one hundred miles east of San Antonio—which would be contrasted by courses of reddish-brown sandstone and a frieze of terra-cotta. Concerns about the durability of sandstone led to a dramatic change: large blocks of Texas red granite from the Hill Country north of Fredericksburg would form the base, and above this the main walls would be of brownish-red sandstone from Pecos. Both of these choices would have been impossible twenty years earlier, before the railroad began to connect Texas. Pecos is 364 miles west of San Antonio, and the Texas and Pacific Railroad had reached the area only in 1881. The quarries of Burnet and Llano had been connected to Austin by rail in the 1880s to provide the granite for the walls of the Texas State Capitol, and San Antonio was another 80 miles to the southwest.

Though the materials changed during the project, the form of the building remained the same (fig. 3.10). The Bexar Courthouse had one of the most complicated floor plans of any Gordon courthouse, with a U shape allowing a courtyard on the east side. The principal entrance was on the north, facing Main Plaza, but the court entrance was carefully planned as well. Gordon was especially concerned with the issue of ventilating his courthouses in an attempt to deal with the Texas heat, and the design allowed for numerous rooms with windows on two walls.

A pair of projecting towers on the north facade framed the entrance, with a segmental arched and open loggia above it. The east tower is seven stories, and the west tower, five stories; there were originally observation decks on floor five of the west tower and floors five, six, and seven of the east tower. In the middle of the building on the east side, the court entrance had steps rising to the north and south porches, which were roofed over and led to a loggia recessed into the walls of the building, a feature repeated on the three floors above. The court itself was on ground level and had a fountain and a large statue in the center. Originally both front towers (and matching rear towers) had steep pyramidal roofs; during the original construction the west tower received an ovoid or beehive dome, which matched the tops of the engaged two-story towers that framed the entrance.

Laub left the partnership while the building was under way and practiced in Washington, D.C. Gordon went on to design many other Texas courthouses before moving his practice to New York City in 1902. The Bexar County Courthouse was enlarged in 1914 and again in 1926. The latter project included gutting the interior and enclosure of the courtyard of which Gordon had been so proud. Further additions were made in 1963 and 1970.[6]

La Villita
Lewis S. Fisher

Villita was fully developed as a neighborhood by the 1880s. The development is clearly documented in Sanborn Insurance Maps created during the ensuing period. The 1888 map shows a tightly developed neighborhood of stone houses and a few commercial uses. Some of the old houses survived into the early twentieth century, while others were demolished for commercial development. The cycle of commercialization and decline continued until the area was considered a slum.

Maury Maverick Sr. was elected mayor of San Antonio in 1939. Mayor Maverick, a former congressman, had the ear of President Franklin Roosevelt and was determined to use the various employment programs of the Depression era to change the face of San Antonio. With other preservation projects under construction (improvements at the Alamo, reconstruction of Mission San José, and the construction of the River Walk), Maverick was concerned about this dilapidated slum along the river and vowed to restore La Villita. He was able to convince O'Neil Ford to come from North Texas to serve as the architect for the project, but he took personal interest, and some control, over the project.

Ford had taken a trip through South Texas with his uncle Homer Jordan in 1923, visiting Castroville, the Texas Hill Country, and the Rio

Grande Valley. Ford said, "I was astonished by the beauty and simplicity of those early Texas houses. . . . They were real, straight to the point, not copied from anything. They fit the land as naturally as the trees."[7] Ford worked for David Williams from 1926 until 1932. They both had fallen in love with vernacular Texas architecture and wrote articles about its simplicity and solidity. This regional spirit would influence Ford throughout his career.

The first restoration of La Villita included only the northwest quadrant of land presently owned by the City of San Antonio. The area was bounded by Villita, Presa, Nacional, and King Phillip V Streets. The project restored six historic houses, built three new structures, and created a plaza (figs. 3.11 and 3.12).

Besides clearing the accumulation of deteriorated building materials and junked automobiles, the New Deal project put workmen and artists to work, often learning new trades. Donated and salvaged materials were used to stretch the limited funds. A kiln was built and used for firing clay pavers and decorative items such as hand-painted plates. Recycled wall bricks were used as paving materials (with limited success), and marble from bathroom stalls and slate fireplace surrounds were also used as paving.

In the 1960s, the southern part of historic La Villita was included within the boundaries of the Urban Renewal Project created to provide land for HemisFair '68, the world's fair held in San Antonio between April 6 and October 6, 1968. Part of the work included widening both South Alamo Street from Commerce to Durango Street, and Nueva Street from South Alamo to Presa Street. The historic character of both streets was destroyed. Alamo Street went from a narrow street to a seven-lane boulevard with planted medians.

Hundreds of houses on the site of HemisFair '68 were demolished, but one was reconstructed at the corner of King Philip V Street and Nueva in La Villita.[8] The Cirilus Gissi house was of *palisado* construction once common in San Antonio but now very rare. The construction technique consists of setting cedar posts closely together vertically in the ground to form the walls. Small wooden slats were attached to the posts to form a lath to protect the wood and fill the gaps between the posts. The wall was then plastered with an adobe or lime plaster. As a finish, the plaster was coated with a whitewash of lime.

In the early 1970s, Maverick Plaza was created as an outdoor venue for parties, conventions, and other gatherings. The plaza was walled with a

Figure 3.11. Isometric rendering of La Villita restoration, ca. 1939. Image by O'Neil Ford. Writers' Program of the Work Projects Administration in the State of Texas, *Old Villita* (San Antonio: The City of San Antonio, 1939). Courtesy of the Texas Collection, Baylor University.

Figure 3.12. Rendering of La Villita restoration in 1939 publication. Writers' Program of the Work Projects Administration in the State of Texas, *Old Villita* (San Antonio: The City of San Antonio, 1939). Courtesy of the Texas Collection, Baylor University.

limestone fence, just as O'Neil Ford had enclosed Plaza Juarez in 1939.

During the nation's bicentennial, the southwestern corner of La Villita was finally renovated. The Joy Kist Candy Company had occupied three of the buildings. Framed construction tied the buildings together to form a maze of interior spaces. Architect William Parrish was hired to rehabilitate five existing structures and provide compatible landscaping.

From 1980 to 1982, Ford (through his firm Ford, Powell & Carson, in a joint venture with Saldana Williams and Schubert) was again asked to head a significant renewal of the historic area. The author of this section served as project manager.

In ensuing years, the growth of the tourist industry and expansion of the city into the outer suburbs have negatively impacted the economic vitality of La Villita. However, recent revitalization of downtown and the redevelopment of the HemisFair '68 site are contributing to an improved economic outlook for La Villita, which remains a significant preservation district demonstrating the vernacular architecture of San Antonio (fig. 3.13).

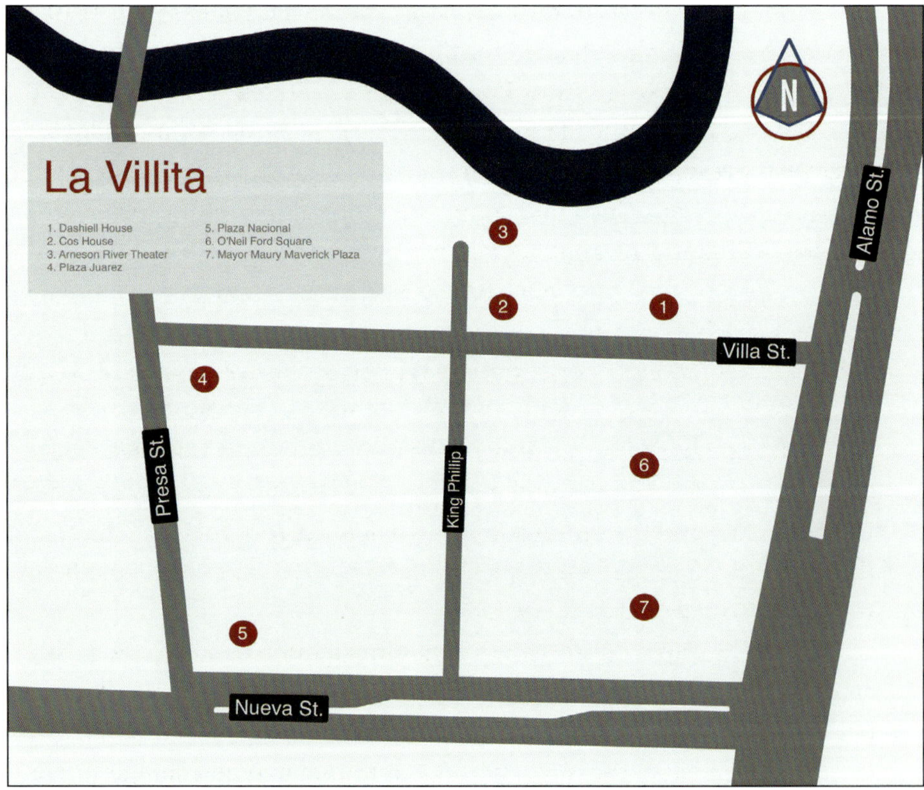

Figure 3.13. Modern map of the extent of La Villita. Image by Brent R. Fortenberry.

Cos House

La Villita

The Cos house is an important historic structure in San Antonio that relates to Texas' fight for independence from Mexico and portrays San Antonio's vernacular architecture. Even though it is an important landmark, the precise history of this house is not known, and the landmark has been modified. According to tradition, within this house the Mexican general Perfecto Cos signed articles of capitulation with the Texian rebels after he was defeated in the Battle of Bejar in December 1835.[9]

The original owner of the house and its date of construction are unknown, but if tradition is correct, the house was built prior to the Texas Revolution. The house is located at the corner of Villita and King Philip V Streets on the south bank of the San Antonio River in La Villita. Historic American Buildings Survey (HABS) drawings indicate that the site extended to the river, where the Arneson River Theatre is now located. It was built abutting the right-of-way of both streets, suggesting the streets were developed before the house was built. Villita Street may have been a pathway between Mission Valero and Villa de San Fernando that led to a ford in the river. Streets in the area were officially laid out around 1810 after a new *cuartel* was planned for this high ground overlooking the town across the river.[10] At this time, Presa and Nueva Streets were laid out and Villita Street straightened to become a proper *calle real*.[11] King Philip V Street was previously known as Womble Alley, named after a woman who ran a boardinghouse in an old adobe building. The street was renamed when La Villita was rehabilitated in 1939 as a way of paying homage to the Spanish king who reigned when San Antonio was founded.

The house is a narrow, three-room rectangular block with a single gable. The two rooms nearest the street intersection are of adobe blocks, while the third room, closest to the river, is of caliche-block construction. Adobe suggests an early, possibly Mexican-era construction date, while caliche blocks were used into the second half of the nineteenth century (fig. 3.14). Beyond the third room are small toilet rooms and a kitchen that were added to the house when it was renovated around 1940. These rooms have since been modified.

The roof is framed of roughly sawn lumber, but the date of the roof is not known. Roof repairs made circa 1982 showed that the roof had previously been of cedar shingles, so at the direction of the Texas Historical Commission, the metal roof was removed and new shingles were installed.

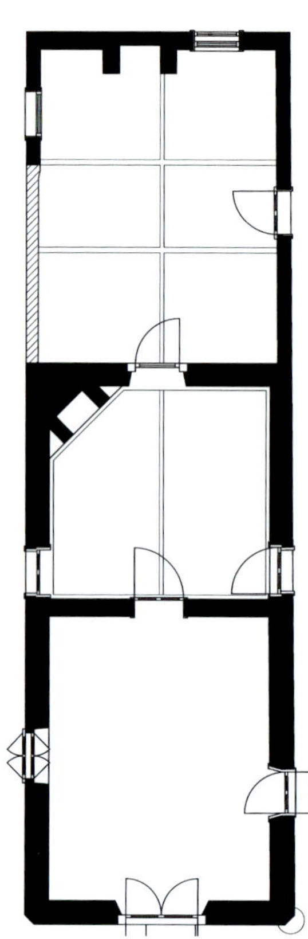

Figure 3.14. Plan of Cos house. Drawing by Hayley M. Field after HABS TX 33 A6.

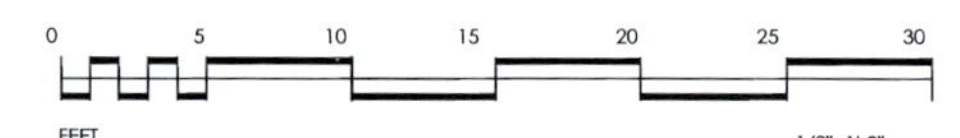

Historic photographs suggest that the house had a pair of French doors facing south to Villita Street. These doors were removed, the opening was made smaller, and the doors were replaced by a wooden casement window. A metal window screen was fabricated that features a copper medallion with a Mexican eagle that was fashioned from an abandoned munition salvaged from a local military base.[12] Along the street on the west side is a door opening to the middle room and a window in the south and north rooms. In a HABS photograph of 1934 showing the east elevation, three single doors opened to the east from each room. These doorways have been widened and double doors installed. A porch has been added to the east elevation, sheltering the new doors.

Dashiell House
511 Villita Street
1856

Jeremiah Yellot Dashiell was born in Baltimore in 1804 and graduated from the University of Baltimore in 1823. He opened a medical practice in

Figure 3.15. Cos house, front elevation. Photo by Kenneth Hafertepe.

Louisville and was one of the nine physicians who founded the Louisville Medical College. In 1846, President James K. Polk appointed him as a paymaster. His position took him to San Antonio in 1849, when he bought this piece of property. He later sent money to his wife and daughter, who were to have the house built. Unfortunately, Dashiell was held responsible for the loss of the military payroll on board a ship that sunk. He was forced to sell the house in 1856 to resolve the debt. He left US military service in 1858 and joined the Confederate army in 1861 as an adjutant general.[13] He lived in San Antonio until he died in 1888 (fig. 3.15).

The house was purchased in 1860 by Augustine Morrisset, who owned it until 1910. The house was heavily damaged by the flood of 1921.[14] The San Antonio Conservation Society purchased it in 1942 and hired architect O'Neil Ford to restore the house,[15] in which he opened his first office in San Antonio.[16] The Conservation Society maintained its offices there from 1953 until 1974, during which time the idea of Preservation Action was conceived during a reception on the grounds of the Dashiell house. The society later used the house for offices for its fund-raising event, "A Night in Old San Antonio." It is presently leased to a restaurant as an events venue.

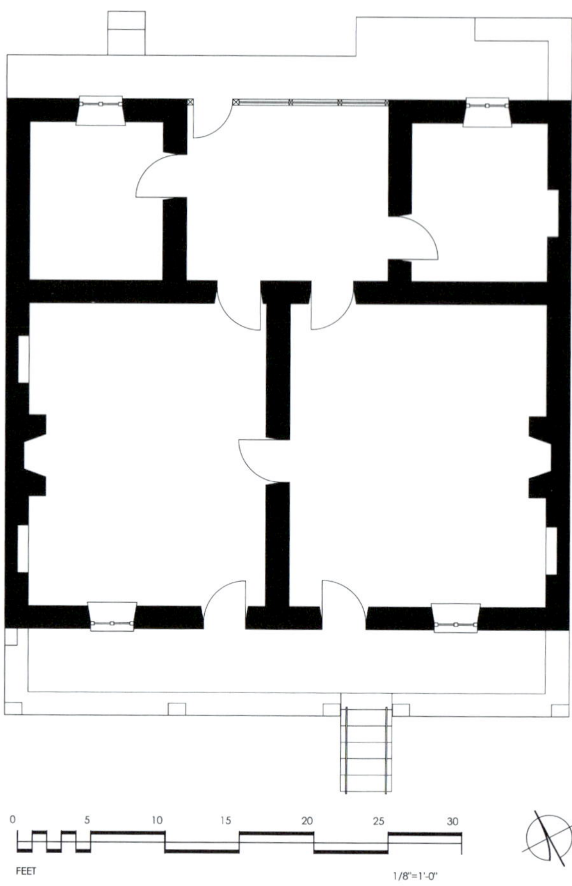

Figure 3.16. Plan of Dashiell house, 1856. Drawing by Hayley M. Field after HABS TX 3169.

The Dashiell house faces Villita Street and backs onto the high bank of the San Antonio River. When it was built, La Villita was in transition from a meager village of small Mexican-era houses to a European-immigrant neighborhood. It must have commanded much attention as the largest house in Villita with a dramatic hipped roof. Early Spanish families of San Antonio often built their houses along the river or creek, but only the Spanish Governor's Palace remains.

The raised cottage is built on a sloping site so that the river side of the building is a full two stories tall. The upper floor has two rooms across the front with three much smaller rooms in back. The center of the rear three rooms is thought to have been a porch recessed under the roof. The two front rooms open into each other with a pair of recessed sliding doors (fig. 3.16).

John H. Kampmann, the most prominent San Antonio builder of his time, constructed the house in 1856 according to a plan he often used. Across Villita Street, the Faville house has a similar plan but is of a single story.

The front porch of the Dashiell house has four bays with an opening centered in each. San Antonio houses of this period often were built without a central hall but with doors opening directly from the front rooms to the porch. In this case the house has four pairs of French doors opening onto the porch. Each door leaf has three glass lights over a flush panel. Each French door is covered with a pair of exterior shutters with louvered blinds above and a single flush panel below.

Arneson River Theatre
San Antonio River Walk
1939

Robert H. H. Hugman envisioned the transformation of the San Antonio River into a charming urban walkway that included European-style shops and businesses. The Arneson River Theatre was a part of Hugman's transformative plan for the River Walk. Although first conceived in 1929, the project was not immediately built. A contentious decade had to pass before ground was broken in 1939. A local improvement district raised $75,000, and Mayor Maury Maverick was able to get $450,000 in funding from the National Youth Administration to fund his vision.[17] Funding was dedicated to the improvement of the riverbank, which the city claimed as public property. The development of the adjacent buildings and entrances off the river had to wait for other business visionaries.

The local utility company owned numerous pieces of property along the river and in the old Villita area, including that where the Arneson Theatre is now located.[18] These were sold to the city for reasonable amounts so that the city could use the land for improvements along the river and in La Villita.[19]

The theater is built into the sloping bank of the river. The terraced seating and the stepped aisles fit nicely into the curve of the river. The stage is located about twenty feet away, across the river. The design of the two buildings that help enclose the theater space reference Hugman's design sense and his romantic taste. The theater is entered from La Villita along King Philip V Street. Patrons pass under a low archway of a building that serves as a concession stand and lighting booth. The stage building has two parts, the limestone backdrop suggestive of a Spanish Mission church and a diminutively scaled house with tiled roof and a dovecote. The sides of the theater are landscaped to provide additional spatial enclosure, which accentuates the romantic feeling of the space.

San Antonio River Walk

Lewis F. Fisher

When Robert H. H. Hugman set out to transform San Antonio's down-town river, he was dealing with a palette that had been evolving for two centuries. A major factor in San Antonio's location in 1718 had been its prospects for an acequia system, a network of irrigation ditches that was soon dug outward from the San Antonio River and served as the city's main water source for more than 150 years. The fifty-mile network was perhaps the most extensive such system within the present-day United States.

The winding course of the narrow, slow-flowing San Antonio River and the convoluted paths of gravity-driven acequias defied placement of an orderly grid pattern of streets and, by the end of the nineteenth century, required two dozen scattered bridges to cross the river. Visitors accustomed to rivers that rushed straight through downtowns were hopelessly confused by San Antonio's twisting river. "You think you have left it behind you," puzzled one, "and there it is before you."

Without the sort of forceful flow that powered mills and factories in river cities elsewhere, San Antonio's riverbanks were not cleared for industrial use but developed in a haphazard fashion. A handful of picturesque small mills sprang up along the banks. They mixed with a smattering of vernacular stone homes looking out above the river, usually a safe twenty feet or so below. Commercial buildings fronting on streets above kept their stone basements sealed against flooding. As development increased the flow of runoff, irrigation walls went up to deflect occasional floodwaters.

By the last quarter of the nineteenth century, arrival of the railroad led to quantum increases in population that outstripped the capabilities of San Antonio's antiquated acequias. Soon artesian wells were serving suburban developments, lowering the water table and the levels of springs feeding the river. Overgrown banks of the now-intermittent stream began to bother citizens who loved their river. In 1904 the street commissioner stepped in to help by doing some tree trimming, only to face ungrateful headlines such as, in the *San Antonio Express*, "Street Commissioner's Men Ruthlessly Lay Axe to Immense Willow Trees That Made the Mill Bridge View Famous." A civic uprising over the desecration led Park Commissioner Ludwig Mahncke to make a fortuitous decision: in the Hill Country he purchased three hundred cypress saplings, which develop deep root structures without disrupting streams. Many survived to become the towering trees that add shade and scale to today's River Walk.

In 1913 a reform city administration adapted a flurry of architects' plans for a beautified river to begin building a river park. The river's flow was channeled by even concrete walls with, on either side, conservative plantings that could survive periodic flooding. In 1919 the city finally hired a major engineering firm, Boston's Metcalf & Eddy, to come up with a comprehensive flood-prevention plan that, contrary to latter-day mythology involving the yet-to-be-founded Conservation Society of San Antonio, did not recommend that the Great Bend be eliminated. Nine months after the report was presented and the city had begun plans to implement it, however, came the September 1921 flood, which inundated downtown, washed away some residential neighborhoods, and caused more than fifty deaths.

Little time was wasted in building Olmos Dam, two miles north of downtown, to block the major source of floodwaters. Next in importance was digging a channel three blocks through the heart of downtown to by-pass the Great Bend during flooding. A dam across the head of the bypass channel was high enough to divert regular flow into the bend but low enough so higher water would drop over the dam into the deep bypass channel and flow on unimpeded.

The Great Bend, thus relieved of threatened devastation from flood-ing, in 1929 attracted the imagination of architect Robert Harvey Harold Hugman, twenty-seven, newly returned to his hometown from New Orleans and believing that San Antonio should capitalize on its Span-ish heritage as New Orleans had on its French origins. He proposed the Shops of Aragon and Romula, a vaguely Spanish-style stage setting involving a narrow street of shops descending from Houston Street and crossing on flagstones into the Great Bend to meet a mix of park-like and commercial development served by Venetian-style gondolas. Hugman's proposal, however, ran afoul of the city's adoption of a master plan by Harland Bartholomew of St. Louis, who believed that those in the hectic downtown would be better served emotionally by being able to gaze from bridge overlooks into the existing quiet, pedestrian-free River Park below.

Bartholomew's plan was rendered moot by the Depression, and Robert Hugman got a job with the Works Progress Administration (WPA). In 1936 hotelier Jack White, eager to improve the unkempt riverbanks past his Plaza Hotel, contacted Hugman and the WPA. White worked out a deal that ultimately achieved municipal and federal WPA funding to replace the old River Park with elements of Hugman's Aragon and Romula. Hugman was hired to plan and oversee the work.

But because of opposition by those upset over elimination of the old River Park's serene features and replacement of its natural setting with fanciful rockwork, Hugman was fired midway through his project. It was too late, however, to undo his key elements. Already completed were the limestone-block channel walls that defined the river's course, not with the sort of previous symmetrical walls that evoked a canal but walls continuing along with a gentle irregular weaving that lent the sense that the banks had been defined by nature and solved the earlier issue of silting by deflecting the flow to prevent buildup of silt.

Sections of concrete walkways appeared as natural flagstones but for the alternating geometric patterns in their designs. These created an ongoing sense of discovery, an anticipation enhanced by upcoming bridges that framed new scenes beyond as they carried streets across the river below. Hugman dealt with one sharp riverside angle by arcing flagstones around it into the stream and gently back so that the River Walk seemed to be floating on the water. Differing styles of street bridges above added eclectic design elements, dating back to three decorative cast-iron bridges installed in the 1890s. In addition to varying designs of stairways down from the street, Hugman designed two narrow stone pedestrian bridges arching the river, one on the northern leg of the Great Bend and the other on the southern, high enough so standing gondoliers could pole their craft beneath.

Existing impediments that could not be removed were incorporated into the design. Underground runoff pipes protruding out to the river were cut back and screened with plantings and rocks. One with a steady discharge was turned into a fountain, its runoff collected into a riverside pool crossed at its edge with separated flagstones, allowing the water to flow between and cascade into the river (fig. 3.17).

Craftsmen features were added. Two signs with wrought-iron letters survive to identify streets above. Passersby have the chance to sit and reflect on occasional heavy cedar benches, which appear only slightly less comfortable than a few high-backed stone benches. A riverside landing or two may still display cedar posts sunk into the river to tie up Venetian gondolas, though such a fleet never materialized. Custom-made lanterns no longer perch on cedar posts, and cedar steps down from one bridge have been replaced with steel.

Figure 3.17. A bare pipe dumping air-conditioning runoff into the San Antonio River was masked by foliage and its runoff diffused into the river between separated flagstones that bend the River Walk's path around a pond. Photo by Lewis F. Fisher.

Despite popularity of the River Walk there was only one long-lasting restaurant, Casa Rio, opened in 1946 and easily reached from the Commerce Street Bridge. Elsewhere, looming above the narrow landscaped ribbon were unsightly backs of buildings fronting on street level above. Danger along the deserted stretches once caused the army to place the River Walk off-limits at night. Without pedestrian traffic there was no incentive for commercial development, and without development there was little incentive for pedestrian traffic.

The impasse was finally breached through the efforts of businessman David Straus. He managed to convince property owners to do simple things such as punch doorways in their riverside basements for picturesque restaurants that, from the aging of interior stone foundations, looked like they had been there forever. Straus's work gained traction with the advent of San Antonio's World's Fair, HemisFair '68, which included an extension of the River Walk into the fairgrounds. Two new hotels opened on to the River Walk, the Hilton Palacio del Rio across from the

Figure 3.18. The original iron conveyor bridge between two towers of the old Lone Star Brewery, now the San Antonio Museum of Art, in background, was relocated and repurposed as a pedestrian bridge when the River Walk's Museum Reach opened in 2009. Image from San Antonio River Authority.

fairgrounds and, farther away on the northern leg, La Mansion del Rio, which included a restored building built in 1867 for a predecessor of St. Mary's University. Large numbers of pedestrians suddenly appeared along the River Walk, and sensitive commercial development soon followed.

To HemisFair's River Walk extension was added another for that rarest of downtown developments, a new shopping mall, oriented around a newly dug lagoon. A later extension beyond passed through an expanded Convention Center. But no expansion exceeded those to the north and the south, as the River Walk quintupled to fifteen miles in length with upgrading of the river's own channel. In 2009 the channel for nearly four miles northward opened as the Museum Reach. Featuring major new public art and enhanced undersides of bridges, the Museum Reach passed the ornate brewery converted into the San Antonio Museum of Art to reach another landmark ex-brewery, the Pearl, centerpiece for a distinctive new development. Soon its banks were being lined with apartment buildings and boutique hotels, and neighborhood renewal was spreading for blocks on either side (fig. 3.18).

To the south, the River Walk had already been improved past the King William neighborhood of Victorian homes. In 2013 a nine-mile stretch of the river on the south opened as the Mission Reach, connecting the four missions within San Antonio Missions National Historical Park. Concrete drainage channels were torn up and replaced with a more natural river channel. Original ecosystems were restored, and in the absence of river-boat service, more than sixteen miles of hike-and-bike trails were built, plus new parks, picnic areas, and public art.

The new River Walk, its three distinct segments regulated with carefully outlined design and zoning controls, now directly supports more than twenty-one thousand jobs and contributes more than three billion dollars annually to San Antonio's economy, as it takes its place in the ranks of the world's great linear parks.

Notes

Material for "San Antonio River Walk" is drawn from Lewis F. Fisher, *American Venice: The Epic Story of San Antonio's River* (San Antonio: Trinity University Press, 2015).

1. The closest analysis of the Comandancia is in two articles by Kenneth Hafertepe: "The Romantic Rhetoric of the Spanish Governor's Palace, San Antonio, Texas," *Southwestern Historical Quarterly* 107, no. 2 (2003): 239–77; and "Restoration, Reconstruction, or Romance? The Case of the Spanish Governor's Palace in Hispanic-Era San Antonio, Texas," *Journal of the Society of Architectural Historians* 67, no. 3 (2008): 412–33. See also Gerald Moorhead, ed., *Buildings of Texas: Central, South and Gulf Coast* (Charlottesville: University of Virginia Press, 2013), 157. Harvey P. Smith's drawings for the reconstruction of the building are at the Alexander Architectural Archives, University of Texas at Austin. Extremely useful are the Sanborn Fire Insurance Maps: 1877, sheet 1; 1885, sheet 8; 1888, sheet 8; 1896, sheet 6; and 1896, sheet 9, Briscoe Center for American History, University of Texas at Austin, and available at http://legacy.lib.utexas.edu/maps/sanborn/s.html.

2. The standard biography is David McDonald, *Jose Antonio Navarro: In Search of the American Dream in Nineteenth-Century Texas* (Denton: Texas State Historical Association, 2010), passim; see also James E. Crisp, "José Antonio Navarro: The Problem of Tejano Powerlessness," in *Tejano Leadership in Mexican and Revolutionary Texas*, ed. Jesús F. de la Teja (College Station: Texas A&M University Press, 2010), 146–68. On the restoration of the house, see Lewis F. Fisher, *Saving San Antonio: The Precarious Preservation of a Heritage* (Lubbock: Texas Tech University Press, 1996), 253–55, 442–43. Primary sources include Bexar County Tax Records, 1842–59, Bexar County Clerk's Office, San Antonio; George Wilkins Kendall to Thomas Falconer, in *Letters and Notes on the Texan Santa Fe Expedition 1841–42*, by Thomas Falconer (New York City: Dauber and Pine Bookshops, 1930), 143–44; US Census for Guadalupe County, 1850, Atascosa County, 1860, and Bexar County, 1860 and 1870; Sanborn Fire Insurance Maps: 1892, sheet 7; 1896, sheet 9; and 1911, vol. 4, sheet 343. The house and adjacent store were documented by the Historic American Buildings Survey (HABS), Library of Congress, HABS TEX,15-SANT, 23- and HABS TEX, 15-SANT, 14-; there are photos and data pages for both but drawings only for the store.

3. Maria Watson Pfeiffer, *School by the River: Ursuline Academy to Southwest School of Art & Craft, 1851–2001* (San Antonio: Maverick Publishing, 2001), 1–55. The

complex is visible on several Sanborn Fire Insurance Maps: 1892, sheet 28; 1896, sheet 60; and 1904, vol. 2, sheet 143.

4. Aspects of the building have been treated in a number of scholarly works: Willard B. Robinson, *Texas Public Buildings of the Nineteenth Century* (Austin: University of Texas Press, 1974), 137, 148; Willard B. Robinson, *Reflections of Faith: Houses of Worship in the Lone Star State* (Waco: Baylor University Press, 1994), 115–16; Pfeiffer, *School by the River*, 7–14; Adán Benavides, "Sacred Space, Profane Reality: The Politics of Building a Church in Eighteenth-Century Texas," *Southwestern Historical Quarterly* 107, no. 1 (2003): 1–30; Richard Cleary, "Texas Gothic, French Accent: The Architecture of the Roman Catholic Church in Antebellum Texas," *Journal of the Society of Architectural Historians* 66, no. 1 (2007): 60–83, especially 77–79; Ann Graham Gaines, "San Fernando Cathedral," *Handbook of Texas Online*, accessed August 11, 2019, http://www.tshaonline.org/handbook/online/articles/ivs01; for more data on the building, see Sanborn Fire Insurance Maps: 1877, sheet 2; 1885, sheet 7; 1896, sheet 11; and 1904, vol. 1, sheet 6.

5. Robinson, *Texas Public Buildings of the Nineteenth Century*, 192–93; and Willard B. Robinson, *The People's Architecture: Texas Courthouses, Jails and Municipal Buildings* (Austin: Texas State Historical Association, 1983), 143. Useful information can be found in Chris Meister, *James Riely Gordon: His Courthouses and Other Public Architecture* (Lubbock: Texas Tech University Press, 2011), 24–25, 283. For primary material, see Sanborn Fire Insurance Maps: 1888, sheet 8; 1892, sheet 6; 1896, sheet 9; and 1904, vol. 1, sheet 6; *Leslie's Illustrated Weekly*, 2nd Texas ed., October 4, 1890, 9; William Corner, *San Antonio de Bexar: A Guide and History* (San Antonio: Bainbridge and Corner, 1890), 39, 129; For obituaries of Otto Kramer, see *Galveston Daily News*, April 15, 1896, 6; and *Architecture and Building* (New York), May 2, 1896, 215.

6. The standard source on Gordon and the Bexar County Courthouse is Meister, *James Riely Gordon*, 54–75, 283–84. For earlier information on the building, see Sanborn Fire Insurance Maps: 1877, sheet 2 (old courthouse); 1885, sheet 7; 1888, sheet 7; 1892, sheet 9 (Giles remodel); 1896, sheet 12 ("old courthouse") and sheet 11 ("New County Courthouse—fireproof construction"); and 1904, vol. 1, sheet 6. See also *San Antonio Daily Express*, May 19, 1891, September 16, 1894, and October 4, 1896; and *American Architect and Building News* 61 (September 10, 1898). In 1968 the building was recorded by HABS.

7. David Dillon, *The Architecture of O'Neil Ford: Celebrating Place* (Austin: University of Texas Press, 1999), 11.

8. Dedication plaque located on the house, 1969.

9. Historic marble plaque on the house, 1917.

10. James E. Ivey, "The Lost Cuartel of La Villita in Colonial San Antonio, Texas," 23, unpublished manuscript, collection of Lewis S. Fisher.

11. Ivey, 27.

12. O'Neil Ford, conversation with the author, ca. 1981.

13. Maggie Valentine, *John H. Kampmann, Master Builder: San Antonio's German Influence in the 19th Century* (New York: Beaufort Books, 2014), 51.

14. A. M. W. Pfeiffer, Dashiell house, historic marker at house, City of San Antonio.

15. Dillon, *Architecture of O'Neil Ford*, 22.

16. Dillon, 54.

17. Fisher, *Saving San Antonio*, 194.

18. "Cos House Site Plan," Historic American Buildings Survey, Library of Congress, 1936.

19. Maury Maverick, La Villita Ordinance, City of San Antonio, City Clerk's files, 1939.

The San Antonio Missions

Paul Ringenbach, with contributions from Kenneth Hafertepe

Beginning in the fifteenth century, a driving force for Spain's worldwide exploration was its desire for gold and silver. In South Texas, however, these precious metals did not exist naturally, blunting Spain's interest there. The real treasure turned out to be the pure and plentiful water that made it possible for the Franciscans to colonize the northern frontier of the Spanish Empire in Texas.

Even though the power of Spain was already in serious decline at the dawn of the eighteenth century, the Crown wanted to protect its assets in Texas and New Mexico. In the 1690s, the main perceived threat was the French, who had moved into the Mississippi River basin. To keep any westward movement by them at bay, the Spanish Crown supported establishment of missions in East Texas in partnership with the Roman Catholic Church. The prevailing thought was that the missionaries could convert the indigenous peoples there and turn them into loyal Spanish subjects. Formed into communities with the missions at the core, these new citizens could serve as a bulwark against the French interlopers.

The need to support the East Texas missions resulted directly in the founding of San Antonio. These missions were never successful, failing to maintain a foothold. One of the main reasons was the long distance from Mexico. Missionaries, soldiers, and settlers were in general agreement that a way stop on the route needed to be established, and the San Antonio River basin soon became the obvious choice. On the Feast of Saint Anthony in 1691, the governor of Coahuila and Texas, accompanied by Father Damián Massanet, had crossed a river that Massanet named "San Antonio de Padua" in honor of the saint. Subsequent expeditions confirmed the efficacy of the San Antonio River basin as a potential mission location. Besides the pure water, the presence of friendly indigenous peoples was positive. These peoples were hunter-gatherers, later known collectively as Coahuiltecans. On May 1, 1718, Father Antonio Olivares founded Mission San Antonio de Valero, later to become famed as the Alamo.

Over the next thirteen years, four more missions found their way to the San Antonio River basin. In 1720, Father Anthony Margil de Jesus received permission to establish Mission San José, just south of Mission

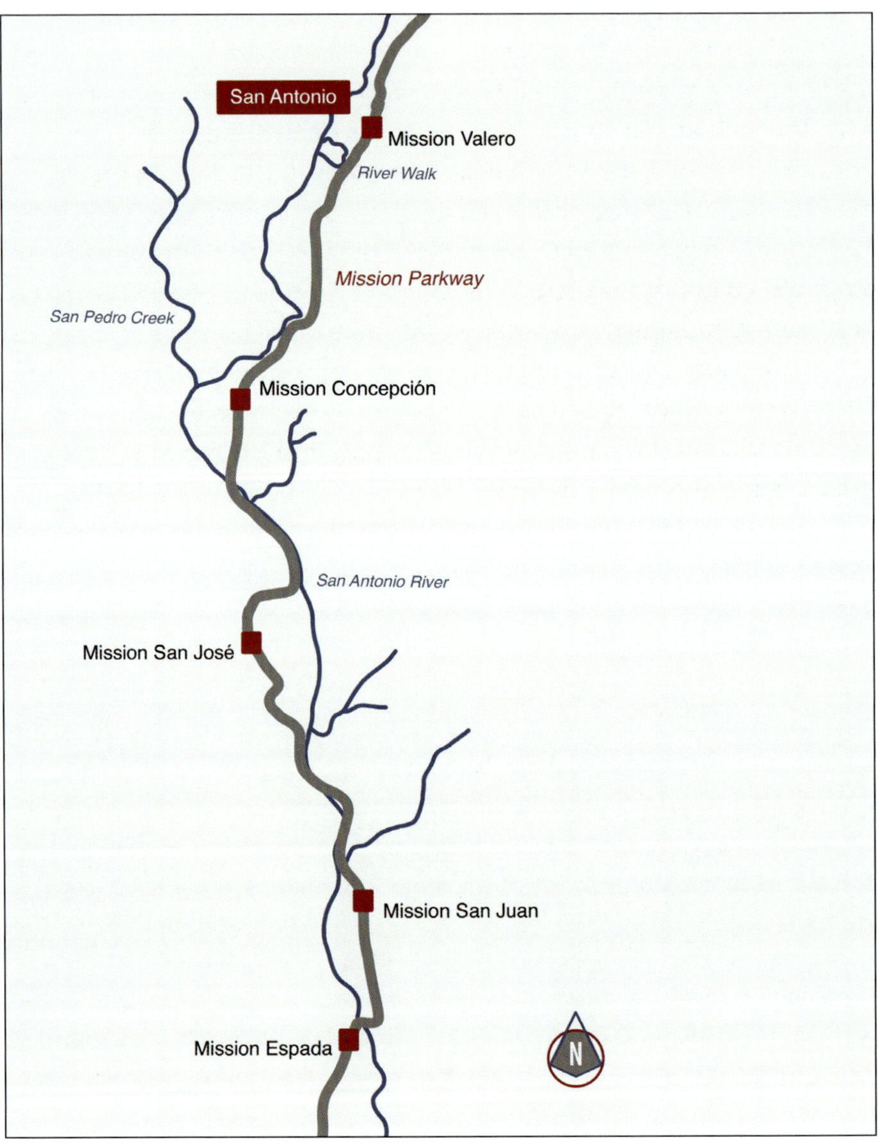

Figure 4.1. Map of San Antonio missions. Image by Brent R. Fortenberry.

Valero. In 1731, three more East Texas missions requested permission to move following the Crown's closure of the presidio that had provided protection to them. The Franciscans established Missions Concepción, San Juan, and Espada along the San Antonio River (fig. 4.1).

Although the Laws of the Indies specified that missions should be at least one day's horseback ride apart, these five were situated along a 7.7-mile stretch of the river. Each of the missions was independent with the goal of becoming self-sustaining. Although the five mission churches differed in appearance, they were all fashioned after the Benedictine Friary Plan, including a *convento* attached to the church. The *convento* housed the missionaries, soldiers, and technical experts. The missions progressed from temporary buildings to limestone structures fashioned out of more than one million metric tons of stone: dug, shaped, transported, and put in place by the indigenous residents. Weir dams shunted the San Antonio River waters into fifty miles of hand-dug acequias (ditches) where gravity flow carried the water to the missions and their more than fifteen hundred acres of farm fields. Other structures included granaries to store produce and buildings for workshops for such things as weaving. Because of raids by Lipan Apaches and Comanches, mission residents constructed fortified stone walls around each of the missions with water wells located inside to protect the residents' water supply in the event of an attack. Each mission also owned a distant ranch capable of hosting mixed herds of four thousand to eight thousand free-ranging cattle, horses, sheep, and goats (fig. 4.2).

Figure 4.2. *Mapa del Presidio de San Antonio de Bexar* (detail), by Luis Antonio Menchaca, March 1764. Courtesy of the John Carter Brown Library, Brown University, Providence, RI.

The Laws of the Indies specified secularization for all missions after ten years. For many reasons, secularization of the San Antonio missions did not occur for decades. The formal process began at Mission Valero in 1793, the other four only partially in 1794 while officials parceled out lands and livestock to remaining mission residents. In 1836, Texas seized all the missions. After a survey found the missions in a dilapidated state, Texas turned the four southerly missions over to the Catholic Church in 1841.

At the turn of the twentieth century, the citizens of San Antonio showed renewed interest in the missions. The Daughters of the Republic of Texas worked with the state to save Mission Valero from commercial development. The group managed the Alamo until 2010, when the state assumed management responsibility. The Conservation Society of San Antonio focused on the four southerly missions. It purchased the granary doors in 1924, followed by the granary and then the lands surrounding the Espada aqueduct. In 1983, the San Antonio Missions National Historical Park opened, including the four southerly missions and Rancho de las Cabras. The Archdiocese of San Antonio retained control and responsibility for the mission churches—all of which continued as active Roman Catholic parishes. A friends group, Mission Heritage Partners, was created in 1984 to supplement the appropriated funds for the park. Las Misiones, a nonprofit organization created to raise funds for the maintenance, preservation, and restoration of the church buildings, successfully raised $15.5 million in 2020. In July 2015, the World Heritage Committee of UNESCO added the San Antonio Missions as the first World Heritage Site in Texas and the twenty-third in the United States.[1]

Mission San Antonio de Valero

The city of San Antonio begins with Mission San Antonio de Valero. Without it, there is no presidio, no other missions, no villa de San Fernando de Béxar—that is, the core of the modern city. The mission and its ground have served not only as an institution for attempting to convert native peoples to Christianity but also as a military installation first for the Spanish army, then the Mexican army, the Texian army, the US Army, the Confederate army, and then the US Army again. Meanwhile, the plaza in front the church and the *convento* became public space, known as Alamo Plaza. After the US Army built Fort Sam Houston, the old church and *convento* declined into retail, but in the early twentieth century they were saved and converted into a shrine to the men who died for Texas independence in 1836. The church and its surroundings remain an icon of San Antonio, but also a lightning rod that still threatens to spark the flames of controversy (figs. 4.3–4.5).

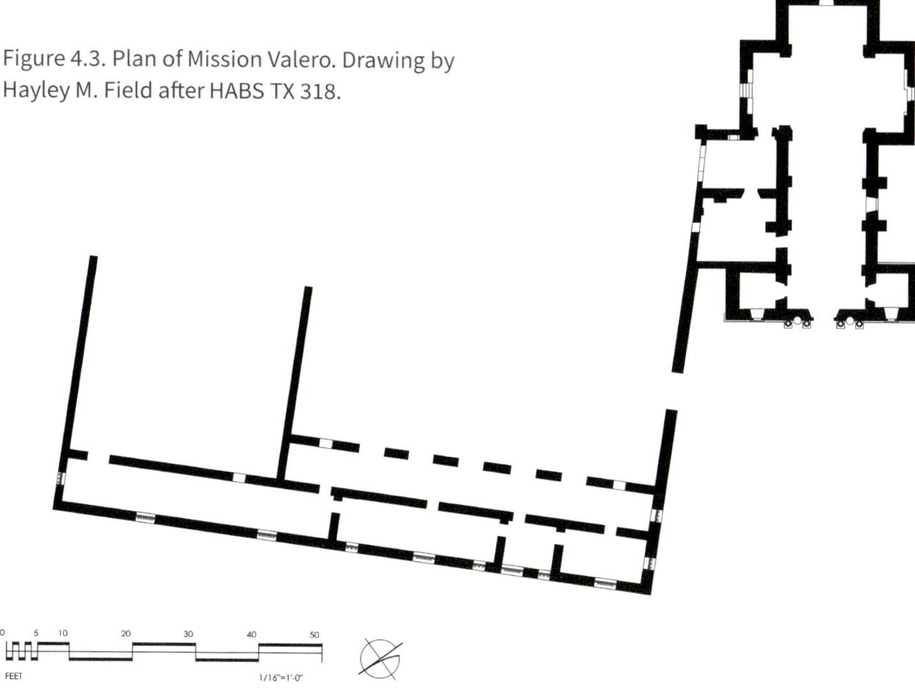

Figure 4.3. Plan of Mission Valero. Drawing by Hayley M. Field after HABS TX 318.

Figure 4.4. San Antonio de Valero, post-1850. Image by Conservation Society of San Antonio.

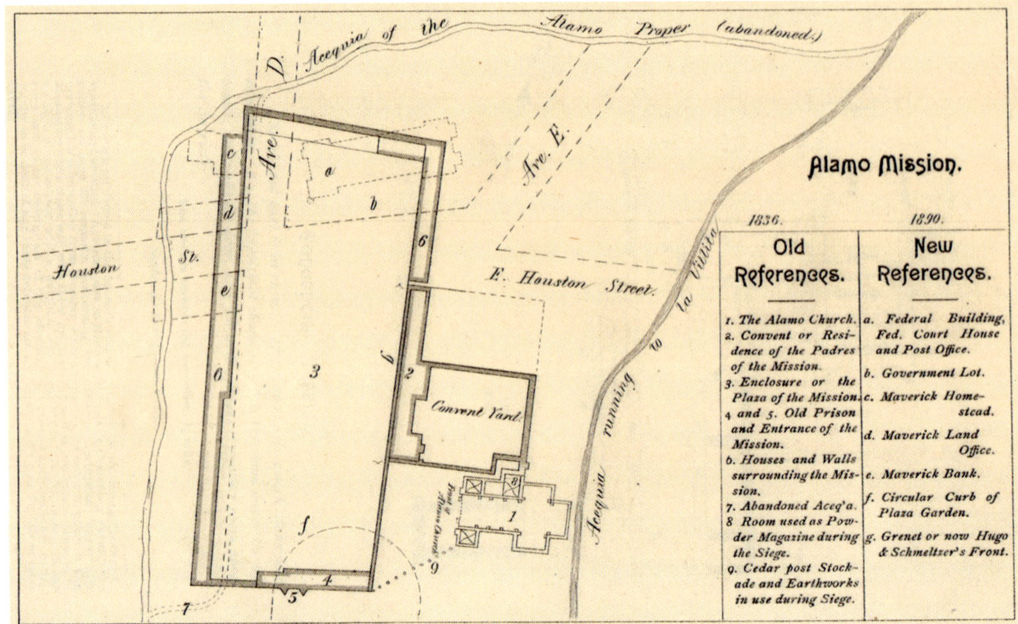

Figure 4.5. Plan of San Antonio de Valero, 1890. Site plan from William Corner, *San Antonio de Bexar: A Guide and History* (San Antonio: Bainbridge and Corner, 1890), after p. 16.

To a modern visitor, it is challenging to understand the physical form of the mission. The modern tourist attraction known as the Alamo includes beautiful gardens to the east of the church, which were not part of the mission compound at all. And in front of the church and *convento* is Alamo Plaza, which was once the plaza of the mission. However, the mission plaza extended into Alamo Street, and the nineteenth- and early twentieth-century commercial buildings on the west side of Alamo Street stand on space once occupied by the quarters for natives. This row of houses extended across Houston Street on both sides of Alamo Street, which includes the site of the US Courthouse north of the *convento* (figs. 4.6 and 4.7). The four rooms of the convento itself, built between 1724 and 1727, have withstood the ravages of time and may well have the oldest walls in San Antonio.[2]

Mission San Antonio de Valero was founded in 1718, but at a site to the northwest of the present location on the west side of the river. That site proved inadequate, as did a second, and the mission moved to its present location in 1724. A one-story stone *convento* and a temporary adobe church were quickly erected; a stone church was begun in 1744, but the roof collapsed in 1756. This led to the decision to start a new

Figure 4.6. San Antonio de Valero, facade of the church. Photo by Kenneth Hafertepe.

Figure 4.7. San Antonio de Valero, portal of the church. Photo by Kenneth Hafertepe.

church building, which was to have a cruciform plan with twin towers and a dome over the crossing. A visitor to the Alamo today will struggle to imagine the planned building, as the facade would be 50 percent taller than the present building. However, a visitor blessed with tunnel vision can focus on the two niches flanking the main door and the matching niches above and see the portal of the anticipated building. One must imagine statues of Saint Francis and Saint Dominic in the first-floor niches—this pair of saints also made an appearance on the facade of Mission San José some twenty years later. However, the careful observer can notice that the keystone of the arch above the double doors is original, with an intertwined "AVMR" for "Ave Maria," that is, "Hail Mary," and with the date 1758 carved beneath it.

The interior can seem a disappointment, given that the church has a later roof that is a distant approximation of the original anticipated barrel vault. However, there are several things worth noting. First, the floor plan is intact to the eighteenth century, with a cruciform plan and small rooms at the base of what would have been a pair of towers, in the manner of Missions Concepción and San José. Second, there are rooms to the east of the north tower room that were planned as a sacristy but in the short term were used as a temporary church. When Father Juan Agustín Morfi visited in 1778, he noted that the temporary rooms were small, "but very tidy and neat."[3] Finally, recent paint analysis has uncovered ample evidence of paint treatment both in the sacristy and in the main body of the church.

San Antonio de Valero was the first of the missions to be secularized in 1793. By 1802 Spanish troops were quartered there: the Second Flying Company of San Carlos de Parras del Alamo. After Mexico won its independence from Spain, the Alamo remained a military post but answered to Mexico City rather than Madrid. When in December 1835 Texian revolutionaries defeated Mexican troops under General Martín Perfecto de Cos, the Mexican army retreated from the city and the Texians occupied the Alamo. Sam Houston, general of the Texian forces, realized the vulnerability of the position and ordered William Barrett Travis to destroy the Alamo and abandon the city. Travis refused and fortified the Alamo. When General Cos returned, accompanied by General Antonio López de Santa Anna, a thirteen-day siege ensued. Because Santa Anna did not recognize the Texians as soldiers of an established country, he overran the fortified mission and killed every man inside, save the enslaved servant of Travis, named Joe, and Susannah Dickinson and her daughter Angelina.

After ten years as an independent republic, Texas consented to join the United States. The US Army was welcomed into San Antonio, as the troops were expected to provide protection against hostile natives. The army quickly created Fort San Antonio on the grounds of the Alamo. As part of that arrangement, they took control of the roofless ruins of a mission church that had been the setting of a Pyrrhic victory less than two decades before. When the army occupied the old mission, it awakened a sleeping giant, the Roman Catholic Church. Bishop Jean Marie Odin filed suit against the City of San Antonio, claiming that ownership still rested with the church. Ultimately, the church prevailed in court. The result was that the army paid rent not to the city but to the church, an arrangement that lasted until 1878.

There was some sentiment within the army command to just demolish the walls of the old church, but Major E. B. Babbitt ordered that carpenters should roof over what was there. As a result the north and south walls were leveled up and a frame roof constructed over it. This roof was hipped at the east end, but on the west end it butted up against open space where the upper part of the facade would have been. This meant that the space was not enclosed. The US Army traveled with carpenters but not with stonemasons; as a result, Babbitt turned to a local stonemason, a native of Germany named Johann Fries. The actual source of the design is unclear; there were no surviving drawings of the original building, but the point was to enclose the structure for its present use. The result was a curvilinear parapet, not drastically different from Spanish Colonial prototypes but imitating none. Created out of necessity in 1849, it became an icon for all time, a form recognized by all Texans even if they have no idea of the complex forces that interacted at its creation.

The next crisis occurred in 1877, when the US Army moved to its new post north of town, which initially retained the name Fort San Antonio but which eventually became Fort Sam Houston. (This was a none-too-subtle poke at former Confederates, as Sam Houston had opposed secession and had been deposed as governor as a result.) The Alamo *convento* was sold to Honoré Grenet, a wholesale grocer who lived just behind the Alamo grounds. The church was leased to Grenet, but ownership remained with the Catholic Church. Grenet created a battlemented elaboration of the *convento*, all but obscuring the remaining historic fabric. Later owners Hugo & Schmeltzer Mercantile Co. retained these dubious additions. In 1883 the State of Texas purchased the remnants of the church building.

The ownership and significance of the *convento* became a hotly contested issue. In the 1890s Adina De Zavala, granddaughter of Lorenzo De Zavala, the first vice president of the Republic of Texas, made the case that the *convento* had been not only an integral part of the mission but also a crucial scene of battle in 1836. As a founding member of the Daughters of the Republic of Texas (DRT) she advocated for preservation based not on aesthetics but on historical significance. She recruited Clara Driscoll to join the DRT and its battle to preserve the Alamo, only to find that Driscoll favored the aesthetic rather than the historic rationale for preservation. Ultimately, Driscoll prevailed and De Zavala left the DRT, only to find new projects with the supposed Spanish Governor's Palace and the supposed Cos house in La Villita. In 1905 the *convento* was acquired by the State of Texas, and the entire complex was placed in the care of the DRT. The Driscoll faction denied that the *convento* dated to the eighteenth century and in 1913 removed the upper floor, leaving only the roofless ruins of the ground floor. Perhaps the most important change to the church in the early twentieth century was the installation in 1921 of a new concrete roof in the form of a barrel vault.

At the Alamo the aesthetic vision of Driscoll and her allies managed to erase changes that had happened to the neighborhood since 1836. Many German immigrants had settled in La Villita and the neighborhood south of the Alamo. On Crockett Street just south of the Alamo grounds was the home of Wilhelm Carl August Thielepape, an engineer, photographer, painter, composer, singer, and, after the Civil War, the first German Texan mayor of San Antonio. The Thielepape house was a good example of a typical German Texan rock house, but it was demolished to make way for an enlarged DRT library. Immediately to the east of the church was the substantial two-story rock house of John M. Carolan, a native of Ireland who became district clerk of Bexar County. Although Rena Maverick Green of the Conservation Society tried to persuade Clara Driscoll, this old rock house was also demolished in the name of beauty.

Also in the 1930s the New Deal made its mark on the Alamo grounds, as did the 1836 celebration of the centennial of Texas independence from Mexico. Federal funds allowed for the creation of a museum to the northwest of the church. Local architect Henry T. Phelps designed a chapel-like building that has often been confused for an actual colonial building. In later years the function of the building shifted from museum to gift shop. Meanwhile, on Alamo Plaza the Italo-Texan sculptor Pompeo Coppini won the commission to sculpt a cenotaph to the heroes of the Alamo, which he called *The Spirit of Sacrifice*. Though commissioned in 1936, it was not dedicated until 1940. In 2019 plans were afoot to move the monument out of Alamo Plaza as part of an attempt to create a new version of what the original plaza looked like.

In recent decades the DRT attempted to come to grips with modernity, but this has proven to be too little too late. Although the remnants of the *convento* were restored to create a museum for HemisFair in 1968, and although the DRT funded paint analysis in recent years, in 2015 control of the Alamo was moved to the General Land Office, a state agency. Soon thereafter the Alamo and the other missions were named a UNESCO World Heritage Site. The General Land Office has moved forward with plans that would close Alamo Street to give some sense of the original plaza. It remains to be seen whether subtraction from the existing historical record will result in a better understanding of the Alamo and the many phases of its history.[4]

Mission Concepción

The church at Mission Concepción is the most intact of the San Antonio missions and the only one that has its original roof. The present building was under construction by 1745 and was dedicated on December 8, 1755. The walls of tufa—a type of freshwater limestone—were originally covered with lime plaster and given a geometrical, multicolored paint treatment. The carving around the entrance is all original to the mid-eighteenth century. The church is cruciform in plan; the roof has a barrel vault, with a forty-four-foot high dome over the crossing. The earth tones of the interior are based on paint analysis. A small portion of the original paint has been exposed on the north wall near the crossing. The baptistry at the base of the south tower has original paint on the east wall. Set into the south wall of this room is an early (if not original) carved stone baptismal font, above which is an arch of Spanish Colonial brick. The room at the base of the north tower has additional painted treatments, as does the sacristy (figs. 4.8 and 4.9).

The several rooms attached to the south tower formed the *convento*, or residence of the priests. These spaces are also barrel-vaulted and were decorated with paint. In one of the larger rooms, known as the library, there is painted decoration around the doors and also in the center of the ceiling, where the sun is given a human face with a mustache. On the south wall of this room is a round-arched bookcase with shelves made from slabs of

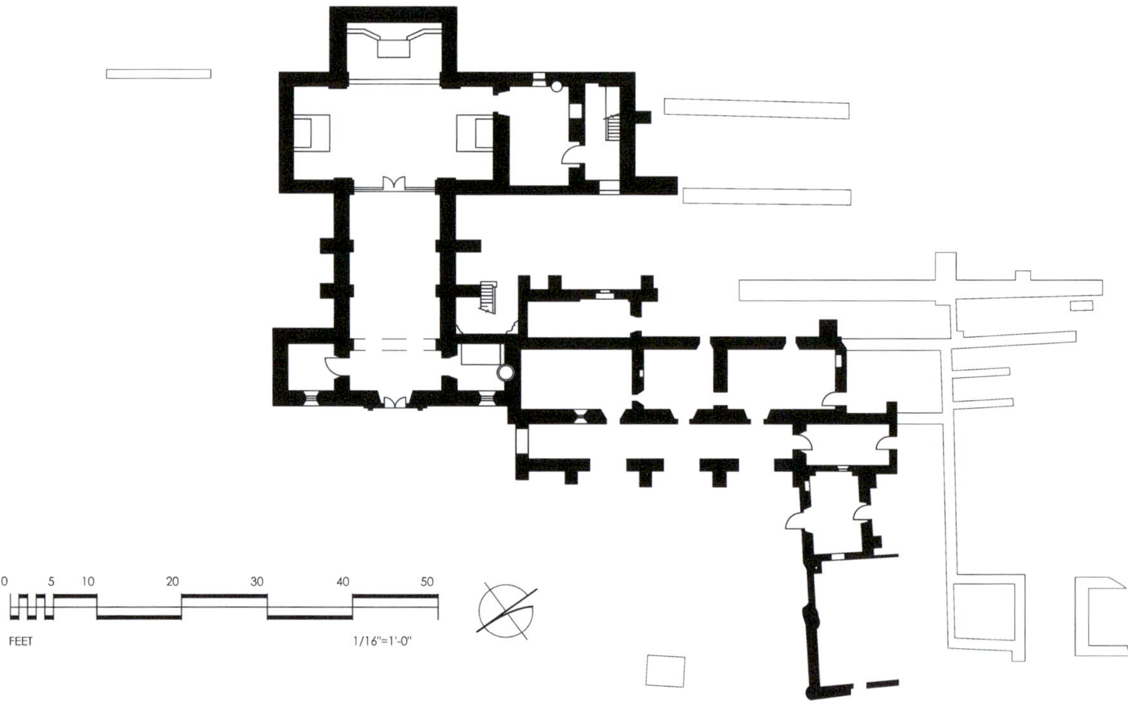

Figure 4.8. Mission Concepción, facade of the church. Photo by Kenneth Hafertepe.

Figure 4.9. Plan of Mission Concepción. Drawing by Hayley M. Field after HABS TX 319.

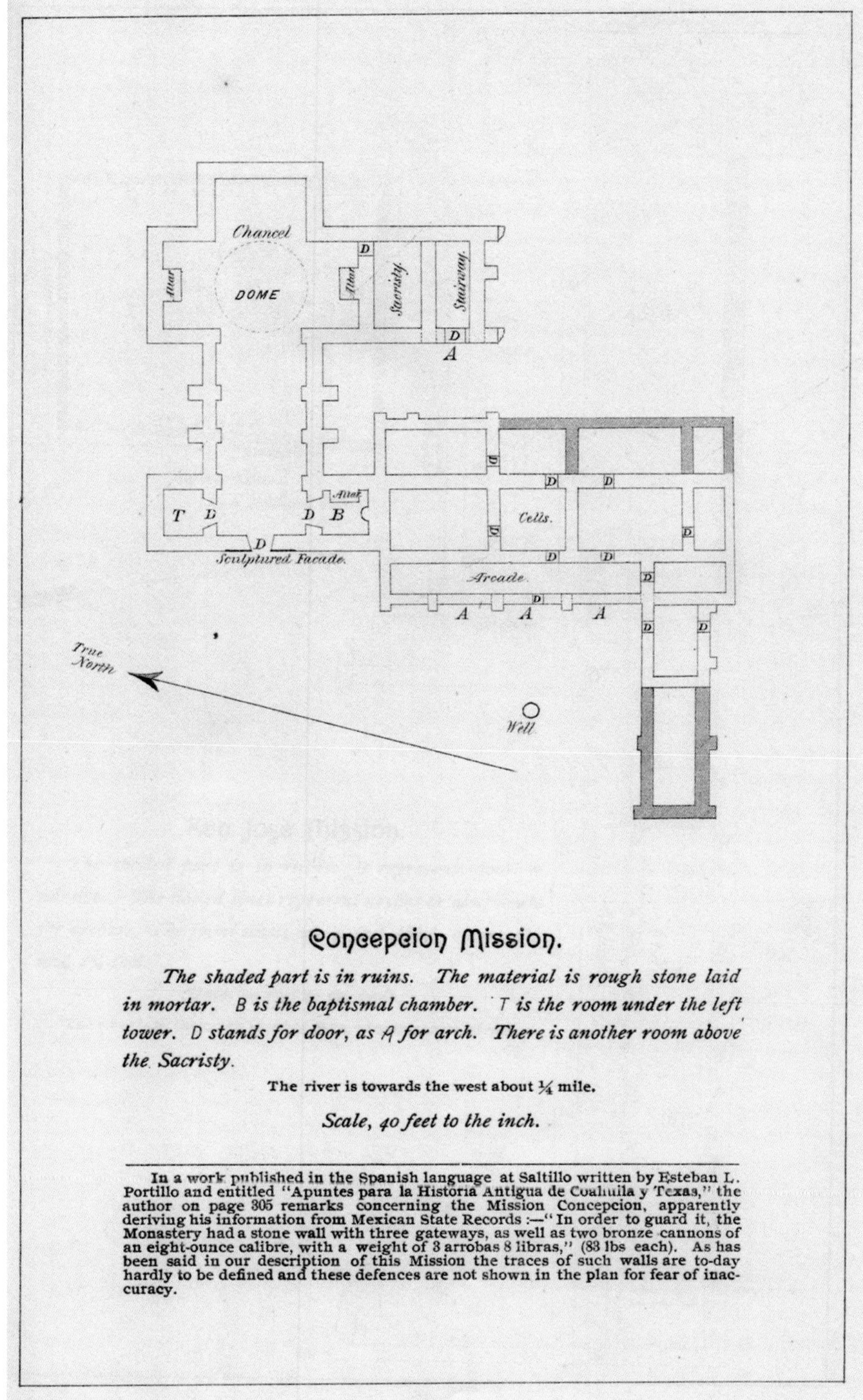

Figure 4.10. Plan of Mission Concepción, 1890. Site plan from William Corner, *San Antonio de Bexar: A Guide and History* (San Antonio: Bainbridge and Corner, 1890), after p. 16.

Figure 4.11. Mission Concepción, looking north of *convento* ruins, south wall of church, and father president's office. Photo by Brent R. Fortenberry.

stone. Architect Harvey P. Smith borrowed this feature for the reconstruction of what is known as the Spanish Governor's Palace (fig. 4.10).

To the east of the *convento* is a wing extended from the south transept of the church. On the first floor is the sacristy, and on the second, the father president's office. The low window in the north wall of the office looks down into the altar end of the church, which allowed the father president to keep watch over activity in the church. (This space has sometimes been interpreted as an infirmary, as the window allows ill congregants to hear Mass.) The staircase to this room remains unchanged since the eighteenth century (fig. 4.11).

All doors in the complex date to twentieth-century restoration, as do the tile floors. Harvey P. Smith installed floors of red tiles, similar to ones that he had found at the Governor's Palace. Smith also designed the punched-tin sconces based on ones visible in the Theodore Gentilz painting *Spanish Dance: Fandango*.

The number of native residents peaked at 247 around midcentury. Most lived in adobe quarters, which have been washed away by centuries of rain and neglect.[5]

Mission San José

If Mission Concepción represents the most intact church of the five San Antonio missions, San José provides the visitor with the best sense of the mission as a collection of many buildings and as a space. This is possible largely because of restoration and reconstruction carried out in the 1930s using New Deal funds. The architect Harvey P. Smith, who had re-created the so-called Spanish Governor's Palace, was in charge of this work and for work at the other three southerly missions (fig. 4.12).

Although the mission was established in 1720, the main church was built much later. As at Mission San Antonio, the earliest physical remains are the first story of the *convento*, behind the present church building. After the collapse of the roof of an earlier stone building, work on the present church was begun in 1768 and completed in 1783. The *maestro albañil* (master stonemason) Antonio Salazar was in charge of the work. The *carpintero* was Pedro Huizar, a native of Aguascalientes in Mexico. After a visit in January 1778, Father Juan Agustín Morfi wrote that "it is, in truth, the first mission in America, not in point of time but in point of beauty, plan, and strength."

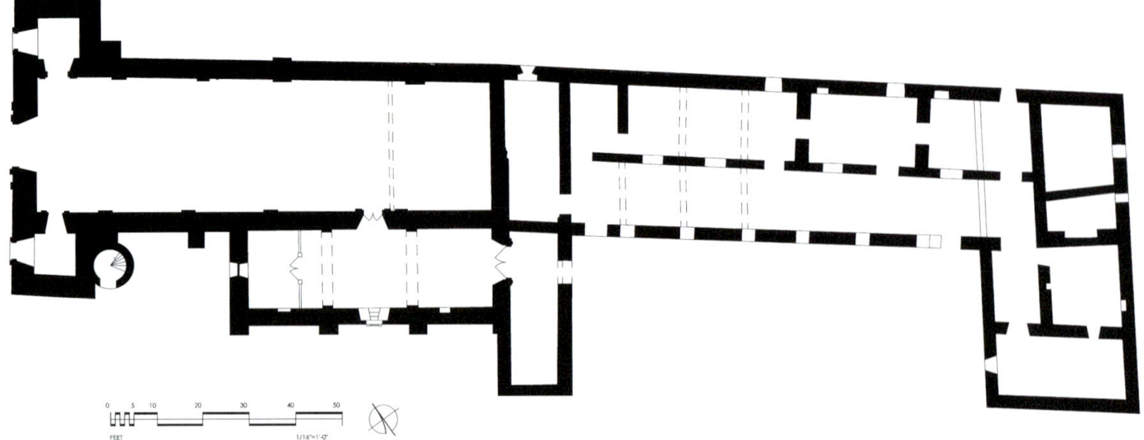

Figure 4.12. Plan of Mission San José. Drawing by Hayley M. Field after HABS TX 333.

Like Concepción, San José was built with two towers—only one of which was completed—and a dome. Unlike Concepción, which has a cruciform plan, the interior of San José is one long rectangular space, roofed with a barrel vault. As at Concepción, the exterior walls were covered in lime plaster and painted with geometrical patterns. In 1932 Ernst Schuchard created a painting (now at the Daughters of the Republic of Texas Library) that suggested the original paint treatment; a small patch at the base of the south tower was repainted in accordance with Schuchard's findings in 1949. Just a few feet west of the church is a small *campo santo* (cemetery); two markers remain in place (fig. 4.13).

The focal point of the facade is the two-story sculptural group. Over the great oval window on the second floor is San José, namesake of the mission, holding the Christ child. To the right is Saint Francis of Assisi, founder of the Franciscan order, and to the left is Saint Dominic, his friend. Above the main door is the Blessed Virgin Mary, in the form of our Lady of Guadalupe—surrounded by beams of light, wearing a crown, and supported by a cherub. Flanking Mary are her parents, Saint Joachim and Saint Anne. The double doors are a restoration, documented by early photographs and paintings. The numerous small panels were carved by Peter Mansbendel, a Swiss woodcarver living in Austin, who had previously fashioned the panels in the door of the Spanish Governor's Palace.

Adjoining the church on the south is a room known as the sacristy, chapel, or baptistry. This space was finished in 1777, several years before the main church. The room has a door on the north opening into the

Figure 4.13. Mission San José, west and south elevations of the church. Photo by Kenneth Hafertepe.

church just outside the altar rail and another door on the east leading to the *convento*. It is also lit with windows on the south and west. The roof consists of three domes. On the exterior the south window is elaborately decorated. This window has been enshrouded in legend, which attributes the stone carving to the carpenter Pedro Huizar, and it is said to be named for Rosa, his supposed fiancée in Spain. Adina De Zavala wrote a book on the missions, *History and Legends of the Alamo and Other Missions* (1917), and stated that "tradition of the oldest settlers gives Huizar as the name of the artist of San Jose" but made no mention of the Rosa legend (fig. 4.14).

The remains of the *convento* include the arcade, the rooms behind the arcade to the north, and the rooms beyond the arcade to the east. The round-arched arcade and rooms to the north, made of tufa, probably predate the present church building. The arcade with pointed arches, formed with nineteenth-century red brick, was added by Benedictines from Latrobe, Pennsylvania, who were in residence from 1859 to 1868. Visible from the *convento* area is a second-story door on the back wall of the church, which once led to the *convento*; this door is outlined in Spanish Colonial bricks, which were smaller and narrower than modern bricks.

Figure 4.14. Mission San José, south window of the sacristy (Rosa's window).
Photo by Kenneth Hafertepe.

The roof of the church, including the dome, and the north wall collapsed in December 1868. The west front along with the portal, the rear wall on the east, and the long south wall were left largely intact. The sacristy, with its famous Rose Window, was also spared. However, the mission continued its decline. By the beginning of the twentieth century, a county road had been built across what had once been the plaza of the mission; this road was not removed until restoration work was begun in the 1930s. Perhaps vibrations from the vehicles rumbling by caused the stone turret enclosing the stair to the bell tower (at the southeast corner of the building) to fall in 1903. (Civic leader Ethel Tunstall Drought gathered the hand-hewn bois d'arc steps and kept them at her home until the turret could be restored.) The tower itself collapsed on March 9, 1928. Atlee Ayres, a local architect best known for suburban houses in the Spanish Colonial Revival style (including the one that now houses the McNay Art Museum) was hired to reconstruct the tower.

Between 1929 and 1931 the Conservation Society of San Antonio purchased the various real estate parcels that surrounded the old granary. They then hired Harvey P. Smith, fresh from his reconstruction of the Spanish Governor's Palace, to reconstruct the barrel-vault roof of the building, which had collapsed. From the inside of the compound the point of transition from the original to reconstruction granary walls was subtly marked with a row of pebbles. The work proceeded slowly, but an infusion of funds from the Civil Works Administration, an early New Deal agency, allowed the work to be completed late in 1933. The interior walls were repainted based on inspection and chemical analysis done by Ernst Schuchard (figs. 4.15 and 4.16).

Harvey P. Smith was retained for the reconstruction of the north wall, roof, and dome of the church. The tufa used on the original church had proven to be porous, so proper limestone was used in the walls in the 1930s. The extant south wall provided a good template for the reconstruction of the north wall, and remnants of the roof at the west end of the building allowed an accurate re-creation of the space. The principal departure from the evidence was the use of flagstone for the main floor of the church. Smith had repurposed such flagstones, formerly used as sidewalks, for the formal rooms of the Spanish Governor's Palace, though evidence had suggested only tile or dirt floors. The same may be true of San José.

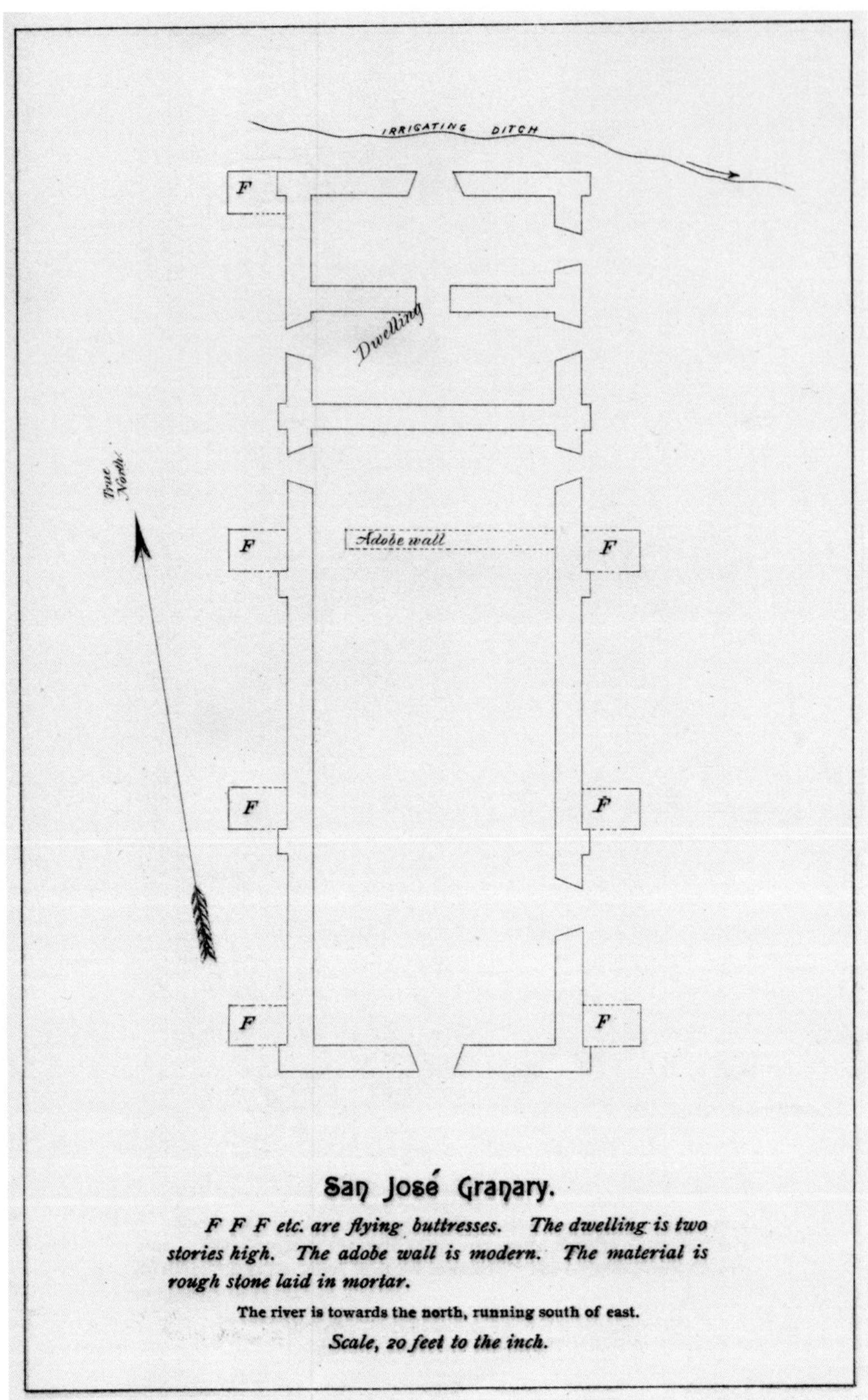

Figure 4.15. Mission San José, plan of granary, circa 1890. Site plan from William Corner, *San Antonio de Bexar: A Guide and History* (San Antonio: Bainbridge and Corner, 1890), after p. 16.

Figure 4.16. Mission San José, interior of granary. Photo by Kenneth Hafertepe.

Originally the mission compound was open, but between 1758 and 1768 new quarters were built around the periphery of the complex, creating defensive walls with a gate south of the granary. On March 16, 1758, Comanche, Bidai, Tejas, and Tonkawa Indians, who were angered that the Spaniards were making overtures to the Apaches, destroyed Mission Santa Cruz de San Saba, which was some 144 miles northwest of San Antonio. Two of the three missionaries were killed, along with four converts. Eighteenth-century records indicate that the new walls were built with stone, creating a fortress-like appearance, but these quarters and the wall they created had disappeared by the 1930s. Harvey P. Smith conducted excavations, looking for the foundation, but it is unclear if the present walls are in their precise original location. Smith also designed the gate on the west wall just south of the granary. Ronald Lee of the National Park Service criticized the gates as too theatrical; Lee also thought that the rock work on the Indian quarters was sloppy.

The rooms along the north wall near the granary were rebuilt as the quarters of presidio soldiers stationed at the mission. The elaborate stove and fireplace that Harvey P. Smith designed recalled his recent design for the *cocina* (kitchen) at the Spanish Governor's Palace, which he created with virtually no evidence of its original appearance.

In 1933 an underground room with steps was discovered just outside the mission walls to the north. It was determined that the room was part of the original mission mill. The Conservation Society traded some of its nearby land to acquire this property; Harvey P. Smith collaborated with Ernst Schuchard, an engineer at the Pioneer Flour Mill, to reconstruct the rest of the building, which was completed in 1938. San José was opened as a state park in 1941 and was part of the National Historical Park that became a reality in 1983.[6]

Mission San Juan Capistrano

Mission San Juan de los Nazonis was founded in 1716 in the borderland between New Spain and New France; when the mission was moved to the San Antonio area in 1731, it became San Juan Capistrano. The San Antonio River was approximately one hundred yards west of the mission walls. The chapel, built in 1756, and *convento* formed part of the west wall of the mission. A granary on the north side was also built in 1756. On the east side can be seen the ruins of another church building, begun in the 1760s and only half finished, which would have been properly oriented (figs. 4.17 and 4.18).

The walls of the chapel are limestone and sandstone rubble. On the east side the wall is given further support by engaged buttresses connected by segmental arches. The most ornamental feature of the exterior is the *espadaña*, a bell tower with three openings in two stages. This is at the north end of the east wall, and the *espadaña* marks the entrance into the chapel. The altar is at the south end of this space, which does not conform with Catholic expectations that the altar would be at the east end. Unlike the missions to the north, San Juan Capistrano did not have a vaulted stone roof but a flat roof supported by boxed beams. The floor is of unglazed tiles, and windows date from the modern era (figs. 4.19 and 4.20).

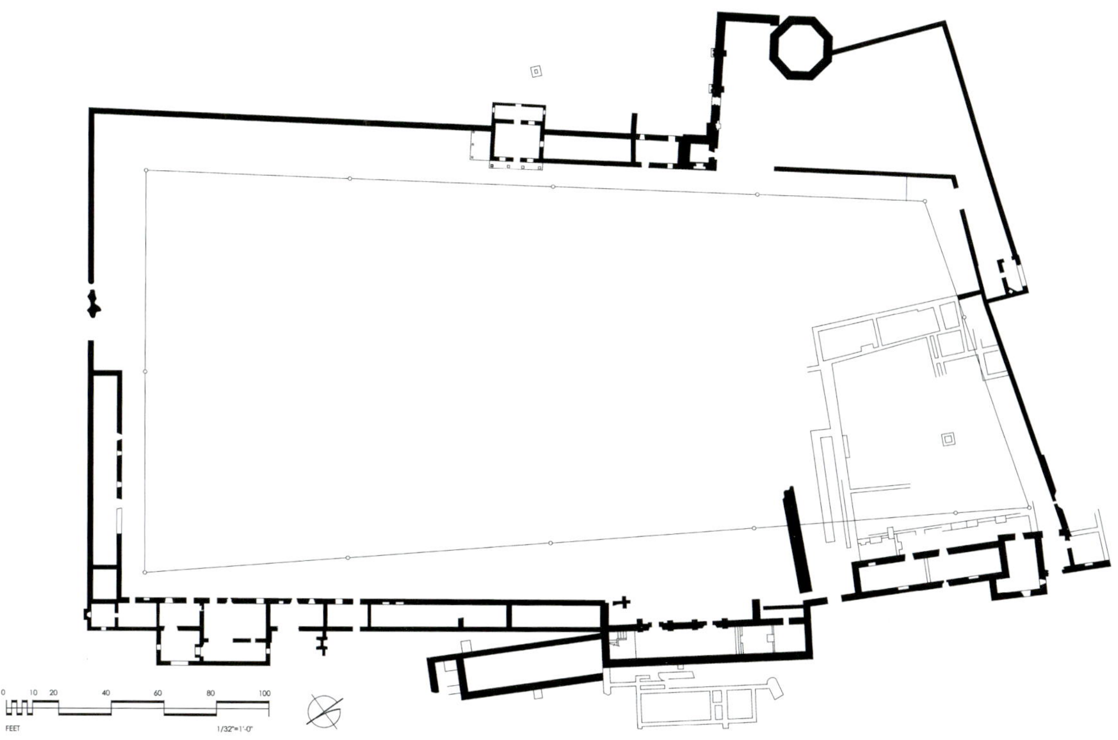

Figure 4.17. Plan of Mission San Juan Capistrano (present church building is at the bottom near the middle). Drawing by Hayley M. Field after HABS TX 321.

Figure 4.18. Mission San Juan Capistrano, grounds with the *convento* and church. Photo by Kenneth Hafertepe.

Figure 4.19. Mission San Juan Capistrano, exterior of the church. Photo by Kenneth Hafertepe.

By 1858 Capistrano and Espada were no longer missions, but they continued as parishes. After the arrival of Father Francis Bouchu, a French-born priest who had come to San Antonio as assistant pastor at the Church of San Fernando, he traveled out to say Mass at the two southernmost parishes. In 1858 he was assigned to them on a full-time basis, and the old *convento* at Espada became his rectory. He considered himself a bricklayer and stonemason and cared for both churches for the rest of his life. However, as he aged, the task became much more difficult. (He was seventy in 1899.) After his death the church underwent extensive repairs. More work was done in preparation for the influx of tourists in 1968 for HemisFair, and the National Park Service has continued restorations since taking charge of the four missions in 1983.

Both Capistrano and Espada are in areas that are less urbanized than the closer-in missions; this lesser state of development allows the visitor to get a better idea of how the missions would have appeared in the eighteenth century.[7]

Figure 4.20. Mission San Juan Capistrano, interior of the church looking south.
Photo by Kenneth Hafertepe.

Mission San Francisco de la Espada

The mission was founded in 1731, but as in the other missions the surviving buildings are later, though the precise date is elusive. A church was built between 1745 and 1756, which is probably the present chapel. Another, larger church was begun in 1762, but it was torn down in 1777. The temporary chapel thus became the permanent church. The chapel and the *convento* were part of the west wall of the mission. Unlike those at Missions San Antonio, Concepción, and San José, the chapel of Mission Espada is not oriented according to liturgical requirements. That is, the chapel faces east rather than west, so the altar is on the west. The San Antonio River is just to the northwest of the mission proper. To the southeast of the chapel are the foundations of a larger church and a stone granary, which stood outside the mission walls. Six stone rooms remain at the southeast corner—their function is unclear. From 1915 to 1967 the two remaining rooms along the east wall were used as a school (figs. 4.21 and 4.22).

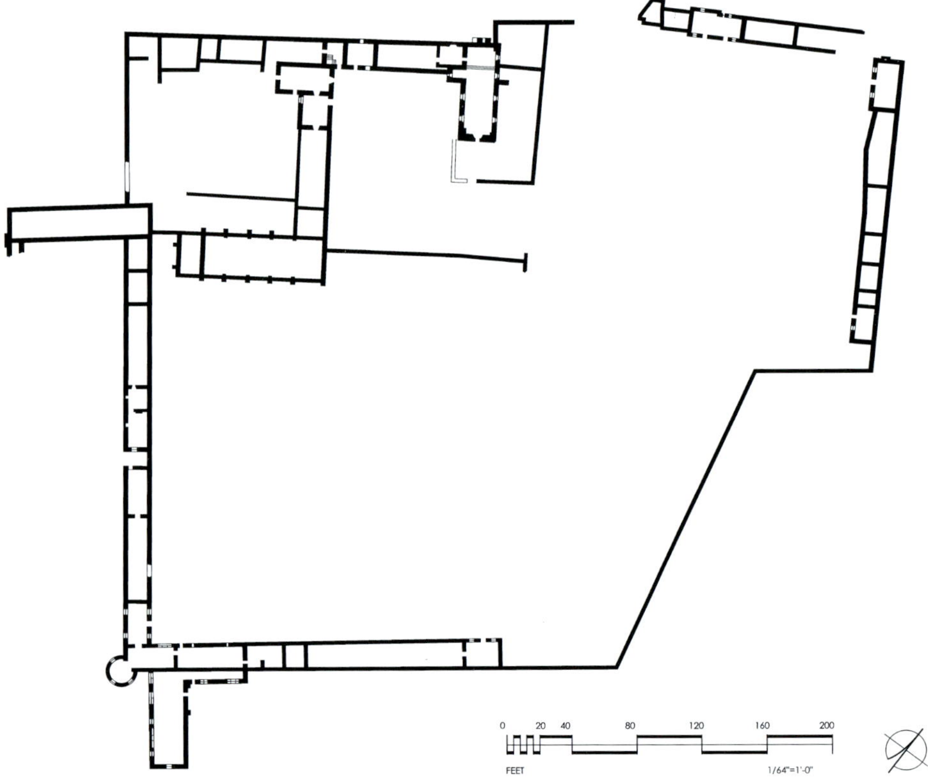

Figure 4.21. Plan of Mission San Francisco de la Espada (present church is at the top near the middle). Drawing by Hayley M. Field after HABS TX 320.

Figure 4.22. Mission San Francisco de la Espada, exterior of the church. Photo by Kenneth Hafertepe.

The chapel is a small building with a cruciform plan. The exterior
is largely intact, except for the windows. The interior is almost entirely
modern. The walls are built of random sandstone rubble. The upper part
of the principal facade has three arched openings containing bells, known
as an *espadaña*. (Mission San Juan Capistrano also has an *espadaña*, but it
is on the north end of one of the long walls.) The only ornamental feature
of the facade is the arched doorway (fig. 4.23). The upper part of the
opening has three scallops; where the curves would meet are right angles
projecting outward. This form is unique in Spanish Colonial architecture
and may well reflect a Moorish influence. Inside the walls are original but
covered with modern plaster. All doors and windows were replaced in
1911. The floors are modern as well, possibly from the 1930s, and consist
of unglazed tiles laid in Portland cement (figs. 4.24 and 4.25).

Figure 4.23. Mission San Francisco de la Espada, portal of the church.
Photo by Kenneth Hafertepe.

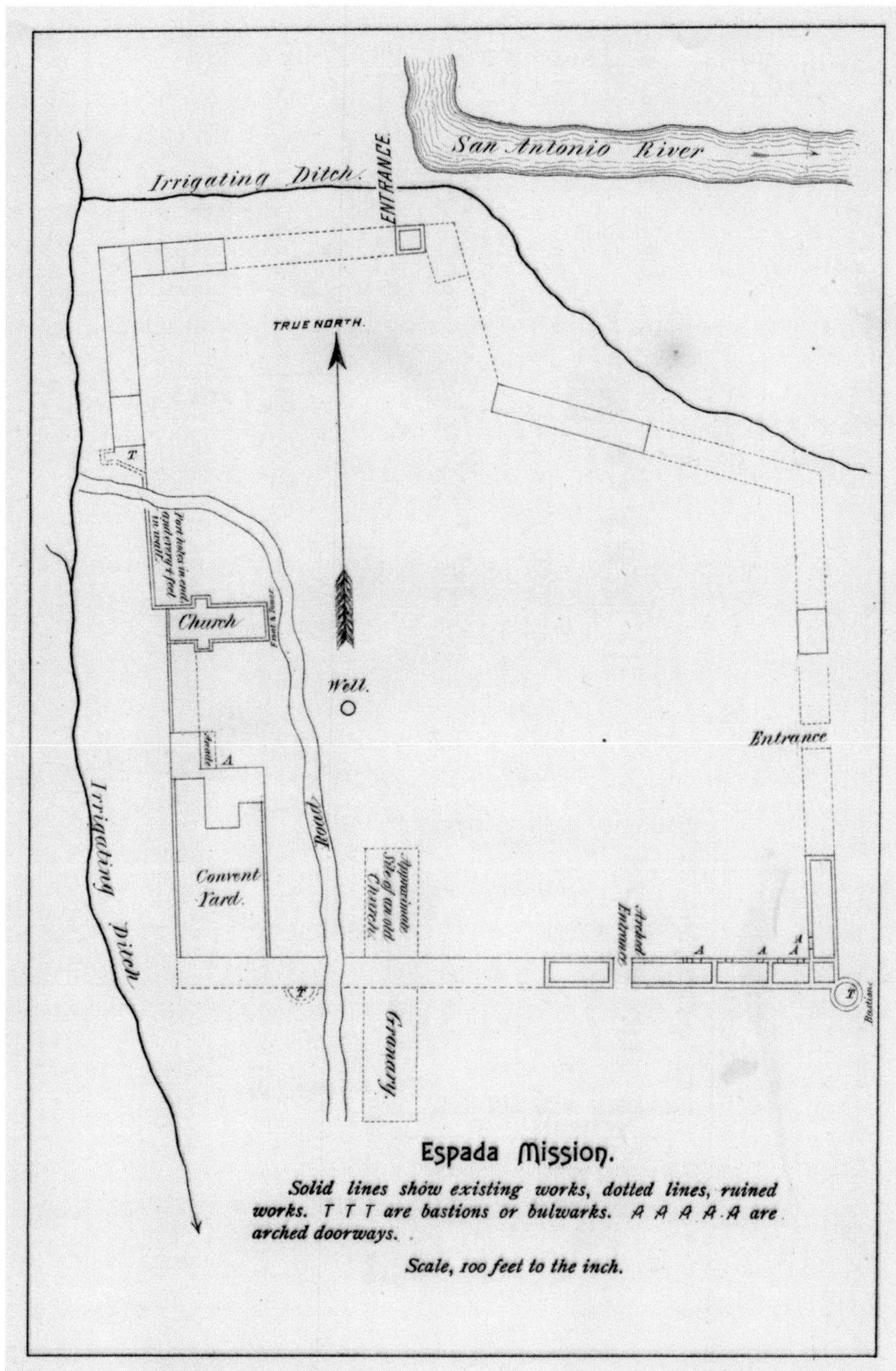

Figure 4.24. Plan of Mission San Francisco de la Espada, 1890. Site plan from William Corner, *San Antonio de Bexar: A Guide and History* (San Antonio: Bainbridge and Corner, 1890) after p. 16.

Figure 4.25. Mission San Francisco de la Espada, interior of the church. Photo by Kenneth Hafertepe.

The fields of the mission were watered by an acequia (an irrigation channel) that included an aqueduct extending over La Piedra Creek for thirty-eight varas, or approximately one hundred feet (fig. 4.26). Also part of the mission was the Rancho de las Cabras, thirty miles to the south, just outside Floresville in Wilson County. From 1731 to 1794 the missionaries and their native converts raised cattle for the mission. The Texas Parks and Wildlife Department purchased the lands that had formed the rancho from several private owners in 1976 and 1977; the National Park Service acquired the rancho in 1995.

In 1858 Capistrano and Espada were assigned to Father Francis Bouchu, who moved to Espada and began repairing the old missions. The church was enlarged in 1856 but by 1858 was showing structural problems. Father Bouchu reroofed the church in 1883. Father Bouchu died in 1097, and between 1909 and 1915 the building was closed for reconstruction, including another new roof. The church was reopened in 1915. Restoration work was done in the 1930s by Harvey P. Smith, who

Figure 4.26. Mission San Francisco de la Espada, aqueduct. Photo by Kenneth Hafertepe.

had previously worked to re-create the Spanish Governor's Palace and to restore Mission San José. Additional restoration work has continued since the cooperative agreement of 1983 in which the National Park Service agreed to provide for the preservation, restoration, and interpretation of Concepción, San José, Capistrano, and Espada.[8]

Notes

1. All material in this introduction has been drawn from *San Antonio Missions: Nomination to the World Heritage List by the United States of America*, January 2014, available at the Library of the Conservation Society of San Antonio or at https://whc.unesco.org/en/list/1466/documents/. Editors' Note: Paul Ringenbach was the lead author and preparer of the document that he and his partners took eight years of voluntary effort to complete.

2. James Ivey, "Comparative Franciscan Architectural Design on the Northern and Central Frontier of New Spain," in *The Spanish Missionary Heritage of the United States: Selected Papers and Commentaries from the November 1990 Quincentenary Symposium*, ed. Howard Benoist and María Carolina Flores (Washington, DC: United States Department of the Interior/National Park Service, 1993?), 182.

3. Jacinto Quirarte, *Art and Architecture of the Texas Missions* (Austin: University of Texas Press, 2002), 48.

4. William Corner, *San Antonio de Bexar: A Guide and History* (San Antonio: Bainbridge and Corner, 1890), 8–12; Benoist and Flores, *Spanish Missionary Heritage*; Anne A. Fox, "Mission Builders: Traces of Texas Archaeology," in Benoist and Flores, *Spanish Missionary Heritage*, 119–22; Ivey, "Comparative Franciscan Architectural Design," 177–99; Arthur R. Gómez, "Romancing the Stones: The WPA Restoration of Mission San José, 1928–1938," in Benoist and Flores, *Spanish Missionary Heritage*, 208–14; Lewis F. Fisher, *The Spanish Missions of San Antonio* (San Antonio: Maverick Publishing, 1998), 26–37; Lewis F. Fisher, *Saving San Antonio: The Precarious Preservation of a Heritage* (Lubbock: Texas Tech University Press, 1996), 40–46, 54–68, 102–16; and Quirarte, *Art and Architecture of the Texas Missions*, 43–64.

5. Corner, *San Antonio de Bexar*, 14–17; Fisher, *Spanish Missions of San Antonio*, 38–53; and Quirarte, *Art and Architecture of the Texas Missions*, 103–30.

6. Corner, *San Antonio de Bexar*, 17–19; Fisher, *Spanish Missions of San Antonio*, 54–75; Fisher, *Saving San Antonio*, 145–79; Adina De Zavala, *History and Legends of the Alamo and Other Missions in and around San Antonio* (1917; repr., Houston: Arte Publico Press, 1996), 123–38; Gómez, "Romancing the Stones"; and Quirarte, *Art and Architecture of the Texas Missions*, 65–102.

7. John C. Garner Jr., "Mission San Juan de Capistrano, Chapel," 1969, Historic American Buildings Survey, TX-321-A, https://cdn.loc.gov/master/pnp/habshaer/tx/tx0000/tx0031/data/tx0031data.pdf; "San Juan Capistrano Mission," *Handbook of Texas Online*, accessed October 5, 2019, http://www.tshaonline.org/handbook/online/articles/uqs25; and Quirarte, *Art and Architecture of the Texas Missions*, 131–47.

8. John C. Garner Jr., "Mission San Francisco de la Espada, Church," January 1969, Historic American Buildings Survey, TX-320-A, https://cdn.loc.gov/master/pnp/habshaer/tx/tx0000/tx0030/data/tx0030data.pdf; James T. Escobedo Jr., "Bouchu, Francis," *Handbook of Texas Online*, accessed October 5, 2019, http://www.tshaonline.org/handbook/online/articles/fbo84; Clint E. Davis, "San Francisco de la Espada Mission," *Handbook of Texas Online*, accessed October 5, 2019, http://www.tshaonline.org/handbook/online/articles/uqs12; and Quirarte, *Art and Architecture of the Texas Missions*, 148–62.

The King William
Neighborhood

Maria Watson Pfeiffer

The fertile fields below the town of San Antonio de Béxar and Mission San Antonio de Valero (later known as the Alamo) were farmed by mission residents who irrigated crops with water from the meandering San Antonio River and an elaborate system of earthen ditches (acequias). East of the river in today's King William neighborhood, water flowed through the Alamo and Concepción (also called the Pajalache) acequias and was diverted into fields in small lateral ditches. This abundant availability of water made the land between the acequias and river some of the town's most desirable real estate (fig. 5.1).

The area that today comprises the King William neighborhood was less than one mile below the town's central plazas, Mission San Antonio de Valero, and the small settlement of La Villita. Roads through the area led to the lower missions—Concepción, San José, San Juan, and Espada—providing access to the rich, irrigated farmland. As new settlers arrived throughout the 1700s, the town and missionary-led communities became well established. The Spanish government's goal of founding a permanent, self-sustaining settlement was therefore fulfilled, and the process of secularizing the missions began in the 1790s. Mission San Antonio de Valero was secularized in 1793, and Governor Manuel Muñoz appointed Pedro Huizar to survey the mission lands for distribution.[1]

The Labor de los Mochos, as the mission's lower farmlands were called, were divided among Indian and Spanish residents. Huizar was awarded a parcel of adjoining land for his services as surveyor.[2]

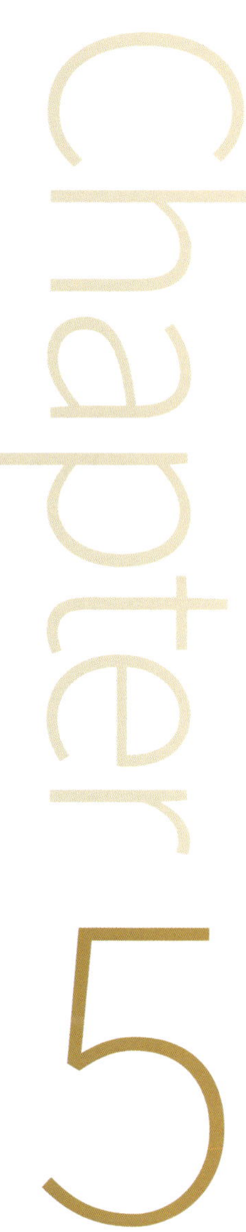

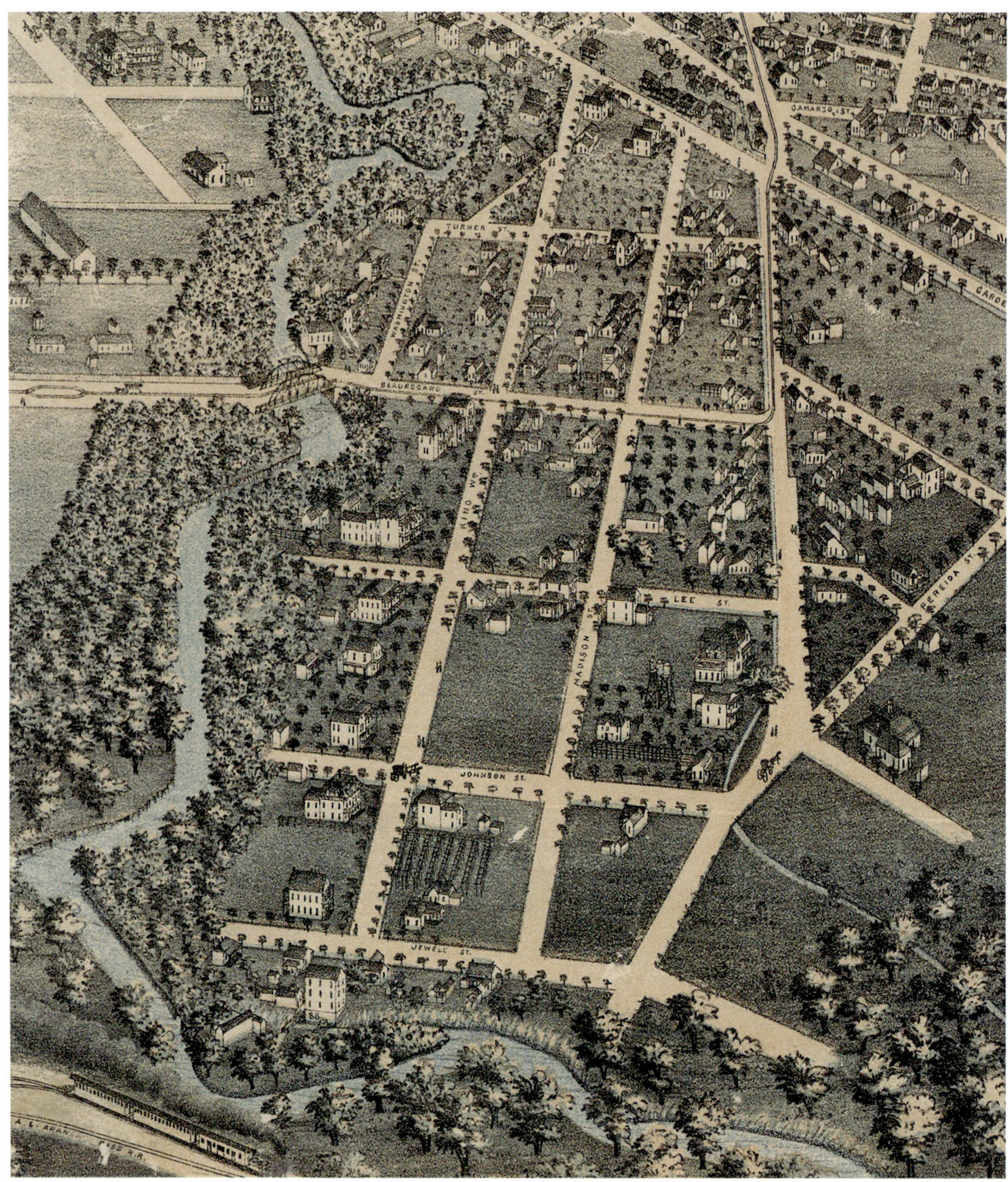

Figure 5.1. King William neighborhood. Detail from Augustus Koch, *Bird's Eye View of San Antonio, Bexar County, Texas, 1886 Looking East*. Image from Wikimedia Commons.

Those who received the former mission lands farmed the irrigated fields and likely constructed small houses or ancillary buildings of fragile *palisado* (post and mud) or soft caliche-block construction, none of which survive. The grantees and their descendants began to subdivide and sell their properties in the early 1800s, and after Texas won its independence from Mexico in 1836, newly arrived immigrants purchased large portions of the former mission fields. They included lawyer Thomas Jefferson Devine and his wife, Helen Elder, who acquired land along both sides of the San Antonio River. Devine and his family first lived in a small, vernacular stone house near the Concepción acequia east of the river before building a Greek Revival residence (now demolished) in 1849 on property they owned west of the river.[3]

The Devines' land east of the river remained a fenced pasture until the mid-1800s. In 1850 they sold tracts at both the north and south ends of their property, retaining the middle parcel, which they platted and sold as individual lots. The six-acre tract at a bend in the river south of Devine's pasture was sold in 1850, and a sixteen-acre parcel to the north was conveyed to Helen Devine's sister, Caroline Catherine "Kate" Elder, in 1853. It was on these riverside tracts that the neighborhood's earliest houses were constructed in the years preceding the Civil War.[4]

Kate Elder and her husband, Newton A. Mitchell, built a two-story, raised stone cottage at the northwest corner of her land in 1858 and subdivided their remaining property according to a plan drawn by surveyor Gustav Freisleben. The lots immediately adjoining their house to the south were acquired by stationery and bookstore owner Gustav Blersch. He hired Freisleben to design his two-story raised stone cottage, which was built in 1860 by contractor John Hermann Kampmann. Below the Mitchell and Blersch houses at the bend and falls in the river, German-born miller Carl Hilmar Guenther acquired the six-acre tract formerly owned by Devine in 1859 and built a two-story, six-room stone house overlooking a mill powered by the swiftly flowing waterway.[5]

The Guenther, Mitchell, and Blersch houses exemplified the work of skilled stonemasons and builders who began working in San Antonio during the antebellum period. These craftsmen had ready access to both hard and soft stone cut from nearby quarries. As the pace of building increased in the postwar years, Devine and others who owned land in the King William area sold lots to individuals who built stone houses in a variety of styles. Lawyer Ernst Altgelt built two houses on the thorough-fare that he named King William. The street was anchored at its south end by Guenther's house and mill and on the north by Anton Wulff's Italianate-influenced home completed in 1870. John and Joseph Ball, both Alsatian stonemasons, built identical gable-roofed, one-story cottages in 1868 on King William. Similar small houses were found on Madison Street, along Mill Street (today South Alamo) that ran south to Guenther's mill, and in the lower part of the neighborhood below Mill.

Stone remained the primary building material for area houses, though with the arrival of the railroad in 1877, brick and milled lumber be-came more readily available and widely used in construction. Beginning in the 1870s, academically trained architects, including Alfred Giles, James Wahrenberger, and Albert Beckmann, designed houses for leading businessmen and their families. Others who left their mark in the 1890s and early 1900s were Leo M. J. Dielmann, Atlee B. Ayres, and James Riely Gordon. As the neighborhood matured, some first-generation stone houses were transformed by the addition of new facades, additional floors, bay windows, and other architectural features. In some instances, large lots were divided and infill houses constructed, a trend that con-tinues in the early twenty-first century. The result is a stylistic milieu of large- and small-scale houses exhibiting vernacular, bungalow, Italianate, Romanesque Revival, Queen Anne, Second Empire, Colonial Revival, and Moderne influences.

The neighborhood's character began to change in the early twentieth century. Many families sold their homes and moved to newer, more mod-ern suburbs such as Monte Vista, Alamo Heights, and Terrell Hills or di-vided their houses into apartments that were rented to meet the housing scarcity during World War I. This trend continued through World War II and the 1950s. Members of some pioneer families remained in spite of the neighborhood's general decline, and in the 1940s, homes were pur-chased by new residents who valued the area's architecture and history. Old and new residents joined together in 1947 to found the King Wil-liam Area Conservation Association, which advocated for protection and preservation of the neighborhood. The society successfully fought zoning battles and a proposed crosstown expressway, laying the groundwork for revitalization.

The restoration of homes and their conversion back to single-family use began in the mid-1960s. This movement was spurred by young design professionals who worked for prominent architect O'Neil Ford at his King

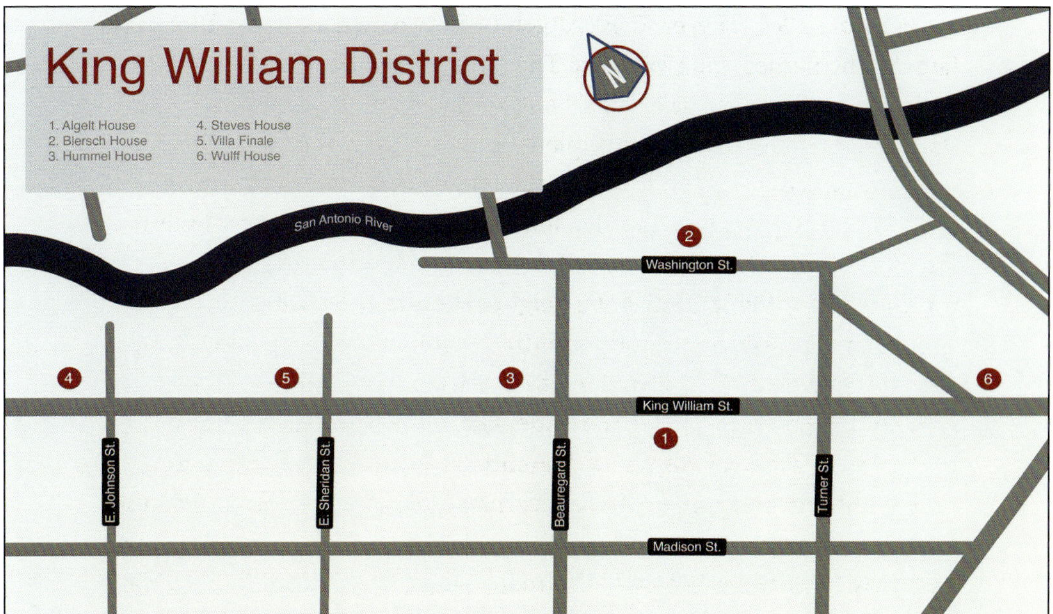

Figure 5.2. King William District. Map by Brent R. Fortenberry.

William Street office. Others included designers and artists associated with nearby HemisFair '68. This fledgling restoration movement gained momentum with the neighborhood's designation as the city's first historic district in 1968 and the first National Register Historic District in Texas in 1972.

The major impetus to recovery was the work of preservationist Walter Mathis, who purchased a house he named Villa Finale on King William Street in 1967. Mathis subsequently bought thirteen more houses that he sold to fellow owner-occupant preservationists. Additional momentum was provided by the Back to the Cities movement that focused attention on inner-city neighborhoods in the 1970s. By the 1980s, many area homes had been restored.

This movement continues in the early 2000s as new residents seeking to live in near-downtown neighborhoods purchase and restore, or "re-restore" the area's diverse housing stock and build new infill structures. Today the King William Association, founded in 1967, continues to advocate for preservation of the neighborhood's residential character and its rich architectural fabric (fig. 5.2).

Figure 5.3. Gustav Blersch house, front elevation. Photo by Brent R. Fortenberry.

Gustav Blersch House
213 Washington Street
1860

Following secularization of Mission San Antonio de Valero in 1793, this portion of the mission's agricultural land was granted to Vicente Amador. He and successive owners farmed the fields on the east bank of the river until 1844, when the property was acquired by prominent local lawyer Thomas Jefferson Devine. The land remained undeveloped until after it was acquired in 1853 by Caroline Catherine "Kate" Elder.[6]

Kate Elder married Newton A. Mitchell, and in May 1859, they hired Gustav Freisleben to survey and subdivide their land. Freisleben laid out wide, unnamed streets that defined three blocks, each containing twenty-two lots measuring 18 × 51 varas (approximately 50 × 142 feet). The Mitchells built their house at the northwest corner of their land (209 Washington Street) and began selling the remaining property, including the lot immediately to the south, which was purchased by Gustav Blersch, a German-born bookseller (fig. 5.3).[7]

Blersch and his wife, Adeline, hired Freisleben to draw plans for their two-story limestone house and paid prominent San Antonio builder John Hermann Kampmann $5,074 to build the house. Blersch's journal also mentions a chicken house and horse stable. Doors and windows were shipped from New York, and wood was supplied by various Texas sources.[8] Writing to his brother in Germany in February 1862, Blersch described the house as "one of the finest here" (figs. 5.4 and 5.5).[9]

Figure 5.4. Gustav Blersch house, 1860. Photograph ca. 1865.
Courtesy of Maria Watson Pfeiffer.

Figure 5.5. Gustav Blersch house, 1860. Photograph ca. 1910.
Courtesy of Maria Watson Pfeiffer.

Freisleben's classically influenced design included three rooms on the main floor raised over a half basement with center passage hall (later enclosed), a floor plan well suited to the hot Texas climate. The east-facing, full-width porch, with jigsaw detailing and box columns supporting a low gabled roof, was accessed by a wide stairway. The secondary facade facing the river also had exterior access.

Blersch moved his mercantile business to Mexico during the Civil War while his wife and children lived in Germany. He returned after the war but sold the house in 1870 to wealthy local banker James T. Thornton. Thornton enlarged the house, adding a bay window and a two-room, two-story wing with open back porch and decorative interior moldings and fixtures. Subsequent owners maintained the house as a single-family residence, and it was acquired by the Clarkson family in 1905. After repairing damage from the 1921 flood, which filled the half basement, the Clarksons added a sleeping porch and enclosed the rear galleries, including the outside staircase. No further changes have been made, and the house remains in the extended family today (fig. 5.6).[10]

Figure 5.6. Plan of Gustav Blersch house. Drawing by Hayley M. Field.

Figure 5.7. Anton Friedrich Wulff house, front elevation, 1870. Photo by Kenneth Hafertepe.

Anton Friedrich Wulff House
107 King William Street
1870

Anton Friedrich Wulff joined vast numbers of his countrymen who left their native Germany in the 1840s for a new life in America. A native of Hamburg, Wulff arrived in New York in 1848 and traveled to Texas, where he found work in San Antonio and the nearby communities of New Braunfels and Fredericksburg.[11] His successful mercantile and freighting business conducted trade in Texas and Mexico. Like other Germans who aligned with the Union cause during the Civil War, Wulff and his family spent the war years away from Texas, living in Mexico, Philadelphia, and Germany before returning to San Antonio. By 1867, the firm of Wulff and Shetelig was conducting a thriving import and commission business (fig. 5.7).[12]

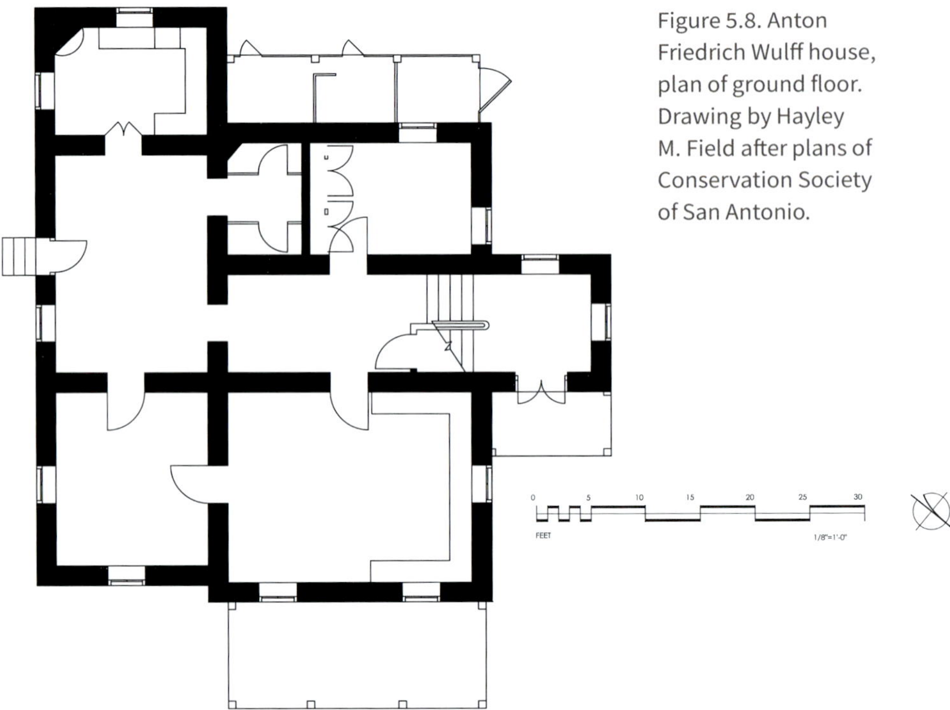

Figure 5.8. Anton Friedrich Wulff house, plan of ground floor. Drawing by Hayley M. Field after plans of Conservation Society of San Antonio.

In November 1868, Anton Wulff paid thirteen hundred dollars for land on the east side of the San Antonio River "about 800 yards below the Main Plaza."[13] The 1.3-acre property was between the river and Concepción acequia, an irrigation ditch that watered the fields of the Spanish mission to the south. Wulff and his wife, Paulita, built a house for their growing family at the head of the still-unnamed and largely vacant street that led to Carl Hilmar Guenther's mill. Built of locally quarried limestone—brick was not readily available in San Antonio at the time—the Italianate-style house with its thick walls, deep verandah, and half basement was well adapted to the hot Texas climate (figs. 5.8 and 5.9). The house is the work of one of the skilled masons or building contractors who transformed postwar San Antonio before the arrival of academically trained architects. Architectural historian Kenneth Hafertepe attributes the sophisticated design to inspiration drawn from period pattern books, specifically Samuel Sloan's design for "A Southern House" published in 1852 in *The Model Architect* (fig. 5.10).[14] While the Wulffs adapted the material, massing, and various other details of Sloan's design, their house shares key features with the "Southern House," including the half basement, verandah, and offset tower. A reporter wrote about the house in March 1871, "Our esteemed friend and neighbor A. F. Wulff is

Figure 5.9. Anton Friedrich Wulff house, showing King William Street before it was paved, ca. 1880. Courtesy of Conservation Society of San Antonio Foundation.

Figure 5.10. Design of the Wulff house may have been informed by the pattern-book illustration of a perspective view by Samuel Sloan, Design 53, "A Southern House," in *The Model Architect* (Philadelphia, 1852). Courtesy of Kitty King Powell and Library Center, Bayou Bend Collection and Gardens, Museum of Fine Arts, Houston.

making a second paradise of his handsome grounds while the style of architecture adapted in the building of his residence is universally admired."[15]

Anton Wulff surrounded the house with beautiful gardens and, as an elected alderman, led efforts to beautify the city's plazas (fig. 5.11).[16] Following Wulff's death in 1894, his family remained in the house until 1902, when it was sold to Arthur and Elise Groos Guenther, both of whom were raised in the King William neighborhood. The house was converted by subsequent owners to commercial use in 1960 and later fell into disrepair. It was acquired by the San Antonio Conservation Society in 1974 and restored as its headquarters. The society continues to use the house. The 1867 August Stuemke limestone barn at the rear of the property was moved to the site in 1982.[17]

Figure 5.11. The Wulff family in their King William Street garden. Courtesy of Maria Watson Pfeiffer.

Ernst Hermann Altgelt House
226 King William Street
1876

Ernst Altgelt was already a well-established figure in nineteenth-century Texas when he purchased land along the thoroughfare that he would later name King William Street. German-born Altgelt surveyed and platted the town of Comfort north of San Antonio in 1854, married Emma Murck in 1855, and established lumber and grist mills. His secessionist-leaning views were unpopular in the German community, and he left his family in Comfort to spend mid-1863 until early 1865 in Germany.[18]

Figure 5.12. Ernst Hermann Altgelt house, front elevation, 1876.
Photo by Kenneth Hafertepe.

After returning to Texas, Altgelt studied law, and in 1866, Emma made their first purchase of land in San Antonio.[19] The couple hired Comfort carpenter Otto Brinkmann to construct their first house, a portion of which was later incorporated into the adjoining house to the south at 236 King William. Emma Altgelt wrote about their 1866 house, "Our house was the first building in the newly laid out street, and by law my husband had the right to name the street. He called it 'King William'" (figs. 5.12 and 5.13).[20]

As the Altgelts' fortunes improved, they purchased the adjoining property and, in 1876, hired local architect and builder Anthony Earhart to construct this more substantial house with a stable. Earhart was one of the city's most prominent craftsmen and at the time was also building the most elaborate house on King William Street to date, the Edward Steves house (at 509).[21] Compared with the Steves house and Anton Wulff house (107 King William), the Altgelts' new two-story residence was a straightforward statement of unadorned limestone construction. The primary facade, with its front-facing gable; paired door and window openings on each floor; and shallow, second-story gallery, contrasted with the decidedly more elaborate homes of the Altgelts' neighbors (fig. 5.14). To the passerby, the only distinguishing details were the arched, paneled

Figure 5.13. Ernst Hermann Altgelt house, rear elevation, 1876. Photo by Kenneth Hafertepe.

Figure 5.14. Ernst Hermann Altgelt house (1876), view from the southwest, October 1961. Photo by Jack Boucher, Historic American Buildings Survey, Library of Congress.

double doors on both the first and second floors that gave a nod to the Italianate style.[22] The house was sited near the north property line, and its south elevation, featuring a deep, full-height gallery and open stairway that wrapped to the second floor, faced a large garden separating the house from the family's first residence. The entry led into a single wide parlor where subsequent owners built an interior stair. It is possible that the two-story ell, which contains the kitchen, was an addition. It does appear on the 1896 Sanborn Fire Insurance Map, the first to document the King William neighborhood (figs. 5.15 and 5.16).

Figure 5.15. Ernst Altgelt, ca. 1860. Courtesy of James Ernest Altgelt.

Figure 5.16. Emma Altgelt, ca. 1880. Courtesy of James Ernest Altgelt.

It is not clear if the house was finished when Ernst Altgelt died in 1878, but his widow settled outstanding accounts with Edward Steves, whose lumberyard provided the building materials, after his death.[23] The house was sold to provisions dealer Theodore Schleuning and his wife, Bertha, in 1882 for five thousand dollars.[24]

After Schleuning's death in 1893, Bertha continued to live in the house until she died in 1932. Her estate conveyed the house to her granddaughter and husband, Elizabeth and Harry Martyn, in 1939. The house was rented and used briefly as a residence and music school before it was acquired by George and Martha Isbell in 1944. The Isbells added the interior stairs and bathrooms and built the stone perimeter wall. The house still remains in the Isbell family.[25]

Edward Steves House
509 King William Street
1876

Edward Steves arrived in Texas with his family in 1849 and settled in New Braunfels, one of the heavily German Hill Country towns north of San Antonio. Though he became a farmer, Steves also trained as a cabinet-maker. After he married Johanna Kloepper in 1857, the couple moved to Comfort, another German community, where he farmed and worked as a carpenter.[26]

Steves and his wife moved to San Antonio following the Civil War in 1866, and he opened a lumberyard that prospered in the postwar years. The arrival of the railroad in 1877 allowed Steves to expand his inventory and speed shipments of material.[27] The Steves first lived in modest houses, but as the business grew and they assumed prominent roles in the community, they selected Alfred Giles, one of the city's leading architects, to design a new residence. Giles later designed King William Street houses for Alexander Sartor (at 217), Albert Steves (at 419), and Carl W. A. Groos (at 335).[28] Their contractors were John Hermann Kampmann and Anthony Earhart, a carpenter and builder who was also working on the nearby Ernst Altgelt house. The local newspaper noted, "Mr. Steves' residence, when it is complete, will be one of the most attractive and substantial in the city" (figs. 5.17 and 5.18).[29]

The two-story house, constructed of smooth-finished, locally quarried stone with a deep, one-story porch, exhibited a variety of architectural influences. The arched windows and doorway reflected the Italianate style,

Figure 5.17. Edward Steves house, front elevation, 1876. Photo by Brent R. Fortenberry.

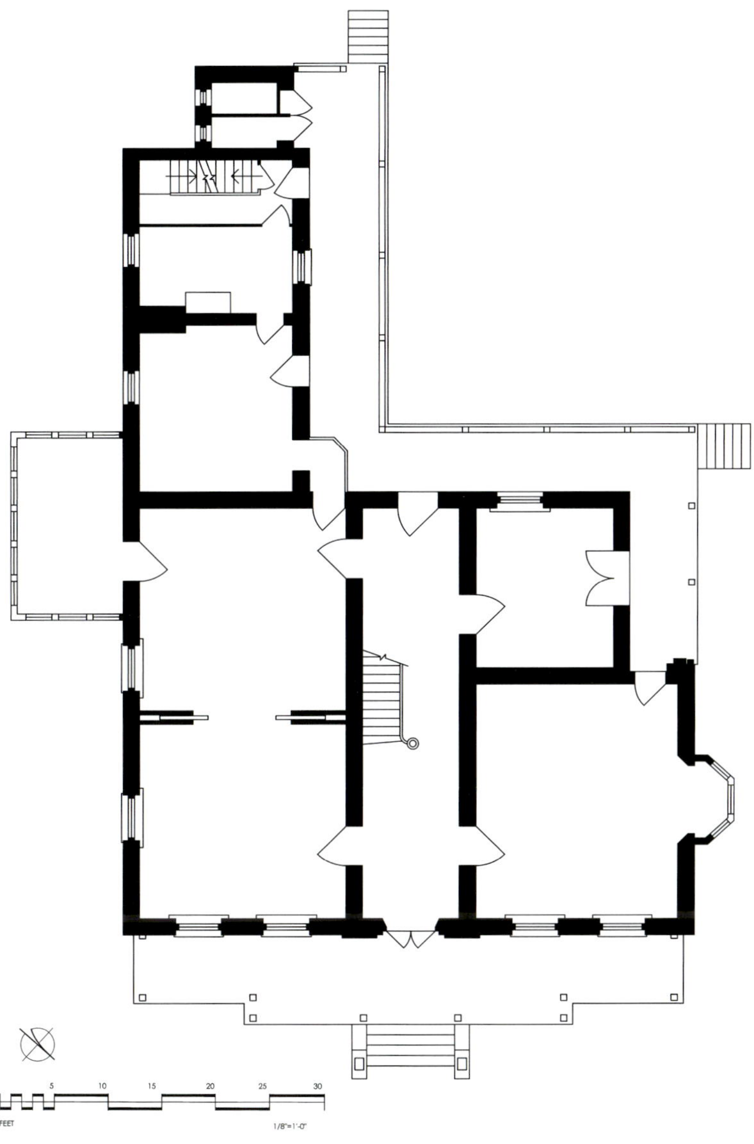

Figure 5.18. Edward Steves house, plan of ground floor. Original drawing courtesy of the Conservation Society of San Antonio, translated by Hayley M. Field.

while the ornate attic dormer windows gave a Second Empire appearance. Writing about the house, Kenneth Hafertepe suggests that the Steves were influenced by pattern books of the period such as A. J. Bicknell's *Village Builder* when planning details such as the rooftop cresting, polychromatic painted shingles, and mansard roof.[30] Their visit to the 1876 Centennial Exposition in Philadelphia, where they purchased some furnishings and a garden fountain, might also have provided inspiration.

Edward Steves applied his knowledge of woods and fine woodworking throughout the interior, using a variety of woods and finishes in flooring, doors, paneling, wainscoting, cornices, and balusters. A reporter visiting the home as it neared completion observed that no residence in Texas "excelled Mr. Steves for beauty of finish, style of architecture and convenience" (figs. 5.19 and 5.20).[31]

Figure 5.19. Photo montage of Steves house, 1878. Courtesy of Conservation Society of San Antonio Foundation.

Figure 5.20. Pattern-book illustration that might have provided architect Alfred Giles and builder J. H. Kampmann with design ideas for the Steves house. Exterior of a house by D. B. Provost of Elizabeth, NJ, in A. J. Bicknell, *Bicknell's Village Builder* (New York, 1872), supp. plate 1. Courtesy of Winterthur Library: Printed Book and Periodical Collection.

Johanna Steves remained in the house following her husband's death in 1900. In 1913, she hired architect Leo M. J. Dielmann to design a natatorium filled by a gushing artesian well drilled behind the house. There Johanna Steves and her neighbors exercised and escaped the Texas heat.[32]

After Johanna Steves's death in 1930, the house was rented but never divided into multiple apartments, a fate suffered by other neighborhood houses. It was donated to the Conservation Society of San Antonio in 1952 and opened as a house museum in 1954. Still owned by the Conservation Society, the Steves Homestead is operated in conjunction with its fellow house museum Villa Finale.

Villa Finale (Norton-Polk-Mathis House)
401 King William Street
1876, 1883, 1899

King William Street was still an unnamed thoroughfare when hardware merchant Russell Cogwell Norton purchased three lots there in 1869, the year after he married Ellen Hayes Whiteley. Both had long-standing ties to San Antonio. Norton's father was a distinguished Texas jurist, and Whiteley's father, Captain (and later, General) R. H. K. Whiteley, oversaw construction of the nearby United States Arsenal, which he commanded until it was relinquished to Confederate troops on February 28, 1861.[33]

Not until June 1876 did the Nortons pay architect and builder Francis Crider three thousand dollars to construct a one-story stone house measuring 46 × 35.5 feet on their property. The house had four rooms, a central hallway, four chimneys, front and back galleries, and a two-room rear wing. The gable roof was metal, and the woodwork, pine. Typical of the period, only the primary elevation was plastered and painted; the secondary facades were unfinished.[34]

Russell Norton experienced financial difficulties and sold the house in 1882 to cattleman Edwin Polk.[35] In 1883, architects Wahrenberger and Beckmann advertised for bids to build a 30 × 36-foot "addition to a soft rock house for Mr. E. Polk on King William Street."[36] Though it has been speculated that Russell Norton added a second floor to the house, bids for the 1883 addition suggest that it was Polk. The 1886 Augustus Koch bird's-eye-view map illustrates a two-story house with no rear addition, and the 1896 Sanborn Fire Insurance Map shows the house with a one-story frame addition (figs. 5.22 and 5.23).

Figure 5.21. Villa Finale, front elevation. Photo by Brent R. Fortenberry.

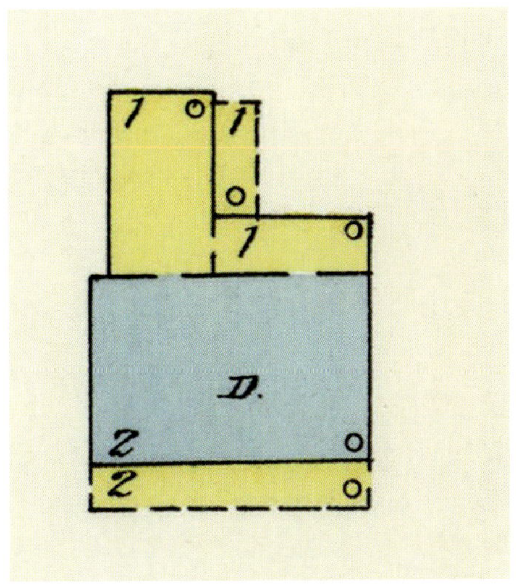

Figure 5.22. Map of Villa Finale, 1896, after purchase by Edwin Polk. Sanborn-Perris Map Co., Limited, New York.

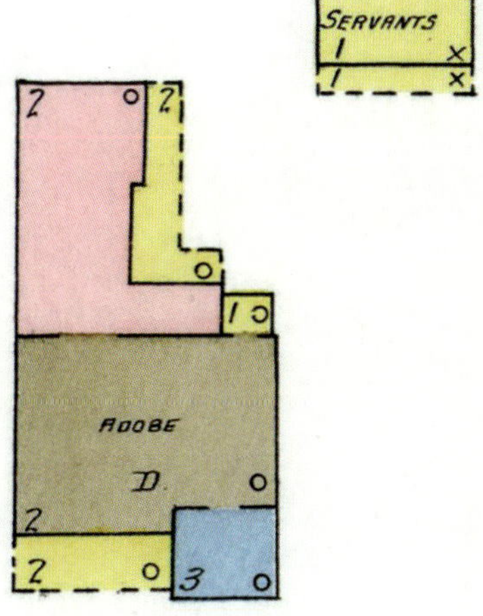

Figure 5.23. Map of Villa Finale, 1904, after additions by Ike and Myra Stafford Pryor. Sanborn Map Company, New York.

After Edwin Polk lost the house to foreclosure in 1895, it was purchased by investors who sold it in 1896 to renowned cattleman, trail driver, and rancher Isaac "Ike" T. Pryor and his wife, Myra Stafford Pryor. In 1899, the Pryors remodeled the house at an estimated cost of eight thousand dollars. The addition of a three-story Italianate corner tower with mansard roof, double gallery, and classical columns and frieze transformed the simple vernacular home into a grand, high-style residence (fig. 5.24).[37]

The Pryors conveyed their home to cattleman and railroad financier Dillard Rucker Fant in 1901, and it was acquired by Eva Brough following Fant's death in 1908. After Brough married banker Dwight E. Potter, the couple named their house "Norwood."[38]

The Brough-Potters sold the house in 1917 just as other neighborhood houses were being subdivided to meet the housing shortage caused by an influx of military families during World War I. In 1918–19, Norwood was used as a dormitory for soldiers' wives and mothers.[39] The house was acquired in 1924 by saloonkeeper William "Billy" Keilman, whose wife, Minnie, a well-known madam, repurposed it as a speakeasy and brothel. A subsequent owner operated the once-grand house as eight small apartments.[40]

Figure 5.24. Villa Finale in its completed form, ca. 1915. From *San Antonio, the City of Beautiful Homes* (San Antonio: Passing Show Printing, 1915).

In 1967, civic leader and collector Walter Nold Mathis purchased the house that he named "Villa Finale" and undertook a two-year restoration. In 2004, Mathis bequeathed Villa Finale and his extensive collections to the National Trust for Historic Preservation, which operates the property as a museum and learning center (fig. 5.25).[41]

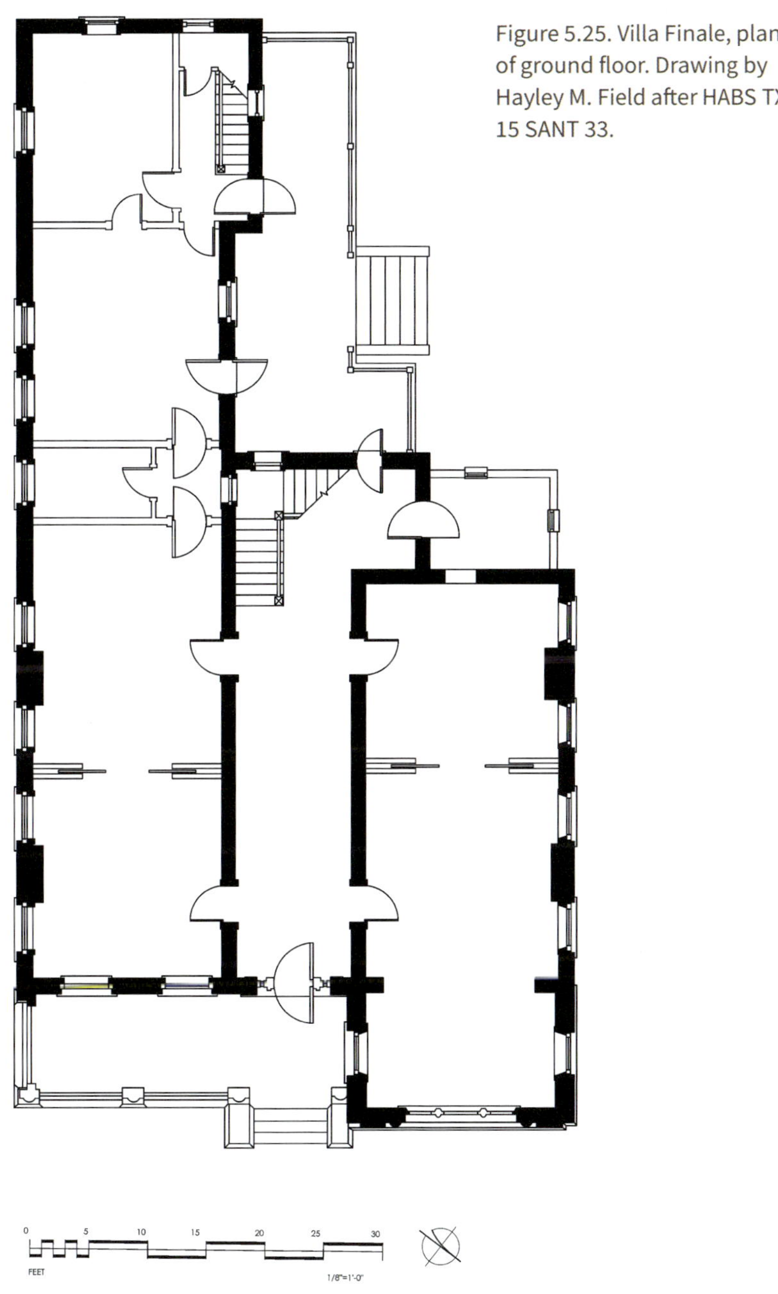

Figure 5.25. Villa Finale, plan of ground floor. Drawing by Hayley M. Field after HABS TX 15 SANT 33.

Figure 5.26. Charles F. A. Hummel house, front elevation, 1884. Photo by Kenneth Hafertepe.

Charles F. A. Hummel House
309 King William Street
1884

Development in the King William neighborhood was well under way when gun and ammunition dealer Charles F. A. Hummel purchased this property in 1883 from Thomas J. Devine. Hummel, his wife, Emilie Wagner, and six children lived above their Commerce Street store until the house was completed. The Wagners hired architects James Wahrenberger and Albert Beckmann to design this Italianate-influenced house facing King William Street, at the time the city's most stylish thoroughfare (fig. 5.26).[42]

The Hummel house was built during the neighborhood's second major construction period following the Civil War. Twelve houses are known to have been completed on King William Street by 1880. When the 1886 Augustus Koch bird's-eye-view map of the city was published, there were approximately thirty. While some were small cottages, others like the

Figure 5.27. Architects James Wahrenberger and Albert Beckmann's design for the Hummel house drew on popular design motifs of the period, as in the W. B. Corneau house, Springfield, IL, by architect E. E. Meyers. From A. J. Bicknell, *Bicknell's Village Builder* (New York, 1872), plate 18, front elevation. Courtesy of US Military Academy Library, West Point, NY.

Hummel house reflected the increased sophistication and financial capacity of their owners and the academic training of local designers.[43]

Wahrenberger and Beckmann designed the Hummel house early in their partnership. The following year they received a commission to design another prominent King William landmark, the Edward Steves Jr. house at 431 King William Street.[44]

The Hummel house is typical of the eclectic Gothic Revival style exhibited in many houses built in the King William neighborhood and throughout San Antonio and Texas in the late 1800s, drawing on eastern pattern books (fig. 5.27). It incorporates Italianate influences as seen in the two-story projecting pavilion that dominates the primary (east) facade, the two-story bay window on the north elevation, and the rusticated quoins. The house is generally L-shaped in plan and built of locally quarried limestone and brick. The deep two-story gallery spans the width of the house and comprises square chamfered wood columns with distinctive jigsaw-cut corner brackets. Finely carved stone quoins and window moldings reflect the same refined craftsmanship evident in other neighborhood houses.[45]

Figure 5.28. The Hummel family on the porch of their King William Street home.
Courtesy of John Doski and Deborah Mueller.

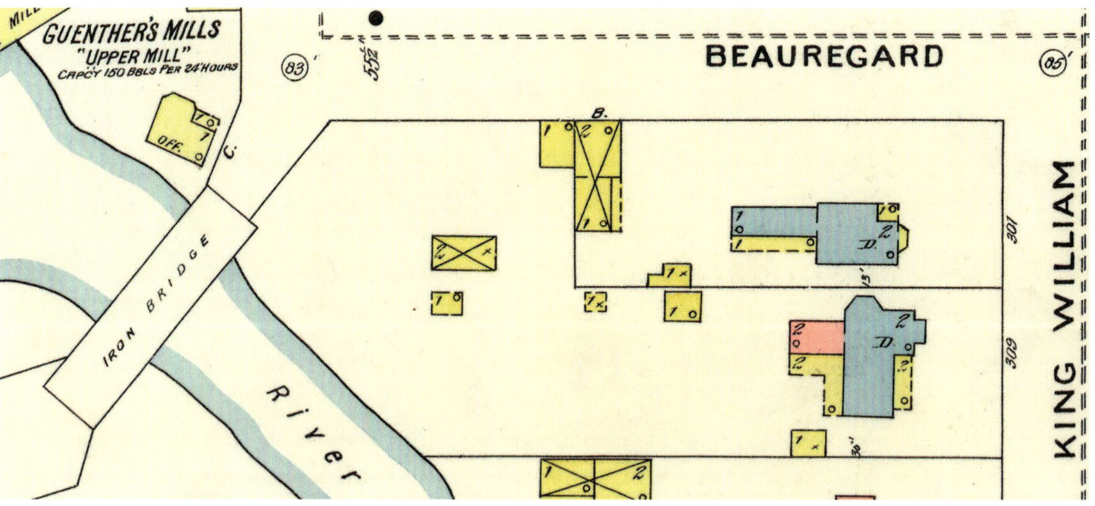

Figure 5.29. Hummel house, 1884, was first illustrated on the 1896 Sanborn-Perris map.
Sanborn-Perris Map Co., Limited, 1896.

As restored, with the exception of a back porch enclosure, the original layout of the house has been retained. The entry hall is dominated by a curving spiral stairway rising to bedrooms on the second floor. The living and dining rooms, separated by operable pocket doors, are located on the north side of the house, while a secondary parlor is to the south of the entry. The kitchen is located in the rear ell (fig. 5.28).

With the exception of a few years, the Hummels lived in the house until their deaths—she in 1927 and he in 1935. It was sold out of the family in 1941 and subdivided into rental units during the neighborhood's prolonged decline from the 1910s to the late 1960s. Walter Mathis, who was largely responsible for renewed interest in the King William neighborhood in the early to mid-1970s, purchased the Hummel house in 1972. He restored the deteriorated exterior and sold it to owners who completed extensive renovations. Subsequent owners have continued to maintain the house, which remains a single-family residence (fig. 5.29).

Yturri-Edmunds Historic Site and House
257 Yellowstone
Circa 1860
Mill foundation, early nineteenth century (?); reconstructed 1964
Louis Ogé Carriage House, circa 1881; relocated 1965
Cristof Postert House, circa 1855; relocated 1984

Traveling south from the King William neighborhood, the road leading to Mission Concepción passes the Yturri-Edmunds Historic Site, owned and managed by the Conservation Society of San Antonio since 1961. The society inherited the property from Ernestine Edmunds, granddaughter of Manuel Yturri de Castillo, who was granted the land in 1824. When the group took possession of the site, it included a furnished vernacular adobe house (ca. 1860) and ruined grist mill (fig. 5.30). Under the society's stewardship, the house and mill were restored and two buildings relocated to the site—the Louis Ogé carriage house (1881) and Cristof Postert house (1855).[46]

Research is ongoing to determine the origin and precise dates of both the mill and house. Recent scholarship suggests a possible association between the mill and one built by Juan Manuel Zambrano at this approximate location about 1807. Prior to twentieth-century channelization, the river ran closer to this site and was a reliable source of water power. After Manuel de Yturri Castillo was granted the land, he repaired an existing

Figure 5.30. Yturri-Edmunds house, front elevation, ca. 1860. Photo by Brent F. Fortenberry.

dam and irrigation ditch to divert water to his fields. Manuel Yturri and his family are not known to have lived on the property. When he died in 1843, there was no mention of the house or mill.[47]

The house represents three building periods—a one-room structure, a two-room addition to the north, and a three-room addition to the west—all of adobe construction. Though the family dated the oldest room to Yturri's acquisition of the property in 1824, John C. Garner, writing for the Historic American Buildings Survey in 1969, places it no earlier than the 1840s and, more probably, in the 1850s.[48] Garner called the Yturri-Edmunds house "without a doubt one of the more significant structures in the San Antonio area" (fig. 5.31).[49]

After she was widowed, Maria Josefa Yturri married Judge Thomas Whitehead in 1847. She died in 1849, and the property passed to her minor children, Vicenta and Mariano. Whitehead became his stepchildren's guardian and managed their assets until they reached adulthood. He is known to have purchased building material in 1859–60, stating he intended to build a mill and other improvements on their property below the city.[50]

Vicenta Yturri received this land when she and her brother divided their inherited holdings in 1863. She had married Ernest Edmunds in 1861, and family tradition maintains the couple began building a house here but stopped because of the Civil War. When building resumed, the

Figure 5.31. Ernestine Edmunds with her mother and friends at the Edmunds homestead. Courtesy of San Antonio Conservation Society Foundation.

Figure 5.32. The Louis Ogé carriage house before its move from 209 Washington Street to the Yturri-Edmunds site in 1965. Courtesy of San Antonio Conservation Society Foundation.

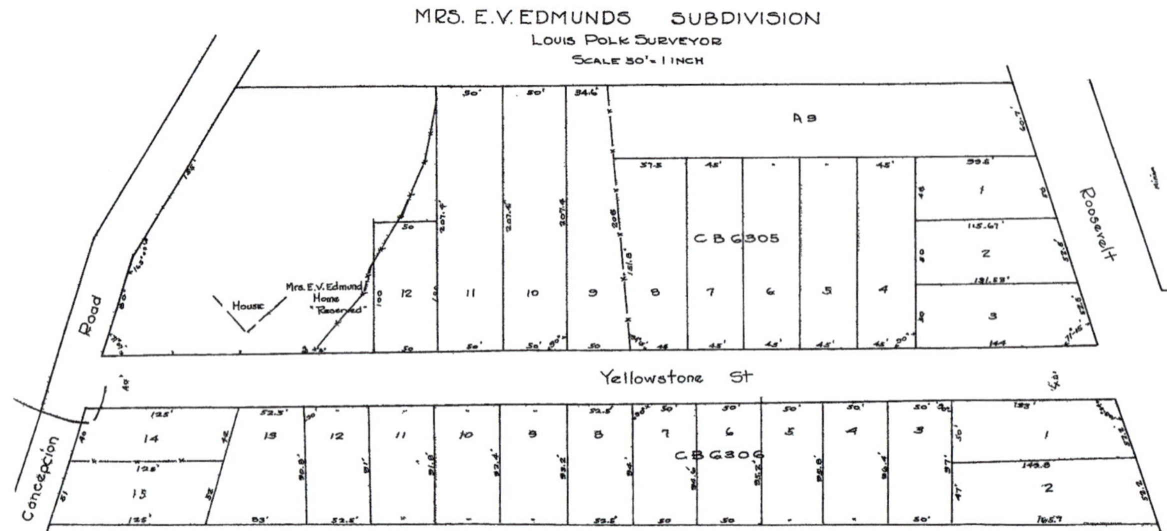

Figure 5.33. The Edmunds family's property was subdivided and developed according to this plat filed in 1923. Bexar County Plat Records, Plat Book 642, p. 124.

result was a triple-pen, rectangular structure with a low-pitched, shingle gabled roof and deep porch extending the full length of the east elevation, with a rear three-room shed roofed addition to the west side of the house. Exterior walls are plastered, and interior walls are finished in whitewashed lime plaster. The house spanned the irrigation ditch running through the property.[51]

When the Edmunds mortgaged their property in 1873, it was described as their homestead. Ernest died in 1874, and it is thought that Vicenta remained in the house. When she leased ten acres for farming in 1879, she reserved the "old mill" for her own use.[52] Vicenta Edmunds lived here until her death in 1924, leaving the property to her three children. Her daughter, Ernestine, died here in 1961, willing the property to the Conservation Society of San Antonio. When the society acquired the site, the only remnant of the mill was an adobe wall and stone steps. The frame mill house and mill equipment were reconstructed in 1964 according to plans by architect Marvin Eickenroht with advice from local millwrights (fig. 5.33).

The two-story, board-and-batten Ogé carriage house, which stood at 209 Washington Street in the King William neighborhood until 1965, was saved from demolition and moved to the Yturri-Edmunds property. The building's exterior was restored and the interior modified to include a meeting room, kitchen, and bathroom on the first floor and an apartment on the second floor. Original openings, including the hayloft door, were repurposed as windows and entry doors, and the decorative roofline trim was restored (fig. 5.32).[53]

The one-room, *fachwerk* Christof Postert house, constructed of cedar posts infilled with limestone and covered with lime plaster, originally stood south of downtown San Antonio at 1604 South Flores. Like the Ogé carriage house, it was threatened with demolition and moved to the Yturri-Edmunds site in 1984. The interior of the house features a raised fireplace.

Notes

1. Edward W. Heusinger, *A Chronology of Events in San Antonio: A Community on New Spain's Northern Frontier* (San Antonio: Standard Printing, 1951), 9; and Jesus F. de la Teja, *San Antonio de Béxar* (Albuquerque: University of New Mexico Press, 1995), 28. Pedro Huizar was born in Aguas Calientes, Mexico, in 1740 but did not arrive in San Antonio de Béxar until the 1770s. Though his popular identity derives largely from his reported carving of Mission San José's facade and Rose Window, Huizar's lesser-known skill as a surveyor contributed to an equally enduring legacy.

2. De la Teja, *San Antonio de Béxar*, 28, 43, 79, 84–86; Bexar County Spanish Archives, MR-2, Bexar County Clerk files. De la Teja's *San Antonio de Béxar* contains a complete account of this transitional period in the city's history. The Indian residents of Mission San Antonio de Valero chose lands below the mission in the area known as the Labores de Abajo. The documentation of Pedro Huizar's grant has not been located; however, it is referred to in other documents, including Bexar County Deed Records (BCDR), LGS #26, Bexar County Clerk files. Huizar's land was bounded roughly by the San Antonio River and today's Turner, St. Mary's, and Nueva Streets. He also owned a second tract farther to the south.

3. BCDR, B2:306–7 (McMullen to Devine, September 4, 1844); "Thomas J. Devine House," Historic American Buildings Survey, Library of Congress, https://www.loc.gov/pictures/search/?q=thomas%20j%20devine%20house&co=hh.

4. BCDR, I1:258–59 (Devine to Roesler, August 12, 1850); L1: 254–55 (Devine to Elder, July 18, 1853). Kate Mitchell's land was described as "the three upper tables of irrigable land on the tract formerly owned by John McMullen." Kate Elder acquired the land together with "buildings and improvements." The extent of the improvements is not known. The sixteen-acre tract is bounded roughly by today's Turner Street on the north, Beauregard Street on the south, Washington Street on the east, and the San Antonio River on the west.

5. Bexar County Marriage Records, D1:150 (N. A. Mitchell and Catherine Caroline Elder, February 12, 1857); "Newton A. Mitchell House," Historic American Buildings Survey; BCDR, H2:321–22 (Mitchell to Pentenrieder and Blersch, January 14, 1860); BCDR, H2:323 (Pentenrieder to Blersch, January 14, 1860); private collection, copy and translation held by Maria Watson Pfeiffer; BCDR, R1:162–63 (Dietz to Guenther, August 26, 1859); and Lewis F. Fisher, *C. H. Guenther & Son at 150 Years: The Legacy of a Texas Milling Pioneer* (San Antonio: Maverick Publishing, 2001), 25–28.

6. BCDR, Spanish Records, 2:60 (Amador to Governor, April 11, 1793); Spanish Records, 2:225 (Amador to Barrera, March 18, 1813); C-1:136 (Barrera to McMullen,

September 16, 1837); B-2:306 (McMullen to Devine, September 4, 1844); and BCDR, L-1:254 (Devine to Elder, July 18, 1853).

7. Bexar County Marriage Records, D1:150 (N. A. Mitchell and Catherine Caroline Elder, February 12, 1857); and BCDR, H2:321–22 (Mitchell to Pentenrieder and Blersch, January 14, 1860). Pentenrieder and Blersch immediately divided their property (BCDR, H2:323, January 14, 1860).

8. Gustav Blersch journal entries, private collection, copies held by Maria Watson Pfeiffer.

9. Gustav Blersch to Ernst Blersch, February 16, 1862, private collection, copy and translation held by Maria Watson Pfeiffer.

10. BCDR, W2:65–66 (Blersch to Thornton, June 6, 1871); BCDR, 239:245–46 (Gaston to Clarkson, September 5, 1905); and BCDR, 2547:461–62 (Groos to Watson, June 11, 1948).

11. Tulitas Wulff Jamieson, *Tulitas of Torreón: Reminiscences of Life in Mexico* (El Paso: Texas Western Press, 1969).

12. Jamieson, 50; "Wulff & Shetelig," *San Antonio Express*, July 1, 1868, 1; and "Death of Mr. Wulff," *San Antonio Express*, July 7, 1894.

13. BCDR, V1:110.

14. Kenneth Hafertepe, *The Material Culture of German Texans* (College Station: Texas A&M University Press, 2016), 172–76.

15. *San Antonio Daily Express*, March 30, 1871.

16. "A Neat Compliment," *San Antonio Daily Express*, March 22, 1890.

17. Anton Wulff House Vertical Files, Conservation Society of San Antonio.

18. Anne Stewart and Mike Stewart, *Ernst Hermann Altgelt, Founder of Comfort, Kendall County Texas* (Comfort, TX: Self-published, 2010), 1–8.

19. BCDR, V1:448 (Devine to Altgelt, April 13, 1868); and T2:666 (Alsbury to Altgelt, April 4, 1866).

20. Quoted in Judith Laufer, "Emma Altgelt: The House on King William," unpublished typescript, 1992, collection of Maria Watson Pfeiffer.

21. BCDR, 1:78 (Nelson to Altgelt, April 30, 1873); Earhart advertisement, *San Antonio Daily Express*, January 15, 1874, 1; and "City News," *San Antonio Daily Express*, January 5, 1877, 4.

22. Hafertepe, *Material Culture of German Texans*, 184.

23. Bexar County Builders and Mechanics Liens, A:112–18 (Altgelt to Steves, July 30, 1878); and BCDR, 14:459 (Altgelt to Steves, February 10, 1880).

24. BCDR, 19:412 (Altgelt to Schleuning, July 25, 1882).

25. "An Old Citizen Dies," *San Antonio Daily Light*, June 23, 1893, 1; "Obituary," *San Antonio Light*, August 8, 1932, 6-B; BCDR, 1711:276–77 (Schleuning to Martyn, August 11, 1939); and BCDR, 2063:536–37 (Martyn to Isbell, August 23, 1944).

26. Ethel Hander Geue, *New Homes in a New Land* (Baltimore: Genealogical Publishing, 1982), 136; and 1850 and 1860 United States Census, Comal County, Texas, https://www.ancestry.com/.

27. Frederick C. Chabot, *With the Makers of San Antonio* (San Antonio: Artes Graficas, 1937), 399–400; and "History of Lumber Business Is Told by Albert Steves Sr.," *San Antonio Light*, May 27, 1923.

28. Mary Carolyn Jutson, *Alfred Giles: An English Architect in Texas and Mexico* (San Antonio: Trinity University Press, 1972), 25, 31, 48–53. Giles was one of only five "architects and superintendents" listed in the 1877 San Antonio City Directory, the first published for the city. See *Mooney and Morrison's Directory of the City of San Antonio for 1877–78* (Galveston: Galveston News, 1877), 205–6.

29. "Fine Buildings," *San Antonio Express*, January 5, 1877, 4.

30. Hafertepe, *Material Culture of German Texans*, 176–79.

31. Donald E. Everett, *San Antonio: The Flavor of Its Past, 1845–1898* (San Antonio: Trinity University Press, 1975), 52.

32. [Leo M. J. Dielmann], *Dielmann's Review* (San Antonio: n.p., n.d.), 31; "Push Work on Pool," *San Antonio Light*, June 15, 1913, 12; and "Going Back to the Days When Everyone Had His Bathhouse," *San Antonio Express*, August 31, 1913.

33. "A Note upon Title 'Phillips' in Appendix to 'Bond's Genealogies of Watertown," *New England Historical and Genealogical Register and Antiquarian Journal* 27 (July 1873): 290–91; facsimile reprint (Bowie, MD: Heritage Books, 1995); and "San Antonio United States Arsenal," Historic American Buildings Survey, 1969. Norton's father, Milford P. Norton, came to Texas in 1839, and Whiteley's father was sent to San Antonio in 1858 to establish and command the United States Arsenal located one block north of Villa Finale. Milford Norton died in San Antonio in 1860.

34. BCDR, 4:468–70 (Agreement between San Antonio Real Estate Building & Loan Association and R. C. Norton and Wife, June 24, 1876).

35. BCDR, 21:348 (Norton to Polk, December 28, 1882).

36. "Contract Bids," *San Antonio Light*, August 31, 1883, 4; and "Building Permits," *San Antonio Light*, September 5, 1883, 4. Bids ranged from $3,355 to $5,650. The winning bidder has not been identified.

37. BCDR, 147:480–81 (Chandler and Franklin to Pryor, October 23, 1896); "Light Flashes," *San Antonio Sunday Light*, October 16, 1898, 4; and "The Hoof and Horn," *San Antonio Daily Light*, May 18, 1899, 5.

38. BCDR, 196:53 (Pryor to Fant, April 6, 1901); BCDR, 290:527–28 (Fant Estate to Brough, September 14, 1908); and Craig H. Roell, "Fant, Dillard Rucker," *Handbook of Texas Online*, accessed February 3, 2020, http://www.tshaonline.org/handbook/online/articles/ffa03.

39. BCDR, 525:63 (Potter to Bacon Investment Company, November 12, 1917); "Shelter for the Night," *San Antonio Light*, March 24, 1918; and "Woman's Home to Be Closed," *San Antonio News*, January 18, 1919.

40. BCDR, 773:211–12 (Gwinn to Keilman, June 23, 1924); and 899:157–58 (Keilman to Keilman, June 17, 1926).

41. BCDR, 5883:336 (Campbell to Mathis, December 27, 1967); and 10541:662–64 (Mathis to National Trust, January 28, 2004).

42. BCDR, 31:291–92 (Devine to Hummel, October 20, 1883); *San Antonio Daily Express*, January 14, 1883; and J. S. Reilly, *San Antonio, Past, Present and Future* (San Antonio: n.p., 1885), 127–28. Wahrenberger and Beckmann practiced together from 1883 until about 1890.

43. Augustus Koch, *Bird's Eye View of the City of San Antonio, Bexar County, Texas, 1873*; and Augustus Koch, *Bird's Eye View Map of San Antonio, Bexar Co., Texas, 1886. Looking North East*, Texana-Genealogy Collection, San Antonio Public Library.

44. Jack R. McGregor, "The King William Section of San Antonio," *Antiques*, September 1975, 451, 453; and Andrew Morrison, *Historic San Antonio, the Alamo City: Her Prosperity and Prospects* (San Antonio: Metropolitan Publishing, 1887), n.p. Morrison states that the partnership was formed in 1882.

45. Just as Kenneth Hafertepe suggests that the Edward Steves house design (509 King William) might have been informed by A. J. Bicknell's *Village Builder*, he also references Bicknell's "Design of Suburban Residence" as a possible inspiration for Wahrenberger and Beckmann's Hummel house. Hafertepe, *Material Culture of German Texans*, 183.

46. Katherine Cruse, "History of the Yturri-Edmunds House and Mill, 257 Yellowstone, San Antonio, Texas," unpublished typescript, Yturri-Edmunds Vertical Files, Conservation Society of San Antonio.

47. Cruse; and Sergio A. Iruegas, *San Antonio Mission Trails Statewide Transportation Enhancement Project*, vol. 3., *Construction Package IV: An Intensive Archeological Survey and National Register Testing at Historic Yturri-Edmunds Mill, Roosevelt Park, and Eagleland Neighborhood, Bexar County, Texas* (Austin: GTI Environmental, 2009), 31.

48. Cruse, "History of the Yturri-Edmunds House and Mill." Further study indicates the house probably dates to the 1860s and later.

49. "Manuel Yturri Castillo Residence," Historic American Buildings Survey Inventory, March 7, 1969.

50. Bexar County Marriage Records, A:123, August 27, 1847; and Cruse, "History of the Yturri-Edmunds House and Mill," 5.

51. Bexar County Marriage Records, D2:294, August 5, 1861; and Cruse, "History of the Yturri-Edmunds House and Mill," 6–7.

52. BCDR, 13:598–600 (Edmunds to Young, October 24, 1879).

53. Yturri-Edmunds Vertical File, Conservation Society of San Antonio.

Vernacular Buildings of the Westside

Sarah Zenaida Gould

The Mexican Revolution broke out nearly seventy-five years after San Antonio ceased to be part of Mexico, but it remains one of the most significant events in San Antonio history. It has had an impact on the local economy, influenced the political scene, and expanded the population with an influx of thousands of refugees. That these refugees descended on San Antonio was not surprising. By the late eighteenth century San Antonio was the center of Spanish (later Mexican) Texas, countless San Antonio families had relatives on both sides of the post-1836 border, and a network of roads and railroads connected interior Mexico to San Antonio, making it easy for San Antonio to maintain its status as the Mexican American cultural capital of the United States.[1] Indeed, the Mexican Revolution started in San Antonio when exiled presidential candidate (and eventual president) Francisco I. Madero issued the Plan de San Luis de Potosí —a call for the overthrow of Mexican president Porfirio Díaz— while staying at the now demolished Hutchins Hotel in downtown San Antonio in November 1910.[2] Though other critics of the Díaz regime, such as Enrique and Ricardo Flores Magón, founders of the Partido Liberal Mexicano, spent their time in San Antonio in homes to the north of downtown, a large percentage of Mexican Revolution refugees landed in the city's west end near the International and Great Northern (I&GN) Railroad line, an area known today as the Westside.[3]

Born out of an area the Spanish established as Villa Guadalupe in 1733, the land was sold off to "incumbent and former councilmen and city officials who held the parcels for speculation" following San Antonio's incorporation in 1842.[4] In the early twentieth century, the

Westside was notable for its diverse population, a result of a lack of racial deed restrictions common to other parts of San Antonio. African Americans, Lebanese/Syrians, Anglos, and others joined earlier waves of Belgian and German farmers and long-established Mexican American families in the Westside. General John J. Pershing's futile 1917 search for Pancho Villa in northern Mexico led to the arrival of an exiled group of Chinese migrants in San Antonio. Some of "Pershing's Chinese," as they were called, also settled in the Westside. This diversity produced a number of notable blended Westside families of Lebanese-Mexican and Chinese-Mexican descent.

The boundaries of the Westside have evolved over time, and even today there is limited consensus on where it begins and ends. Cultural geographer Daniel Arreola described the emergence of a "dual landscape," following the overthrow of Mexican rule in 1836, with separate Mexican and Anglo downtowns by the early twentieth century.[5] The Mexican downtown was located to the immediate west of San Pedro Creek. As described in a 1938 city guidebook, "the Mexican District of San Antonio is a city all to itself, existing side by side with the gringo city across San Pedro Creek."[6] Alternately called Laredito or the Mexican Quarter, this area encompassing roughly Houston Street to the north, Nueva (formerly Monterey) Street to the south, San Pedro Creek to the east, and Pecos Street to the west was the pre–urban renewal commercial center of the Westside, including dozens of Mexican American–owned businesses and Spanish-language theaters, but the Westside stretched as far west as Zarzamora Street or even West Twenty-Fourth Street. Throughout the 1920s and early 1930s residents could travel across the Westside via streetcars along Ruiz, West Commerce, Guadalupe, and Laredo Streets.[7] When the streetcars stopped running in 1933, buses took their place (fig. 6.1).

The 1960s began an era of pushing the Westside's boundaries farther west, beyond Interstate 10 and extending as far west as Callaghan Road, and today there are only a few remnants of the old Westside. These include the Alameda Theater, a grandiose Spanish-language movie palace dating to 1949; the Mercado (Market Square), the old produce row where many *Mexicanos* sold their goods and which remains an important cultural touchstone for many Mexican American San Antonians but now is primarily promoted as a tourist destination, resulting in a tension in identity; and Casa Navarro, the former Laredito home of José Antonio Navarro, a signer of the Texas Declaration of Independence and Texas statesman, and now a National Historic Landmark (fig. 6.2 ; see also fig. 3.4).

Figure 6.1. The Westside, from Map of the City of San Antonio, Bexar County, Including Suburbs Both North and South, 1924. Image by Nic Tengg.

Figure 6.2. Casa Navarro, ca. 1962, with the new county jail being erected behind it. Courtesy of Harvey Belgin Photograph Collection, B-021-D-01, UTSA Special Collections.

The Westside has no singular dominant residential architectural style. Rather, the built environment is a reflection of successive waves of settlement as well as periods of often destructive urban renewal. In the mid-nineteenth century, the area was notably home to jacales, an indigenous architectural form typically made of vertical mesquite posts, horizontal mesquite branches, walls plastered with mud or adobe, and a thatched roof. Though jacales had relatively short life spans because it was relatively easy and affordable to repair and replace them, they persisted in the area through the first half of the twentieth century.[8] Following the I&GN line's arrival in San Antonio in 1881, the Westside neighborhood of Prospect Hill was founded in 1884 (roughly West Martin [formerly Lakeview] to the north, Cesar Chavez [formerly Durango] to the south, Zarzamora to the west, and Alazán Creek to the east) and flourished with small to medium-sized Victorian homes (folk and Queen Anne) dating from about 1890 to 1910.[9] In the aftermath of the outbreak of the Mexican Revolution, more modest bungalows and craftsman-style homes were built throughout the Westside, primarily from 1910 to 1925, the period to which most of the area's historic homes date. Additionally, with a heavy concentration of working-class laborers simple shotgun houses, typically one room wide and several rooms deep, as well as *corrales*, groupings of typically wooden houses or single-story barrack-style apartments around a common outdoor area, flourished in the 1920s–30s.[10] Other types of homes found in the Westside include late nineteenth-century farmhouses not dissimilar to those found in the Texas Hill Country, as well as Spanish Eclectic and Mission styles.

While many of the residential architectural styles found in the Westside are not unique to the area, distinctive characteristics mark many of the homes. As defined by Daniel Arreola in his classic study on Mexican American housescapes, Westside homes are painted in every color of the rainbow, the front yards are generally enclosed by a fence, and the yardscapes are frequently adorned with religious shrines. Arreola traces these design patterns to pre-Columbian Mexico as well as Moor-inspired Iberian practices.[11]

He further claims that because San Antonio has remained a receiving point for new migrants from Mexico, cycles of reinvigoration of Mexican culture flow through the city, keeping the Mexican culture fresh, thus largely staving off assimilation of the Westside's cultural aesthetics.[12]

Westside commercial buildings similarly run the gamut of styles, including Beaux-Arts, Classical Revival, Romanesque, Mission, and

Spanish Colonial. Perhaps the most important commercial architectural styles in the Westside are those used for pecan-shelling factories and small stores, called *tienditas*. San Antonio sits at the center of Texas' commercial pecan-growing industry, and in the early twentieth century surrounding counties sent their pecans to San Antonio to be shelled at factories that primarily employed Mexican Americans for pennies an hour. Pecan-shelling factories ranged in size and design, but several in the Westside occupied two-story brick warehouse-style buildings (fig. 6.3). Similar buildings were used for garment factories, such as the Basila Frocks building at 500 North Zarzamora. *Tienditas* are especially distinctive in design and far more common in the Westside than in other working-class areas of San Antonio (fig. 6.4). Built of wood, brick, or stone, *tienditas* are typically small, narrow buildings, sometimes with a residence attached to the back, sometimes existing as a detached building located in the front yard of a residence. They often have a false-front facade in the form of a stepped gable, creating an upside-down "T" extending across the upper front of the structure (fig. 6.5).[13]

Elongated octagonal windows and decorative tile work are distinctive ornamental features of a number of twentieth-century Westside commer-

Figure 6.3. Workers striking outside a Spanish Revival pecan-shelling factory that once stood at 1927 Guadalupe Street, 1938. Courtesy of San Antonio Light Collection, L-1759-P, UTSA Special Collections.

Figure 6.4. Basila Frocks building. Courtesy of Zintgraff Collection, Z-0239-B-01, UTSA Special Collections.

Figure 6.5. La Perla, front facade, 1500 Guadalupe Street. Photo by Kristel Puente.

cial buildings. Offering relatively inexpensive flair, such windows were likely custom-made, as a variety of sizes can be seen in the neighborhood and some of the tiles would have been locally made at the San Jose Mission Potteries, including those seen on the exterior of the Guadalupe Theater (fig. 6.28).

The Great Depression hit the Westside particularly hard, as did the automation of pecan shelling, which resulted in underemployment in the community.[14] Father Carmelo Tranchese of the Westside's Guadalupe Catholic Church lobbied for years to bring public housing to San Antonio. His efforts resulted in construction of the Alazan-Apache Courts, the first authorized and largest public housing project in San Antonio. The International style–influenced Los Courts, as they are sometimes called, still stand in the Westside, a testament to community activism and decades of local government underinvestment in the area.[15] Noted local architect N. Straus Nayfach, a native San Antonian and Jewish Texan, trained at the University of Texas and spent most of his career designing homes for the middle class but also maintained a connection to the marginalized Mexican American community. He designed the Courts in the late 1930s along with several Westside Spanish-language theaters, including his masterpiece, the Alameda.

Beginning in the 1960s, urban renewal mercilessly hit the Westside, resulting in removal of large swaths of homes and businesses to make way for Interstate 10, the county jail, and later the city jail.[16] Today, the Westside continues to find itself threatened by unfettered development. Though the Westside is arguably one of the richest cultural areas of the city of San Antonio, it is also one of the poorest. Median household income in the Westside is $24,766; however, there are pockets where that number slips much lower.[17] Meanwhile, San Antonio is one of the fastest-growing cities in Texas (and the United States), with particularly aggressive city-incentivized, mostly market-rate, downtown residential development. With relatively low property values coupled with close proximity to downtown, the Westside is currently facing a crisis of land speculators, house flippers, and looming gentrification. The current encroachment of development was further fast-tracked in September 2018 when the University of Texas at San Antonio announced plans to expand its downtown campus into the Westside. Even in the course of writing this chapter, I have had to remove buildings from the listed sites because of demolitions. While many of these demolitions were fueled by a desire to sell vacant land to developers, others were the result of multiple code violations that the property owner could not afford to address. As one community member puts it, the Westside is the most valuable land in the poorest neighborhood, and the developers know it. Community members are presently working toward a historic district nomination in the hopes of staving off more erosion of our proudly working-class, mostly Mexican American neighborhood (fig. 6.6).

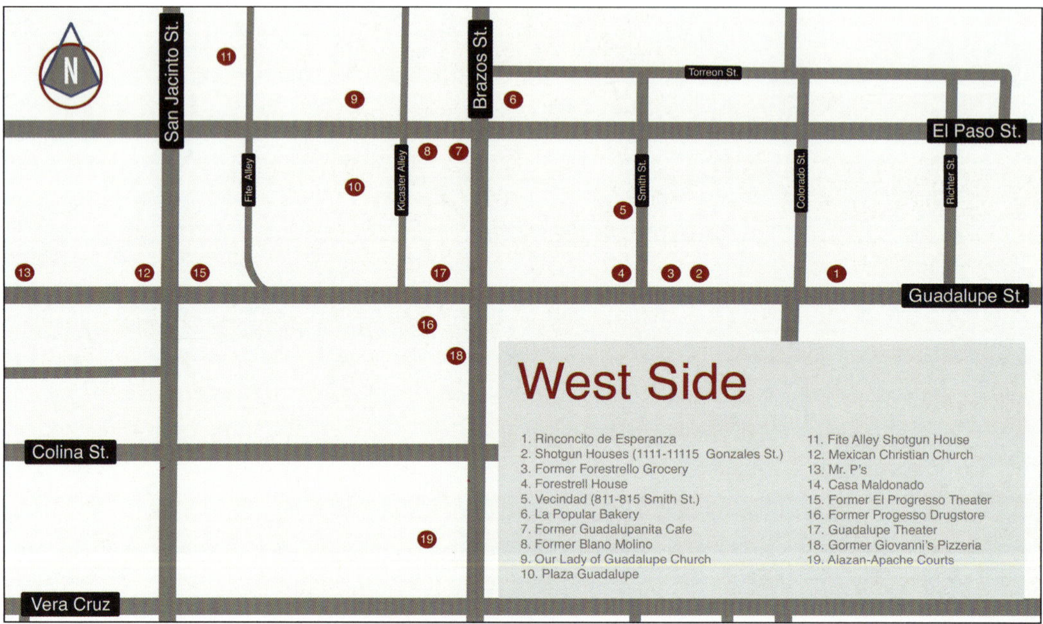

Figure 6.6. Map of the core West Side vernacular buildings.

Figure 6.7. Esperanza Peace & Justice Center. Photo by Sarah Gould.

Guadalupe Corridor Tour Highlights

Rinconcito de Esperanza
816 South Colorado Street

The Rinconcito de Esperanza is the Westside location of the Esperanza Peace & Justice Center, an arts and social justice organization that incorporates historic preservation into its community work. This site was formerly listed as 816 and 820 South Colorado (fig. 6.7).

Figure 6.8. Casa de Cuentos, south elevation, Rinconcito de Esperanza. Photo by Brent R. Fortenberry.

Casa de Cuentos

This folk Victorian house dates to approximately 1906. It has served as a home and as a small business, including Torres Grocery (1938–48) and three different dry cleaners (1951–63). In 1994, Emilia Sánchez owned the house and was known for taking care of the poor of the neighborhood. Community members called the house La Casa de Misericordia. In earlier times, up to four smaller structures existed behind this house, including the existing casita and a small bakery run by Manuel and Luisa Cazares (ca. 1931). The Esperanza Peace & Justice Center purchased the house in 2001 and has since operated the Casa de Cuentos as a community gathering space (fig. 6.8).

Casita

At only two hundred square feet, this 1920s casita is an example of a typical poor Westside family's home during that era. When the Esperanza acquired the three-room casita, the last of three casitas that once stood on the property, the seller offered to demolish it, and many thought it could not be salvaged. The original exterior cypress boards were too damaged to remain in their original location but were trimmed and reused for sections of the interior walls. New cypress boards were used to re-create

Figure 6.9. Casita, south elevation, Rinconcito de Esperanza. Photo by Brent R. Fortenberry.

the original exterior, and reclaimed lumber from stadium bleachers that were being dismantled at the nearby St. Mary's University were used in the floor and ceiling. A ductless mini-split air-conditioning system was installed along with new electrical wiring to make it a comfortable and functional space once again. Originally, the property included an outhouse, and the casita remains without a bathroom both to preserve the earlier layout and serve as a reminder of how many Westside families lived in the past. Today, the casita is used for programming as well as guest quarters (fig. 6.9).

MujerArtes Adobe Studio

Since 1995, the MujerArtes Clay Cooperative has offered training in clay arts to working-class women of all ages. Through sculpting, drawing, painting, and the telling of their stories, the women reflect in their clay creations their lives as *Mexicanas*, Chicanas, Latinas, and Westside residents. This "green" compressed earth-block (adobe) structure—the first to be built in the Westside in a century—was completed in 2017. It is an example of how the old ways are still good ways. The building is a long rectangle with two bathrooms and a small kitchen at the north end, a large studio space in the center, and a kiln room at the south end. The

Figure 6.10. MujerArtes Adobe Studio, west elevation, Rinconcito de Esperanza. Photo by Brent R. Fortenberry.

space is heated and cooled with a ductless mini-split system, which, coupled with the naturally insulated walls, keeps energy costs low. Members of MujerArtes designed the decorative tiles and murals that adorn the building's interior and exterior (fig. 6.10).

Ruben's Ice House

This structure began with the southern wooden half of the building, which dates to the 1930s. It was transformed from a home to the M&E Grocery Store (named for Manuel and Elida Reyes) around 1950. The narrow building was one big room with shelves on both sides and additional product displays along the length of the middle of the room. About 1959, owner Manuel Reyes constructed the concrete block addition, where he operated Ruben's Ice House (named after his son), a longtime community gathering space that closed in 1987. Another narrow rectangle, the addition was divided into a front room where beer was served (to men only), a walk-in cooler, and a kitchen at the back where burgers were served through a sliding window. Two small bathrooms were accessible from the outside west wall, and an enclosed patio (for women and families) sat at the back on an extant concrete pad. The once-common Texas icehouse—a combination convenience store and beer joint—is an endangered species, and fortunately this one still has the original walk-in cooler.[18] In 2007, the Esperanzas acquired Ruben's Ice House with the support of the Reyes children. It will be transformed into the Museo del Westside, a community participatory museum focusing on the rich history and culture of the Westside. Design plans by architect Dwayne Bohuslav call for rehabilitating the original structure and expanding the building with a compressed earth-block addition at the rear (figs. 6.11 and 6.12).

Figure 6.11. Ruben's Ice House, north elevation, Rinconcito de Esperanza. Photo by Brent R. Fortenberry.

Figure 6.12. Proposed rehabilitation of Esperanza Peace & Justice Center. Image by Arthuro Vilchis.

Figure 6.13. Shotgun houses at 1111–1115 Guadalupe Street, south elevation. Photo by Brent R. Fortenberry.

Shotgun Houses
1111, 1113, and 1115 Guadalupe Street

Three identical wooden straight shotgun houses, currently painted blue, lime-green, and yellow, exemplify the Westside color palette as well as the historic density of the neighborhood. The minimal setbacks bring the front doors of these houses nearly to the sidewalk (fig. 6.13).

Former Forestello Grocery Store
1203 Guadalupe Street

Dating to 1910, this wood and stucco storefront with residence originally housed the Forestello Grocery Store. Its rectangular plan is distinguished by the corner entry, curved gable, and wraparound awning. The Forestello family lived in the house next door for three generations (fig. 6.14).

Forestello House
1211 Guadalupe Street

This eclectic Neoclassical-inspired Victorian building has a stucco exterior, hipped roof, gable bay extensions, and wraparound porch with Corinthian columns. It remained in the Forestello family until 2016 (fig. 6.15).

Figure 6.14. Former Forestello Grocery Store, front elevation. Photo by Brent R. Fortenberry.

Figure 6.15. Forestello house, front elevation. Photo by Brent R. Fortenberry.

Figure 6.16. *Vecindad* houses in Smith Street, front elevation. Photo by Brent R. Fortenberry.

Vecindad

811, 811½, 813, and 815 South Smith Street

One of the few remaining examples of a *vecindad*, a cluster of homes on a shared lot, in the Westside, straight shotgun houses face the street, and additional houses are located behind them, facing each other. The wooden houses have small inset porches with concrete decks and corrugated metal roofs (fig. 6.16).[19]

La Popular Bakery

1225 El Paso Street

Formerly called La Chiquita Bakery, this location has served as a neighborhood bakery for more than forty years. Typical of the many family-owned bakeries around the Westside, they specialize in Mexican *pan dulce* (sweet bread). The corner entry opens into a small customer area dominated by long glass displays filled with *pan dulce*. The rest of the building, hidden behind a wall, houses the kitchen. The concrete-block exterior features one of the Westside's dozens of murals. San Anto Cultural Arts, a Westside youth arts program, created this one, titled *Familia y Cultura es Vida*, with Mary Agnes Rodriguez, a prolific Westside artist, serving as the lead artist (fig. 6.17).

Figure 6.17. La Popular Bakery, front elevation. Photo by Brent R. Fortenberry.

Figure 6.18. Former Guadalupanita Café, front elevation. Photo by Brent R. Fortenberry.

Former Guadalupanita Café
1310 El Paso Street

This wooden commercial storefront with a false-front facade and sidewalk awning was home to the Guadalupanita Café for thirty-seven years. Here Luis and Juanita Mata served up what many believe was the best salsa in town. The exterior details include stone veneer wainscoting along the front facade along with a hand-painted sign. Inside, the building features a small open dining area and enclosed kitchen. Today the building belongs to the Guadalupe Cultural Arts Center, which plans to rehabilitate and reopen it (fig. 6.18).

Figure 6.19. Former Blanco Molino, front elevation. Photo by Brent R. Fortenberry.

Former Blanca Molino
1316 El Paso Street

A former mill for Nix-Tamal, corn masa for making tortillas, this otherwise simple rectangular structure features a large window on either side of its double doors and a transom window above each opening. All are framed with decorative orange-and-white painted tiles. The Blanca Molino is also remembered for selling *barbacoa*, *carnitas*, and *chicharrones* on the weekends (fig. 6.19).

Our Lady of Guadalupe Church
1321 El Paso Street

Right Reverend John W. Shaw, coadjutor bishop of San Antonio, founded Our Lady of Guadalupe Church to serve the area's Spanish-speaking families. Leo M. J. Dielmann, a San Antonio native, designed the Romanesque Revival church in 1921. In 1932, the church was transferred to the

Jesuits, who appointed Father Carmelo Tranchese as its pastor. Father Tranchese worked tirelessly on behalf of the parish, leading the struggle to bring public housing to the Westside and championing Mexican American culture through his annual production of *Las Posadas*, a traditional Mexican Christmas play. The Jesuits left the church at the end of 2018, but it continues to serve the predominantly Mexican American community. The building features a common side-aisle plan common to Catholic interiors, with a ribbed barrel-vaulted ceiling that springs from the simple pilasters. The blue-painted ceiling is pierced by two compass-headed windows in each bay. The longitudinal plan terminates in an apsidal chancel with a raised step. A chancel rail is absent, and the altar is now pushed forward from the eastern wall, a product of the many reforms of Vatican II. The side aisles are covered by similar ribbed barrel vaults, terminating with chapels at the eastern ends of each (fig. 6.20).

Figure 6.20. Interior of Our Lady of Guadalupe Church. Photo by Brent R. Fortenberry.

Plaza Guadalupe
1329 Guadalupe Street

Plaza Guadalupe is an open-air plaza created in 1984 in the traditional style of the Spanish plaza located opposite the church. It was designed by Reyna/Caragonne, one of a few Latino architectural firms in San Antonio at the time. The El Paso Street side of the plaza features a statue of General Ignacio Zaragoza, who was born outside Goliad, Texas, and later led

Figure 6.21. Plaza Guadalupe, north entrance. Photo by Brent R. Fortenberry.

the Mexican army's victory over France at the Battle of Puebla—what we now celebrate as Cinco de Mayo. Adjacent to the plaza on the Guadalupe Street side is Westside artist Jesse Trevino's ten- by forty-foot tile mosaic *vela* (candle) depicting the Virgin of Guadalupe (fig. 6.21).

Shotgun Houses
300 block of Fite Alley

This original grouping of shotgun houses with Victorian and Neoclassical influences demonstrates the narrow lots and massing common in parts of the Westside that were developed in the 1930s. Slightly wider setbacks than seen in the shotguns on Guadalupe Street allow more room for plantings and front yard fences that are typical of the Westside (fig. 6.22).

Mexican Christian Church
1501 Guadalupe Street

This church in the Spanish Colonial Revival style opened in 1925. The stucco exterior features cast adornments, including finials and door surrounds; the windows and doors feature decorative wrought iron. The nave's ceiling is varnished wood with exposed timber trusses. The raised first floor sits on top of a full basement, a rarity in San Antonio (fig. 6.23).[20]

Figure 6.22. Shotgun houses on Fite Alley, front elevation. Photo by Brent R. Fortenberry.

Figure 6.23. Mexican Christian Church, front elevation. Photo by Brent R. Fortenberry.

Mr. P's

1601 Guadalupe Street

This eclectic commercial and residential structure has seen multiple additions as well as artistic interventions in its lifetime, including a mosaic tile Virgen de Guadalupe on the second floor looking over the street, mosaic tile benches planted in the sidewalk on either side of the walk-up service window, colorful metal rooster atop the wrought-iron accented

Figure 6.24. Mr. P's, front elevation. Photo by Brent R. Fortenberry.

patio cover, and metal dragon mounted on top of the business's sign pole. It currently serves as a popular taco, hamburger, and *raspa* (snow cone) eatery (fig. 6.24).

Casa Maldonado
13120 Guadalupe Street

Dating to the mid-1920s when it was Albino Maldonado's home, this structure is primarily associated with his son Bill Maldonado, a community leader active from the mid-1930s to 1960s. At a time when Mexican Americans were largely disenfranchised from local politics, Bill Maldonado organized meetings for Progressive Democrats and headquartered his Mexican American baseball league in this building. In 1948, Maldonado was the only Mexican American candidate for county commissioner in Bexar County and one of three Mexican Americans running for election in Texas. Though he never won an elected government position, many future elected officials learned the ropes at 1312 Guadalupe Street. Later, the building was transformed into a job training center and then Speedy's, a popular diner remembered for its burgers. The Maldonado family owned the building, a simple rectangle with a storefront parapet and sidewalk awning, from 1910 to 1997. In 2009, the property's new owner made a request to demolish the building, citing its age and condition. Thus began a two-year community-led battle to save the building. The two-story rear addition dating to the 1930s did not survive, but today, the rehabilitated one-story building is a reminder of the power of community organizing (fig. 6.25).[21]

Figure 6.25. Looking west on Guadalupe Street: Progress Drugstore (far left), Progress Theater (center), and Casa Maldonado (right), 1937. Courtesy of Zintgraff Collection, ∠-1216-L-01, UTSA Special Collections.

Former El Progress Theater
1306 Guadalupe Street

Built in 1931, the Progress Theater was an early Spanish-language theater in this part of the Westside. A single-floor structure built at two-story height to house an open auditorium, it was constructed from concrete and

Figure 6.26. Looking west on Guadalupe Street: Progress Drugstore (far left), Progress Theater (center), and Casa Maldonado (right), 2019. Photo by Kristel Puente.

the facade was stuccoed. The main entrance originally had an arched metal canopy overhead (fig. 6.26).[22]

Former Progress Drugstore
1300 Guadalupe Street

The existing concrete-block structure with stucco veneer mostly dates to 1941 but is built on an earlier 1920s structure; the current exterior reflects a mid-1940s renovation. The second story's Mexican tiled exterior walls mask the differences between the various construction phases of the building and are punctuated by hand-painted tile panoramas. The exterior walls of the first floor feature a skirt of black-and-white checkered tile and ribbed glass-block windows along Guadalupe Street and elongated octagonal windows along Brazos Street.[23] The recently renovated building currently belongs to the Guadalupe Cultural Arts Center and has served as offices (fig. 6.27).

Guadalupe Theater
1301 Guadalupe Street

Part of the Lucchese family Spanish-language theater empire in San Antonio, the Spanish Colonial–inspired Guadalupe Theater was designed by

Figure 6.27. Progress Drugstore, front facade. Photo by Kristel Puente.

Figure 6.28. Guadalupe Theater, south elevation. Photo by Brent R. Fortenberry.

N. Straus Nayfach in 1942 and anchored the area's entertainment district. The local San Jose Mission Potteries made the decorative tiles on the building's exterior. The corner entry is topped by a three-sided marquee and neon spire. The theater fell into decline in the 1960s and was rehabilitated by Reyna/Caragonne as part of the Guadalupe Cultural Arts Center in 1984. Today, the theater is a frequently used performance space for dance, theater, music, and film (fig. 6.28).

Former Giovanni's Pizzeria
913 South Brazos Street

Originally a wood-frame shotgun house dating to about 1900, the structure was converted to a *tiendita*, a small neighborhood grocery store, and at least four additions after 1912 resulted in the building's current footprint. By the 1980s, it was a stucco-over-wood siding structure housing the Courts Food Market, a store that primarily served the residents of the Alazan-Apache Courts, and most recently was a beloved neighborhood pizza shop. The side of the building features the mural *La Gloria en los Brazos de Guadalupe* (2010) by David Blancas. The mural depicts the Virgin Mary extending her arms around Westside landmarks that have been demolished or threatened, including La Gloria (1928–2002) and Casa Maldonado.[24] The building now belongs to the Esperanza Peace & Justice Center, which plans to reopen it as a healthy food store. Currently the closest grocery store is more than a mile away, and most Alazan-Apache Courts residents do not own a car (figs. 6.29 and 6.30).

Alazan-Apache Courts
1011 South Brazos Street

Built between 1939 and 1942, the Alazan-Apache Courts were the first approved public housing in San Antonio and remain the largest public housing project in the city. Constructed during the era of segregation for Mexican American residents, Los Courts, as they are known, were built to alleviate the substandard living conditions of some of the city's poorest residents. Originally housing nearly five thousand people, today the Courts have been substantially thinned out to about eighteen hundred residents. N. Straus Nayfach, who also remodeled the Guadalupe Theater and now-demolished Teatro Nacional, as well as designed the famed

Figure 6.29. Former Giovanni's Pizzeria, east elevation. Photo by Brent R. Fortenberry.

Figure 6.30. Mural on former Giovanni's Pizzeria, north facade. Photo by Brent R. Fortenberry.

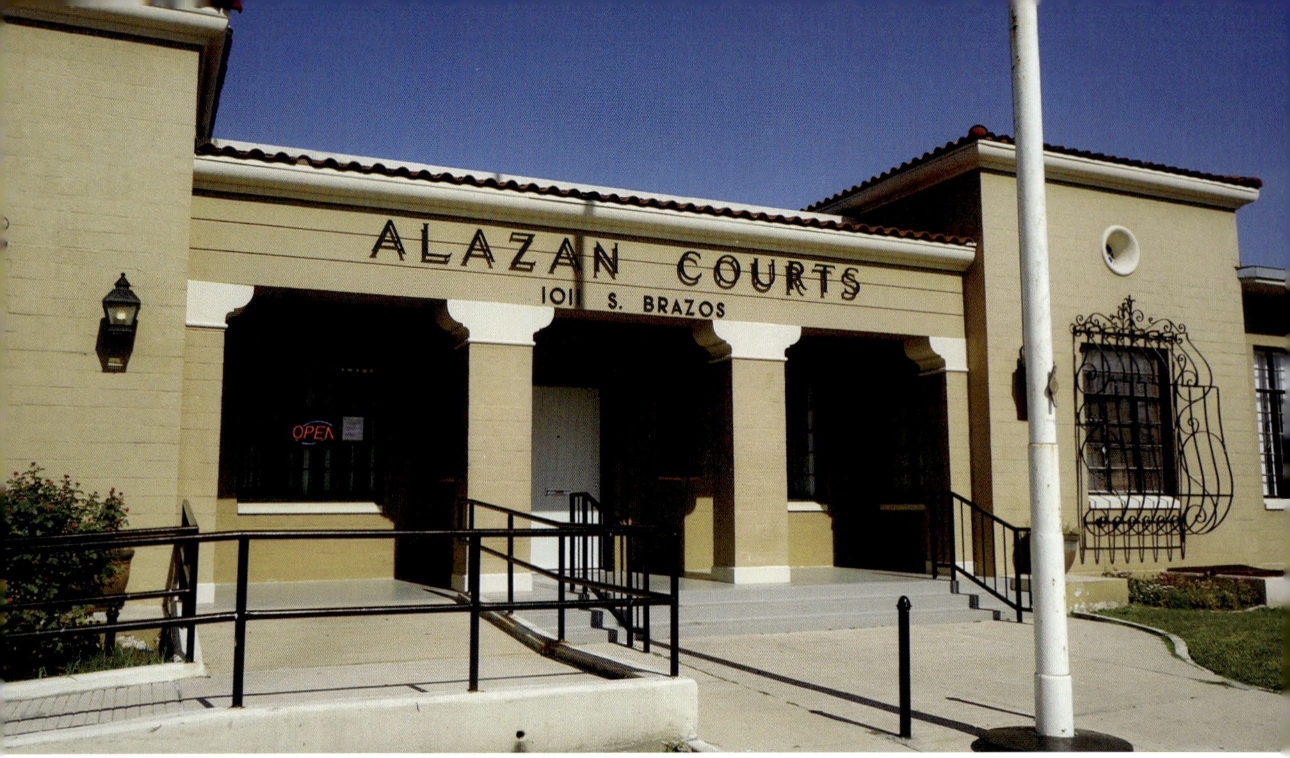

Figure 6.31. Alazan-Apache Courts, east elevation. Photo by Brent R. Fortenberry.

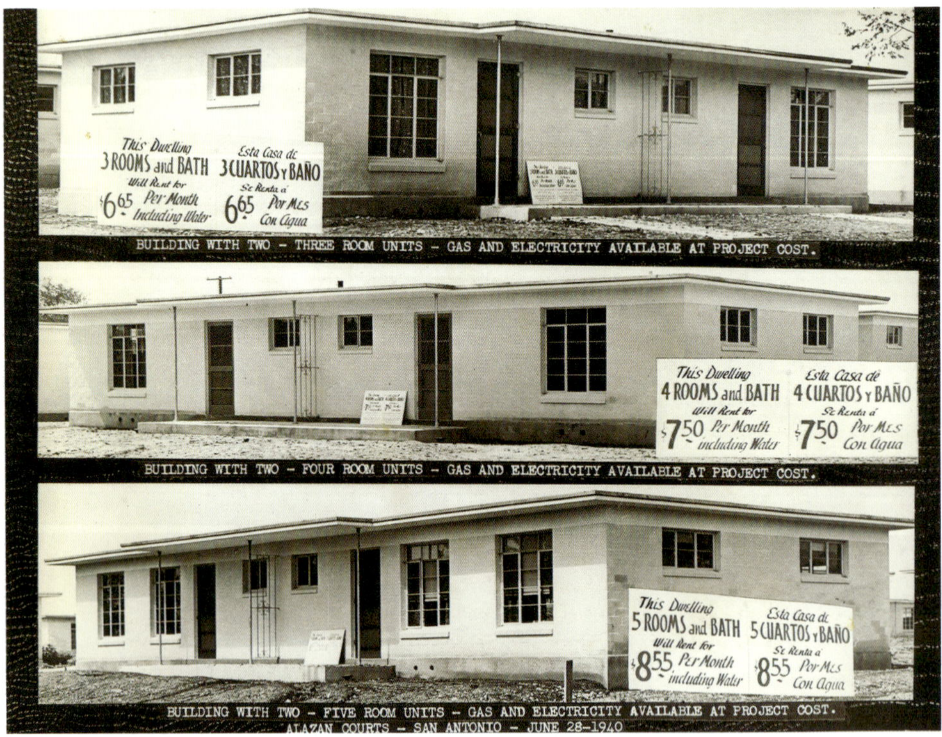

Figure 6.32. Alazan apartments from "USHA Housing in San Antonio, Texas June 1940: A Pictorial Supplement to the 1939 Annual Report." Image from San Antonio Housing Authority.

Alameda Theater, designed the Courts. To develop his design, Nayfach studied the worker housing project at Bal Buena in Mexico City, which predated the US public housing system (figs. 6.31 and 6.32).

Notes

1. Daniel Arreola, "The Mexican American Cultural Capital," *Geographical Review* 77, no. 1 (1987): 17–34.

2. Paula Allen, "Hutchins Hotel Linked to Mexican Revolution," *San Antonio Express-News*, October 8, 2010.

3. For information on the Westside, see Rogelio Agrasanchez Jr., *Mexican Movies in the United States: A History of the Films, Theaters, and Audiences, 1920–1960* (Jefferson, NC: McFarland, 2006); Andrew Perez Associates Architects, *Villa de Guadalupe: Historic Resources Assessment* (San Antonio: Historic Preservation Office, 1986); Daniel Arreola, *Tejano South Texas: A Mexican American Cultural Province* (Austin: University of Texas Press, 2002); Arreola, "Mexican American Cultural Capital," 17–34; María Antonietta Berriozábal, "Una Historia de una de Muchas Marias," *Frontiers: A Journal of Women Studies* 24, no. 2–3 (2003): 155–67; Julia Blackwelder, *Women of the Depression: Caste and Culture in San Antonio, 1929–39* (College Station: Texas A&M University Press, 1984); William Clayson, "'The Barrios and the Ghettos Have Organized!': Community Action, Political Acrimony, and the War on Poverty in San Antonio," *Journal of Urban History* 28 (January 2002): 158–83; Christine M. Drennon, "Social Relations Spatially Fixed: Construction and Maintenance of School Districts in San Antonio, Texas," *Geographical Review* 96 (October 2006): 567–93; Richard Garcia, *Rise of the Mexican American Middle Class: San Antonio, 1929–1941* (College Station: Texas A&M University Press, 1991); Robert A. Goldberg, "Racial Changes on the Southern Periphery: The Case of San Antonio, Texas, 1960–1965," *Journal of Southern History* 49 (August 1983): 349–74; Gabriela González, "Carolina Munguía and Emma Tenayuca," *Frontiers: A Journal of Women Studies* 24, no. 2–3 (2003): 200–229; Patricia E. Gower, "Unintended Consequences: The San Antonio Pecan Shellers Strike of 1938," *Journal of South Texas History* 17 (Fall 2004): 88–103;, Raquel R. Marquez, Louis Mendoza, and Steve Blanchard, "Neighborhood Formation on the West Side of San Antonio, Texas," *Latino Studies* 5 (2007): 288–316; Ana Luisa Martinez, "Pablo Cruz and 'El Rigidor': The Emergence of a Bicultural Identity in San Antonio, 1888–1910," *Journal of the West* 45 (Fall 2006): 21–28; J. Gilbert Quesada, "Towards a Working Definition of Social Justice, Father Carmelo A. Tranchese, S. J. and Our Lady of Guadalupe Parish, 1932–1953," *Journal of Texas Catholic History and Culture* 4 (1993): 44–64; Heywood T. Sanders, "Empty Taps, Missing Pipes," in *On the Border, an Environmental History of San Antonio*, ed. Char Miller (Pittsburgh: University of Pittsburgh Press, 2001), 141–68; Harold A. Shapiro, "The Pecan Shellers of San Antonio, Texas," *Southwestern Social Science Quarterly* 32 (March 1952): 229–44; Zaragosa Vargas, "'Tejana Radical': Emma Tenayuca and the San Antonio Labor Movement during the Great Depression," *Pacific Historical Review* 66 (1997): 553–80; Kenneth P. Walker, "The Pecan Shellers of San Antonio," *Southwestern Historical Quarterly* 69 (July 1965): 44–58; and Donald L. Zelman, "Alazan-Apache Courts: A New Deal Response to Mexican American Housing Conditions in San Antonio," *Southwestern Historical Quarterly* 87 (October 1983): 123–50.

4. Andrew Perez Associates, *Villa de Guadalupe*, 5.

5. Arreola, *Tejano South Texas*, 134.

6. Arreola, 136.

7. Hugh Hemphill, "Missouri Pacific Railroad in San Antonio," Texas Transportation Museum, accessed April 1, 2019, https://www.txtransportationmuseum.org/history-rr-missouri-pacific.php.

8. Joe S. Graham, "Texas-Mexican Vernacular Architecture," *Handbook of Texas Online*, accessed September 9, 2019, http://www.tshaonline.org/handbook/online/articles/cbtut.

9. Nic Tengg, *Map of the City of San Antonio, Bexar County: Including Suburbs Both North and South* (San Antonio: Nic Tengg, 1924), Library of Congress, https://www.loc.gov/item/2010593158/; and Andrew Perez Associates, *Villa de Guadalupe*.

10. See John Michael Vlach, "Afro-Americans," in *America's Architectural Roots: Ethnic Groups That Built America*, ed. Dell Upton (New York: Wiley, 1986), 42–47.

11. Daniel Arreola, "Mexican American Housescapes," *Geographical Review* 78, no. 3 (1988): 299–315.

12. Arreola, *Mexican Cultural Capital*, 34.

13. A loose definition of *tiendita* can be found in Devon G. Peña, "Toward a Critical Political Ecology of Latina/o Urbanism," Acequia Institute, accessed September 30, 2019, p.http://www.acequiainstitute.org/assets/Toward_a_political_ecology_of_Chicana-o_sustainable_urbanism_Draft_of_June_47068.pdf, p. 20. Pictorial examples of *tienditas* in San Antonio can be found in "Westside Designated Landmarks Phase II, June 2014," City of San Antonio Office of Historic Preservation, https://www.sanantonio.gov/Portals/0/Files/HistoricPreservation/Westside_Phase_II.pdf.

14. Gower, "Unintended Consequences," 88–103.

15. Parts of the Westside were without city water and sewage connections and paved streets through the early 1960s.

16. Lewis F. Fisher, *Saving San Antonio: The Preservation of a Heritage*, 2nd ed. (San Antonio: Trinity University Press, 2016), 253–55.

17. Darcy Sprague, "San Antonio's Generosity, ZIP Code by ZIP Code," *Folo Media*, January 11, 2018, https://www.folomedia.org/san-antonios-generosity-zip-code-zip-code/.

18. Rick Lyman, "Icehouses in Texas Vanishing like Their Frosty Beer on a Warm Afternoon," *New York Times*, August 23, 1998.

19. Andrew Perez Associates, *Villa de Guadalupe*, 175.

20. Andrew Perez Associates, 147.

21. Westside Historic Preservation Group, *Casa Maldonado, Aka the Pink Building: 1312 Guadalupe St., San Antonio, Texas* (San Antonio: Esperanza Peace & Justice Center, 2011); and Andrew Perez Associates, *Villa de Guadalupe*, 227.

22. Andrew Perez Associates, *Villa de Guadalupe*, 229–30.

23. Andrew Perez Associates, 231–32.

24. For more about La Gloria, see "Save La Gloria," Esperanza, accessed February 10, 2020, http://esperanzacenter.org/esperanza-projects/save-la-gloria/.

The Hill Country Vernacular

Kenneth Hafertepe

According to the noted Texas cultural geographer Terry G. Jordan, "Hill Country" is a vernacular term applied to a region including all or part of twenty-five counties near the geographical center of Texas. It is especially identified with settlement by immigrants from the various German states in the mid-nineteenth century. Their houses, churches, schools, dance halls, and other buildings still dot the landscape. In recent years it has become such an appealing concept that many small towns in Central Texas have attempted to brand themselves as "the gateway to the Texas Hill Country."[1]

The Hill Country is bounded on the east and south by the Balcones Escarpment, which runs just west of Dallas, Waco, Austin, and San Antonio. On the eastern side of the escarpment is Blackland Prairie, ideal for raising cotton; on the west are limestone hills with a thin layer of soil above, which is much better suited for ranching. The western border of the Hill Country is the Edwards Plateau, which is also where West Texas and the Great High Plains begin. The Hill Country is, by and large, a dissected plateau, that is, a plateau that has been eroded to the point that there are many hills and valleys (fig. 7.1).

The vegetation of the Hill Country was determined by the light soils and the relatively infrequent rain. The tallest trees, especially cypress, line the banks of rivers and creeks. Away from such sources of water, several types of oak are prevalent. Mesquite and Ashe juniper (known locally as cedar) have always been present but have expanded as soils were disrupted first by attempts at farming and grazing and then when farms were abandoned. In recent years there have been some attempts to cut back Ashe junipers to try to restore balance to the regional ecosystem.

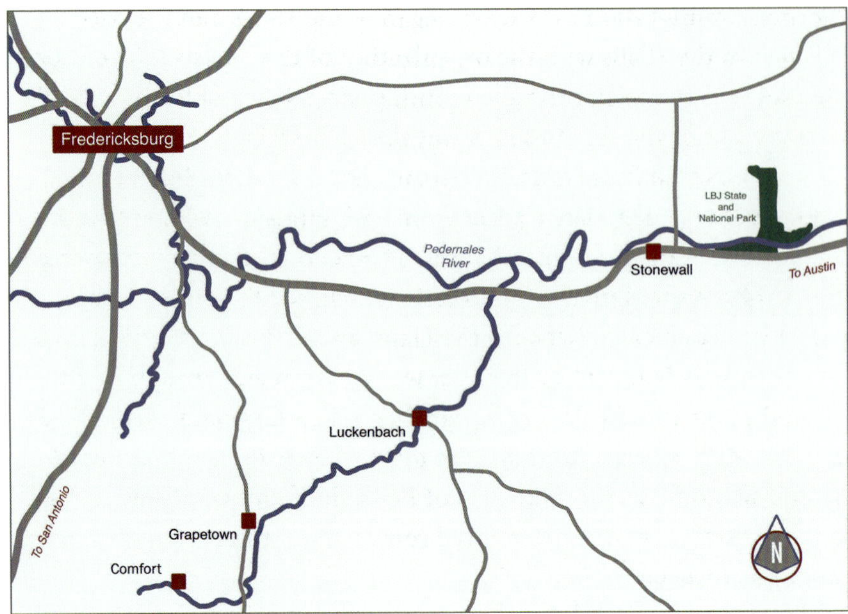

Figure 7.1. Map of the Hill Country including Fredericksburg, Comfort, and Stonewall. Image by Brent R. Fortenberry.

The land was home to Native Americans for centuries; in the nineteenth century Lipan Apaches, Comanches, and Kiowas lived or hunted there. (On the other side of the Balcones Fault, groups such as the Wichita and Waco Indians were agriculturalists and thus more permanently settled.) Indeed, so assertive were the Comanches in defining this as their hunting ground that it was known to Spaniards and later European settlers as the Comanchería. This became the setting for many battles between Native Americans and settlers in the late nineteenth century. After Texas entered the Union in 1845, the US Army created a number of forts, including Fort Martin Scott near Fredericksburg, which drove the natives farther and farther west and ultimately onto reservations by the end of the century.

The Hill Country was settled by Anglos from the Upland South, especially Tennessee, Missouri, and Arkansas, and by immigrants from northern Europe, especially Germany but also Alsace and Silesia along the border between Germany and Poland. Anglos settling in the Blackland Prairie brought with them African American slaves to work the fields, but very few African Americans lived in the Hill Country, and those were brought there by their Anglo-American owners. Although San Antonio was the cultural hearth of Mexican Texans (known as Tejanos), few Tejanos moved into the Hill Country.

German immigration into Texas began in the 1830s, but the pace quickened in the 1840s with the organization of the Adelsverein, or Society of Noblemen, which promoted immigration. Few noblemen actually had intentions of moving to Texas, but they were happy to encourage land-poor German farmers and others to move. In May 1842 they sent representatives to negotiate a grant from Sam Houston, who at that time was president of the Republic of Texas. The negotiations did not succeed, but in 1844 representatives of the Verein purchased the Fisher-Miller tract, which was located between the Llano and Colorado Rivers. This was a monumentally bad deal, as the tract was far from any European settlement and in the middle of the Comanchería. Few Germans ever settled there. In 1845 the Verein founded the town of New Braunfels north of San Antonio and, in 1846, the town of Fredericksburg northwest of San Antonio. Ultimately the Adelsverein brought more than seven thousand immigrants to Texas.[2]

Although the lands to be settled were rural and suited for agriculture, many settlers had little experience at farming or ranching. Many craftsmen, particularly cabinetmakers, left Germany because the Industrial Revolution and furniture factories made it difficult for craftsmen to remain financially viable. Further, the failed political revolution of 1848 convinced many that democracy in Germany was at best a distant dream. Many German political radicals and intellectuals found themselves living in tiny towns in the Texas Hill Country. However, Germans in the Hill Country looked to San Antonio when they desired a big-city experience, given that in the 1850s roughly one-third of the population of San Antonio was German.

Some German immigrants to Texas were *Freidenkers*—free thinkers who opposed a state religion and chose not to belong to any organized religion. Indeed, Comfort was an agnostic enclave for several decades. However, most Hill Country Germans, including some residents of Comfort, were religious. The population of Fredericksburg was roughly two-thirds Lutheran (or Evangelical Lutheran), one-fourth Roman Catholic, and one-tenth Methodist. Areas that were strongholds of Lutherans and Catholics, such as Gillespie County, had many dance halls, saloons, and ethnic clubs; areas with a higher concentration of Methodists, such as southeastern Mason County and western Llano County, frowned on dancing, drinking, and playing cards.

There were very few African American enslaved workers in the Hill Country. In the 1860 slave schedule of the US census there was a total of fifty-two slaves in Kerr County (including Comfort) and thirty-three in Gillespie County (including Fredericksburg). Although some prominent German Texans, notably Ernst Hermann Altgelt of Comfort and San Antonio and Wilhelm von Rosenberg of Round Top and Austin, were supporters of the Confederacy, most German Texans did not approve of slavery or secession. This is not to say that German Texans were vocal about such beliefs or that they were free of racist attitudes about African Americans or Mexican Americans—especially about perceived differences in work ethic. However, they had not been raised in a culture that embraced slavery or systematically looked down on nonwhites.

When the Civil War broke out, many refused to take an oath of loyalty to the Confederacy, much less enlist in the Confederate army. The closest thing to a compromise was for Germans to promise to serve in a "home guard," which was supposed to protect the Hill Country from any Union invasion. In spite of such measures, many German men were lynched during the war. German Texans even coined a term for their tormentors: *die Hängerbande*. Some families moved to Mexico or back to Germany for the duration of the war. One group of German men, lightly armed civilians who were attempting to make it to Mexico, were attacked by Confederate soldiers. Nineteen German Texans were killed in the immediate attack; over the next few days another nine to eleven who had escaped the scene of the attack were captured and either hung or shot in the head. Confederates referred to this as the "Battle of the Nueces"; most Germans called it the "Nueces Massacre."

The earliest buildings were log houses; within five or ten years, new houses were built of *fachwerk* or stone. Although the technology of building with logs originated in central Europe, familiarity with this technique had been lost to the immigrants to Texas. They had to learn from Southerners—or African American slaves—how to build with logs. German log buildings usually were constructed using the V notch, which Terry Jordan associated with the Upland South. However, within ten years of their arrival Hill Country Germans had devised their own type of log house. Instead of hewing the logs, fitting them as close together as possible, and then filling the gaps with mud and rock, Hill Country Germans alternated between logs and complete rows of mortared stones. This was more airtight, required less maintenance, and was extremely durable.[3]

Fachwerk houses utilized a long-standing European building tradition: a heavy frame, usually with downbraces, infilled with brick, stone, or, in some cases, adobe. The latter infill, presumably picked up from Tejanos in San Antonio, was cheaper to install but also required an outer covering of plaster to protect against rain. Most houses with adobe infill were early, and the material was quickly abandoned. Brick was the most popular infill in New Braunfels and San Antonio; stone infill predominated farther out in the Hill Country.[4]

Rock houses ("rock" being the preferred term for stone in the Texan vernacular) began to be erected in the early 1850s, simultaneously with *fachwerk* houses, and continued to be built for at least half a century. These could be one, one and a half, or two stories. The story-and-a-half house achieved a sort of iconic status in the Hill Country, especially with the addition of a back room in a lean-to, giving it a "saltbox" profile.[5]

In terms of floor plans, scholars have struggled to link German Texan houses with European prototypes. At the level of rooms, the three key rooms were the *stube* (a sitting room and best bedroom), *kuche* (kitchen), and *kammer* (bedchamber). Often a log house combined all these functions into one room. When the family upgraded to a *fachwerk* or rock house, the log house was retained to serve the more specialized function of kitchen. Usually a *stube* was a squarish room, and a bedchamber more rectangular—not unlike their equivalents in a Pennsylvania *flurkuchenhaus* plan. In a story-and-a-half house where there was no existing log house, the front room would be the *stube*, the back room the *kuche*, and the room upstairs the *kammer*.[6]

Because many of these communities had trained carpenters and cabinetmakers, doors could often have handsome raised panels. In the Victorian era doors began to feature panes of window glass. Early windows tended to be casement windows, a form with which the settlers had been familiar back home. Starting in the 1850s double-hung sash windows started to gain popularity and were an early indicator of the adoption of outside ideas. Some Hill Country houses featured built-in cabinets in the front room. When there was a single front room, the typical pattern was window-door-window.

Central passages were exceedingly rare, though at least one Fredericksburg house originally had a dogtrot (*durchgang* in German). When there were two front rooms, there could be one or two front doors. The lack of a central passage meant that staircases were either inside a room or were external. In a two-room plan staircases were usually in the back room on the wall shared with the front room; exterior staircases were usually on a side wall, though in San Antonio a few were found on the back wall.

There were few buildings that might be considered Victorian in the

Hill Country until around 1880, and usually this was a sign of German Texans beginning to merge into the American mainstream. In 1879 the Comfort merchant August Faltin hired the English-born San Antonio architect Alfred Giles to design a two-story building, a store with a residence above. Giles went on to design several other buildings in Comfort, both commercial and residential. In Fredericksburg he designed the Gillespie County Courthouse (now the Pioneer Memorial Library), a house for the prominent Bierschwale family, and the Bank of Fredericksburg. When in 1894 August Faltin decided to build a new house not above his store, he hired not Alfred Giles but another, younger San Antonio architect, Albert Beckmann. (Subsequent to his early work for Faltin, Giles had designed several buildings for the Ingenhuett family, and the Paul Ingenhuett house of 1895 is attributed to Giles as well.)[7]

Other Hill Country residents could also visit the King William District in San Antonio to get ideas for their new houses. Only in the 1890s did Hill Country residents adopt houses with T- or L-plans. This was also the era of one or two gables sitting on the front side of roofs with a transverse ridge. Gingerbread decoration was extremely rare until the 1890s.

After the Civil War, some of the former slaves remained in the area but represented a tiny part of the population. An African Methodist Episcopal Church was built at the eastern edge of town in 1887. This remains the most prominent evidence of African American residence in Fredericksburg. Few Tejanos settled in the Hill Country, preferring San Antonio and Bexar County. During and after the Mexican Revolution of 1910–20 a large number of migrants fled the civil war and settled in Texas; many came to Fredericksburg. Again, the most prominent surviving marker of this immigration is religious: Our Lady of Guadalupe Catholic Church, built in 1917.[8]

The early twentieth century saw the quicker adoption of mainstream American architectural ideals. Bungalows predominated in the 1910s and 1920s; these could be either brick or frame. And in the 1920s the occasional period house could be found, even the Spanish Colonial Revival. Another distinctive localism was buildings of concrete blocks. Of course, this was a national trend, but citizens in Fredericksburg adopted it with enthusiasm. Locally these were manufactured by Henry and Hugo Basse at the Basse Brothers Cement Yard; their product become known as Basse blocks. At the same time railroad connections (with Kerrville as the closest depot) allowed the use of bricks made in San Antonio, D'Hanis, and elsewhere.[9]

Churches began to resemble others found in San Antonio and elsewhere in Texas. Two Fredericksburg congregations turned to San Antonio architects. James Wahrenberger designed the new Holy Ghost Lutheran Church, built 1888–93, and Leo M. J. Dielmann designed the new St. Mary's Catholic Church in 1905–6. Both men were Texas natives but spoke German and were sent back to Germany to study their profession. St. Mary's was also notable for its interior decoration, which led to its being included in a National Register thematic nomination among the "Painted Churches of Texas."[10]

Residents of the Hill Country still take great pride in their German heritage, though things have changed in the last thirty years. Fredericksburg has been converted from a sleepy county seat to a tourist destination. In the 1980s there were virtually no wineries in the Hill Country; now US 290 from Johnson City to Fredericksburg is lined with wineries and the vineyards that support them. The soil and climate of the Hill Country are good for growing some varieties of grapes, but others are shipped in from other parts of Texas and beyond.

The Hill Country has also seen the construction of new and large mansions and the remodeling of old houses. The rapid rise of bed-and-breakfast inns has given a new and relatively sympathetic use for many old houses. However, many owners are faced with the temptation to make houses look older than they actually are on the assumption that older is better and that a *fachwerk* house is best of all. Many older residents mourn the loss of peace and quiet of their Hill Country towns and object to the traffic problems that have come with the tourist boom. The Vernacular Architecture Forum (VAF) meeting comes at a time when the Hill Country is struggling with its future even as it attempts to preserve its past.

Comfort

August Faltin General Store, now Comfort Crockery and Goldbeck-Faltin House

402 Seventh Street

1879, 1907 (store); 1854 and after (house)

The August Faltin General Store may seem to be oriented away from the center of town, but this complex is so old that it predates the commercial development on High Street. Indeed, the Faltin store is on Main Street and initially faced one of two public squares, this one now known as Altgelt Field. However, chronic flooding of Cypress Creek pushed settlers who located on Water and Broadway Streets to higher ground, specifically Front Street and the appropriately named High Street.

The site was originally developed by Theodore and Fritz Goldbeck. Born in Verden in the Kingdom of Hanover, the brothers came to Texas with Prince Carl of Solms von Braunfels, who founded the settlement of New Braunfels in 1845. Not content with being original settlers of one German community, the brothers moved on to Comfort in 1854. The only remaining evidence of the Goldbeck brothers is the one log room of the Goldbeck-Faltin house behind the store and facing Seventh Street. They opened a store at the corner of Main and Seventh, probably one room initially, though it was expanded along Main Street over the years.

The one-room house was built in 1854 or 1855, as the Goldbecks soon moved on. The room was what Terry Jordan would call "nearly square"— roughly fourteen and a half by thirteen and a half feet. The front had a door and window; there was also a window on the south side and, ultimately, doors on the west and north. The log corners were V-notched, which Terry Jordan saw as evidence that Germans were learning their log-house building skills from Upland Southerners. (Another Comfort house with V notching is the Wilhelm Heuermann log house on High Street.) Not learned from Upland Southerners was the practice of alternating the logs with a row of mortared rocks, which ensured greater stability and airtightness than typical log houses. The room had a cast-iron stove in the back left corner, indicated by the flue set between stones on the south side wall. The roof was originally covered with cypress shingles, though by 1936 the covering was standing-seam tin.

The Goldbecks soon decided to move to San Antonio, which had its own thriving German community. (Theodore Goldbeck, a strong Unionist, spent the Civil War in Mexico but returned to Texas after the war, working in Austin at the General Land Office during Reconstruction.) They sold the house and store to a new arrival, August Faltin. A native of Prussia, his father was a merchant in Danzig, and August soon opened his own store in Leipzig. In 1856, he married Clara Below, the daughter of a senior officer in the Prussian army, and the newlyweds soon moved to Texas.

The Faltins quickly expanded the house, first with a room to the rear and then with two additional rooms to the north, which more than doubled the size of the building. All three rooms were built using the *fachwerk* technique—a heavy frame infilled with stone, brick, or adobe. In the

Faltin house, the room to the rear of the log-and-rock room was infilled with sunbaked adobe bricks. As was typical with *fachwerk* houses infilled with adobe, the entire house was plastered over. This had the practical effect of weatherproofing the adobe and the aesthetic effect of unifying the look of the exterior. In New Braunfels the typical infill was brick, but the Faltins (or their builders) seemed to have adapted the use of adobe bricks from Tejano builders in San Antonio.

When a second front room was added, it was twenty feet, seven inches, much wider than the original log-and-rock room. This and the new room behind it were infilled with limestone, perhaps suggesting that the Faltins had learned that adobe walls required frequent maintenance. The front room had a central door flanked by a window on each side; this was a fairly typical arrangement in German Texan houses, especially for a *stube* (parlor). On the north side wall was a chimney, which for an unknown reason was later removed. There were doors into the log-and-rock room and into the new back room. Both back rooms were rectangular and probably served as bedchambers. With the creation of the *stube* the original log-and-rock room could be used in a more specialized manner as the kitchen.

In 1860 the family consisted of August and Clara; two small daughters, Helena and Elisa; Clara's younger brother, Max Below, who worked in the store; and one servant, Minna Stieler. (Minna would later marry Henry Heinen; her younger brother Adolph would become a prominent stock raiser who declared himself the "Goat King of Texas.") August reported that he owned real estate worth eighteen hundred dollars and personal property worth forty-four hundred dollars. The latter certainly reflected the stock-in-trade; the figure of eighteen hundred dollars was fairly substantial for a pioneer settlement, suggesting that both the house and store had been enlarged. (Faltin also engaged in stock raising, which would also affect his real and personal property.) Ten years later the Faltins had five children (one more followed), and the household also included a clerk in the store and a domestic servant. Faltin's real estate had increased in value to six thousand dollars, though his personal estate had declined to seventeen hundred dollars.

In the 1870s Faltin associated with another merchant, Charles Schreiner of Kerrville, in a store in that town; Faltin sold his interest in the Kerrville store in 1879, but in the 1880s the pair created a new store, Faltin & Schreiner, in Junction City, west of Fredericksburg. In 1878 Faltin hired Alfred Giles, the English architect working out of San Antonio, to design an addition to the store with a residence above, which was completed the next year. Within a couple of years, Schreiner hired Giles to design a store, a hotel, and a residence in Kerrville. The drawings for the Faltin store and residence were on linen tracing paper; the drawings for the 1907 addition, which replaced the original store, were blueprints. All the linen drawings are signed by Alfred Giles, and all are dated 1878, except for the drawing of the shelves for the store, which is dated 1879. The blueprints are all signed "Alfred Giles, architect," but the date 1907 appears only on the pediment at the angled southeast corner.

The two-story limestone block of the new Faltin building was attached to the west end of the original store. Like the original store, it faced Main Street and the original square. The limestone on the main facade was finely worked, with segmental arches above the centered double doors and flanking windows; the side walls were limestone rubble. The heavy cornice had a nearly semicircular pediment in the middle, with August Faltin's name and the date 1879. Behind the cornice was a hipped roof with two-by-eight rafters meeting at a ridge board. In 2003 August Faltin III reported that he had discovered that one of the windows had the mark of J. H. Kampmann, the San Antonio builder who also had a sash and door factory, which would have added to the impressive character of the Comfort building.

Inside there were shelves on both side walls, much of which survives. In front of this was a U-shaped counter; a clerk would be responsible for pulling items from the shelf. The rear third of this space was raised a few feet above the main floor; presumably this functioned as the counting room before the creation of a separate office in the 1907 addition. On the west side wall was a staircase to the basement and, at the rear corner, a stair to the second floor.

Below the store was a large basement lit by two light wells on the front wall, another on the west side wall, and two windows on the back wall. Steps on the east wall behind the original store building facilitated deliveries into this space. (These steps were retained in the 1907 addition but were later replaced by an elevator, which is nevertheless quite old.) Some of the window frames and other woodwork have numerical calculations written in pencil, and the post by the stair is painted "Schryner San Antonio."

Upstairs were two front rooms (presumably double parlors), the larger one being on the west. Between the two rooms were pocket doors (Giles called them sliding doors) that rolled on six-inch wheels. Projecting forward from the front wall was a two-story frame porch. The upstairs porch, accessed through three triple-hung sash windows (six over six over six) was welcome additional living space and was later screened in. Behind the west parlor was a hall, with access to the principal staircase, a toilet room (certainly one of the earliest in the Hill Country), and a back room that may have been a dining room, if the kitchen was in an outbuilding. (It lacked the accoutrements that Clara Faltin, or a domestic servant, would need for cooking, such as a dry sink or an adjoining pantry. Perhaps the kitchen remained in the log-and-*fachwerk* house.) Behind the east parlor were three bedrooms, each with a built-in washstand, similar to one still in Giles's Steves house on King William in San Antonio. In between the front and middle bedrooms was a bathroom, which had a built-in bathtub (again, one of the earliest in the Hill Country).

August Faltin retired in 1889; his sons Richard and August renamed the firm Faltin Bros. & Co. After a couple of years living in retirement over the store, which may not have seemed like much of a retirement, August and Clara decided in 1894 to build a new two-story house on the west side of town. They did not hire Giles but instead chose Albert Beckmann, a Texan born to German-immigrant parents, who lived in the King William District and designed a number of houses there. Apparently August Jr. moved into the residence above the store, as in 1895 his brother Richard built a house facing Sixth Street at the end of the block. The elder August died in 1905, but Clara lived until age ninety-five, dying in 1930.

In 1907 the younger August hired Giles to design a new stone building to replace the store of the 1850s, adjoining the store he had designed in 1878–79. The original store had faced Main Street, but for the new building Giles designed double doors flanked by large plate-glass windows on the Seventh Street facade, as well as an angled wall at the corner of Main and Seventh with a second set of double doors and, above the cornice, a pediment inscribed with the date 1907 and "Aug. Faltin." The Main Street elevation was definitely secondary, and the 1879 Giles building was also deemphasized in the bargain. As in the 1879 building, Giles called for coursed stone on the front elevation and rubble stone on the sides. The ground floor was largely commercial space, with three cast-iron columns running down the middle of the room. At the northwest corner was an office with doors into both the 1879 and 1907 spaces that was lit by two windows on the north wall. A separate exterior door at the west end of the 1907 building opened onto a staircase abutting the 1879 store, which led to five second-story offices and a "lodge room," possibly for local singing societies.

As larger and finer residences were built, the old log-and-rock and *fachwerk* house was used for storage. Parts of the exterior were covered with board-and-batten siding. Later it was lived in by August Faltin III, who restored the house to something like its original appearance. One departure from the original was his decision to replace the adobe brick with large blocks of limestone, because the adobe was just too difficult to maintain. In the 1990s vandals lit a fire in the 1878–79 Faltin store, doing considerable damage. Faltin later restored the structure and at that time turned the second floor into apartments. In spite of such changes, this is one of the most significant surviving nineteenth-century commercial buildings in Texas (figs. 7.2–7.7).[11]

Figure 7.2. Faltin Building, east and south elevations, 1879. Courtesy of Alexander Architectural Archives, University of Texas Libraries, University of Texas at Austin.

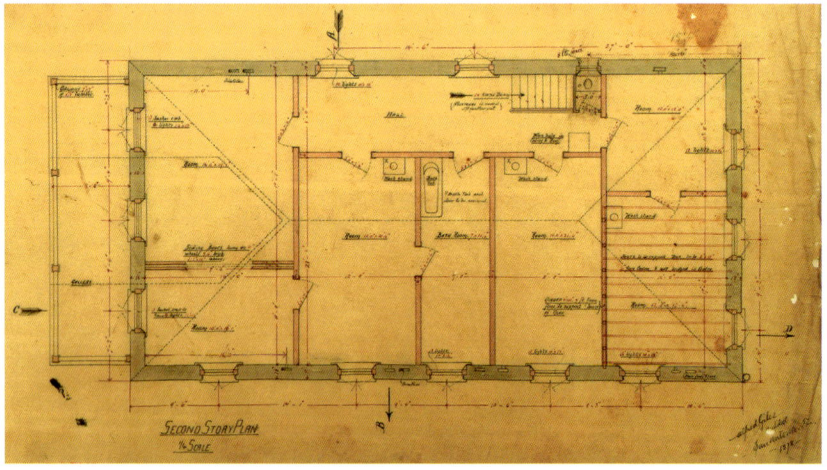

Figure 7.3. Faltin Building, second-floor plan. Courtesy of Alexander Architectural Archives, University of Texas Libraries, University of Texas at Austin.

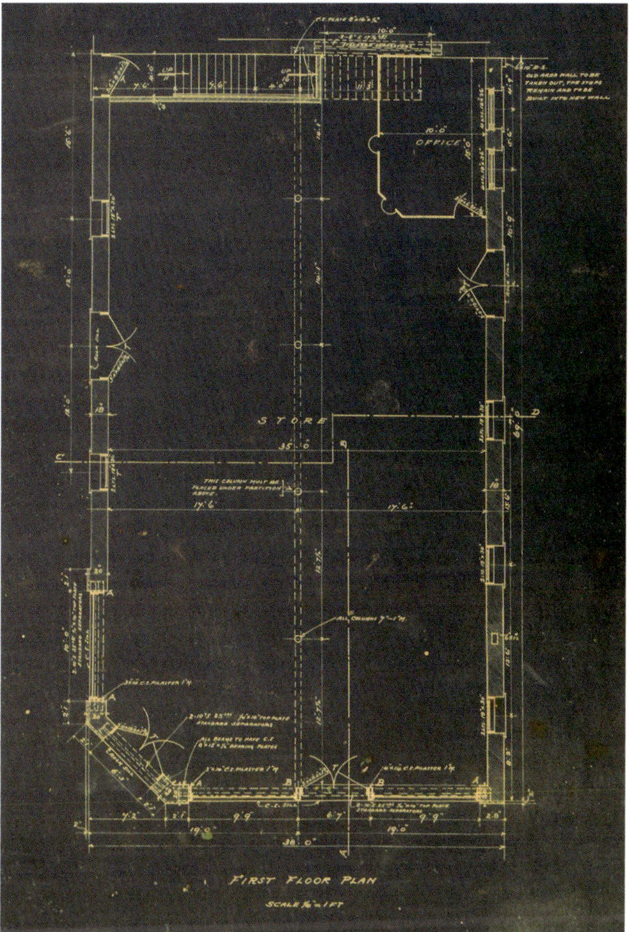

Figure 7.4. Faltin Building, first-floor plan. Courtesy of Alexander Architectural Archives, University of Texas Libraries, University of Texas at Austin.

Figure 7.5. Goldbeck-Faltin house. Photo by Kenneth Hafertepe.

Figure 7.6. Faltin General Store. Photo by Kenneth Hafertepe.

Figure 7.7. Goldbeck-Faltin house, front elevation. Photo by Kenneth Hafertepe.

Figure 7.8. Ingenhuett-Faust Hotel, 1880–81, 1893–94. From J. E. Grinstead, *South-West Texas: From the Mountains to the Sea* (Kerrville: J. E. Grinstead, 1904), 39.

Ingenhuett Hotel, now Faust Hotel
717 High Street
1880–81, 1893–94

Since its founding Comfort had been a stopping place on the road from San Antonio to Fredericksburg. After the Civil War this road became the route for supplies to the western US Army forts as well as for commercial traffic. (Many Hill Country Germans had government contracts to cart materials for the army.) The original Ingenhuett Hotel was the eastern part of the present building. The site was previously occupied by the Ingenhuett store, which was demolished after the construction of the new store a few doors down. The new hotel was built of very regular limestone blocks and was five bays wide with a centered door, two-story porches with turned columns, scroll-saw brackets, and balusters on both the front and rear sides. For a dozen years the hotel was operated by Marie Ingenhuett's brother, Charles Karger, and his wife, Alwine (figs. 7.8 and 7.9).

By the 1890s the conflict with Native Americans was winding down and so, too was the construction of army posts. After Comfort became a stop on the San Antonio and Aransas Pass Railroad in 1887, many in Comfort began to reframe the community as a summer resort. Peter Ingenhuett turned to Alfred Giles of San Antonio to enlarge the hotel and update its style. (Ingenhuett family stories attribute both the store and

Figure 7.9. Ingenhuett Saloon, 1891. Photo by Kenneth Hafertepe.

the 1880 structure to Giles as well, but Giles did not mention them in two advertisements; he did, however, list the hotel in his 1899 advertisement.)

Giles designed a new wing on the west side of the existing hotel, with the ridge of the roof running perpendicular to the street, creating a T-shaped plan. The porch was extended one bay to accommodate a new segmentally arched opening for double doors. The steps to the original central door were removed, and a balustrade was installed. Stone steps marked the new main entrance, and the far left window was converted to a door; the balustrade in front was removed and steps installed. The 1893–94 enlargement continued the porch on the west side of the courtyard, creating a porch with an L shape. The new wing, like the old, was made of limestone but now had a standing-seam metal roof.

Inside was a front room that served as a parlor, with a large elliptically arched tripartite window looking out onto High Street. This room had a fireplace with a heavily rusticated mantel on the west wall. Earlier generations of Germans had shunned open fireplaces in favor of cast-iron stoves, which they valued as more efficient and economical; this new fireplace probably fulfilled a more ceremonial function than a utilitarian one.

The new innkeeper was Ernst Ingenhuett, son of Peter and Marie. (One of their older sons, Paul, had taken over the store.) By June 1898 Ernst was advertising in the *Houston Post*, noting for coastal readers that

Comfort was 1,437 feet above sea level and was "one of the best summer resorts in Texas. Fine stone hotel building. Special rates to families by the week or month. No consumptives taken." Two years later Ernst was advertising in the *San Antonio Express* and stated that the Ingenhuett was the "only first class hotel in town. Entire rock building. Hot and cold baths and electric lights. Centrally located."

In 1904 J. E. Grinstead of Kerrville published a pamphlet about all the towns from San Antonio to Kerrville, titled *South-West Texas: From the Mountains to the Sea*. He noted that in Comfort "well equipped hotels cater to the wants of visitors. Worthy of special mention among these is The Ingenhuett . . . which is a modern stone building, well equipped throughout." He also noted that there were two saloons nearby for thirsty travelers.

Louis and Mathilda Faust purchased the hotel in 1909. It remained in business as the Faust Hotel until Mathilda's death in 1946. Subsequently the property went into decline, though it has been used as an antiques cooperative and a bed and breakfast. The current owners have restored the building to its original function as a hotel.[12]

Ingenhuett Saloon

725 High Street

1891

Both the Menger Hotel in San Antonio and the Nimitz Hotel in Fredericksburg operated breweries to wet the whistles of thirsty travelers. (It was a very dry 498 miles from Fredericksburg to El Paso!) In 1891 Peter Ingenhuett built this saloon between his store and his hotel. Like the store, it was three bays wide, but here there were three pairs of French doors rather than the single door of the store. All three French doors had fanlights above with segmental tops; second-floor windows had round arches. The cornice was applied only to the front of the building, not the sides or back; a pediment above indicated the pitch of the roof and also named the owner and date of construction. Inside was one large open space, except for the staircase to the second floor, built into the east wall. Opposite the staircase was the bar, which incorporated a segmental arch framed by squat columns. Behind the bar was a large tripartite mirror.

The Ingenhuett family claimed this to be an Alfred Giles design, along with the hotel, store, post office, and the house of Paul Ingenhuett. This may be true, but the building was not listed in Giles's advertisements.

(The Ingenhuett Hotel was definitely by Giles.) Better documented are the contractors: the building does have a stone on the lower left side of the main facade into which is carved "Davey & Schott / Contractors." Davey and Schott were Benjamin Abraham Davey (from England) and Wilhelm Bruno Schott of Kerrville (from Germany). Davey came to the United States in 1855 at age nine; Schott immigrated in 1882 at age eighteen. Their first building together seems to have been the 1890 Weston Building in Kerrville; this was originally a saloon but has served many functions over the years.

Their work on a saloon may have recommended them to the Ingenhuetts; like the Weston Building the saloon is a simple two-story limestone structure. Davey & Schott may well have been the contractors for phase two of the Charles Schreiner mansion in Kerrville, which was designed by Alfred Giles; this, however, was several years after the saloon in Comfort. Paula Ingenhuett later identified Bruno Schott as the builder of the house in which she was born.

Hubert Ingenhuett, who operated the saloon in the 1890s, called it the Capitol Saloon. From 1900 to the beginning of Prohibition, there were a number of owners. In 1904 the saloon was advertised as having a good pool table. In the 1910s Ernst Karger advertised that he sold "Beer, Wines, Liquors and Fine Cigars." By 1918 it was a confectionary and ice-cream parlor and later a restaurant.

Behind the saloon is the Ingenhuett-Real Halle, or Opera House (1890). Built for Peter Ingenhuett, it resembles many Texas dance halls; it is unusual for having a limestone facade. Ernst Karger advertised it as a "rock dance hall, with splendidly furnished stage." In 1925 Paul Ingenhuett began to use the building for storing wool and mohair.[13]

**Jacob Gass Blacksmith Shop and Residence,
later Comfort Museum**

High Street at Eighth Street

1891–92

This sober rock building was a blacksmith shop on the first floor and a residence on the second. The original owners were Jacob Gass and his wife, Louise. Phillip Jacob Gass was born in Bicken, Nassau (now part of Hesse) in 1845; he came to the United States with his family when he was seven. Jacob apprenticed as a blacksmith with the Theis family in Boerne (his sister Wilhelmine had married Jacob Theis in 1862). The original

Figure 7.10. Jacob Gass Blacksmith Shop and residence, 1891–92. Photo by Kenneth Hafertepe.

master blacksmith of Comfort, Herrmann Wille, died in 1870, which created an opportunity for Jacob. In 1873 the twenty-seven-year-old Gass married sixteen-year-old Louise Wille and took over the blacksmith shop (fig. 7.10).

The historical marker and all written accounts state that it was built in 1890 by a stonemason from Sisterdale, J. Gottlieb Lorbeer; it took him nearly a year to build the first floor, and the second floor was built in a matter of weeks using mechanized equipment. Little is known about Lorbeer, but his story-and-a-half rock house still stands in Sisterdale. The initials JGL and the date 1887 are carved into the lintel above the front door.

A granddaughter of Jacob and Louise Gass, Viola Gass Frizzell, dated the building to 1891 because when it was built, her father was around nine years old. Karl (aka Charles) Gass was born in 1883, which would actually put the date at 1892. The historical marker application of 1986 suggested that the contractor who hoisted the stones to the second story was Bruno Schott, who in 1891 built the Ingenhuett saloon with his partner, Benjamin A. Davey. Paula Ingenhuett also mentioned Schott as the contractor for the Paul Ingenhuett house nearby.

The building had a hipped roof resting on the rock walls; the roof also projected to the north to cover a central pediment on the main facade. The roof was fashioned of standing-seam tin from the start. On the north, east, and south elevations there was a door flanked by a window on each side. On the west elevation there were only two windows. Apparently there was no internal staircase originally; rather, there were external wooden stairs on the rear (south) elevation. (It should be noted that there were three exterior doors on the second floor. Perhaps there was some anticipation of a wraparound porch, or perhaps that the upper floor would be used for the storage of wool or other commodities.)

The building was purchased by Paul Ingenhuett in 1904. In 1910 Jacob and Louise were still living on High Street along with three of their nine children and Louise's seventy-six-year-old mother, Marie, and Jacob was still running a blacksmith shop, so perhaps they rented from Ingenhuett. After the Gass family departed, Ingenhuett used the building for storage of flour to be sold in the adjoining store.

Paul Ingenhuett died in January 1932. The next year his widow, Ida, agreed to let the building be used as a museum and library—much as would happen in Fredericksburg just three years later with the reconstruction of the Vereins-Kirche. She had the external stair removed and built one inside at the southeast corner. By 1933 the windows had been covered over with sheets of galvanized iron, but soon these were replaced with window sash. Vincent J. McAteer, editor of the *Comfort News*, commented that the building, "with its massive walls of stone and its primitive simple style of architecture will present an appearance suggestive of a public building, and will provide a worthy setting for any collection of historical relics, records and documents." McAteer urged his readers not to be discouraged by an incremental approach, noting that the collections of the American Wing of the Metropolitan Museum of Art, Mount Vernon, and Monticello were built up over time. In 1979 a new metal roof was installed, and in 1981, after the building passed from Paula Ingenhuett to her nephew Roy O. Perkins III, beams were strengthened, the chimney was rebuilt, and central heating was installed (fig. 7.11).[14]

Figure 7.11. Jacob Gass Blacksmith Shop, west elevation. Measured by Brent R. Fortenberry. Drawing by Hayley M. Field.

Figure 7.12. Paul Ingenhuett house, 1897–98. Photo by Kenneth Hafertepe.

Paul Ingenhuett House
420 Eighth Street
1897–98

Paul Ingenhuett was the second son of Peter and Marie Ingenhuett and the one who seemed to inherit the mercantile instinct. He was born on this block and lived here his entire life. When the census taker arrived in 1880, his parents reported that the occupation of the twelve-year-old Paul was "merchant." He took control of the Ingenhuett store at age eighteen, and, presumably, he lived over the store once his parents moved to their new Victorian cottage down the street in 1888. He married Ida Flach in 1891. She was born in Texas, but her father was from Hesse and her mother from Westphalia (figs. 7.12–7.14).

In September 1897, Paul purchased this lot from his older brother, Hubert. Paul and Ida's daughter Paula, who was born in the house in 1902, remembered hearing from her parents that Alfred Giles designed the house and that Bruno Schott of Kerrville, who built the Ingenhuett-Karger saloon with Benjamin A. Davey, was the contractor. The house is not listed in Giles's 1899 advertisement, but the Ingenhuett Hotel, on which he worked just three years earlier, was. However, the floor plan of the house shows a typically Gilesean concern with adequate ventilation, an important issue in the hot Texas climate.

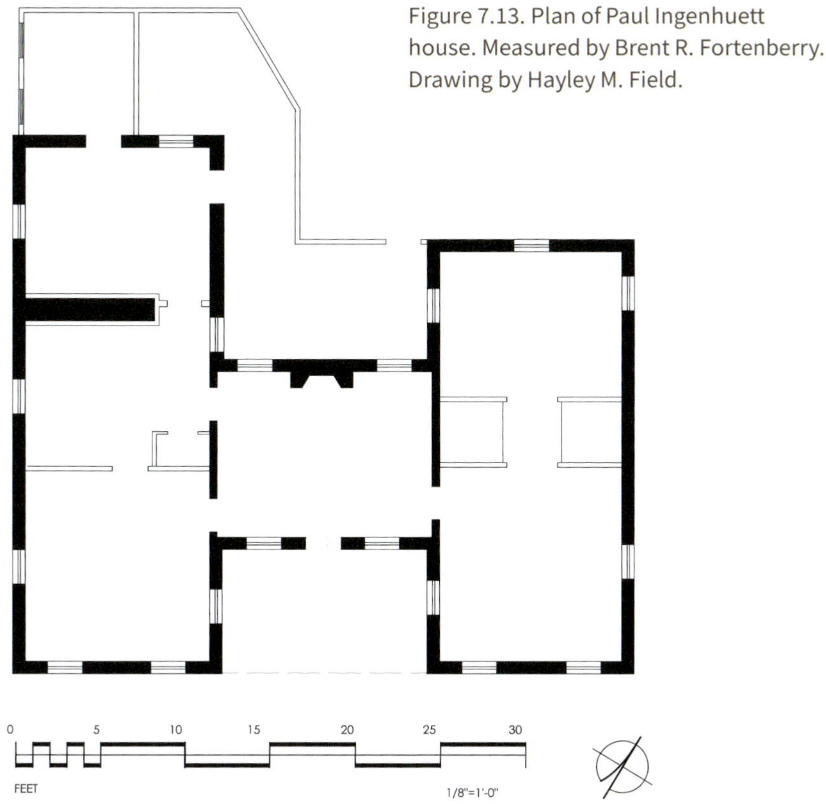

Figure 7.13. Plan of Paul Ingenhuett house. Measured by Brent R. Fortenberry. Drawing by Hayley M. Field.

Figure 7.14. Paul Ingenhuett house, historic photo before April 1922, courtesy of Roy O. Perkins III.

The house was built of sturdy limestone, quarried two miles from town. Still visible in the blocks are indentations that allowed a crane to lift them into place. The front porch originally had turned wooden columns, which were replaced in 1914 with the present squarish stone piers. (Paula also remembered that Ernest Palmer Giles [1894–1986] designed the new porch. Palmer was the son of Alfred Giles.) The roof was originally covered with tin, but a hailstorm in 1936 led to a new roof, which Paula Ingenhuett stated was of "English tile." All chimneys are original, except the brick chimney added in 1935, visible from the rear.

The house was roughly H-shaped in plan, with gables at both ends of the facade. This was a highly unusual floor plan for Texas, but it retained the German Texan preference for direct entry into a room of living. The recessed porch had a centered door, another on the right side wall, and a window on the left side wall. The house had no passages, central or otherwise. The door led into the living room, which was heated by the preferred cast-iron stove until a fireplace was built on the back wall in 1935. The room had two large windows on the front wall and another pair on the back wall.

The right side wall had one door, which led into a large dining room. This room also had access from the front porch, two windows on the front wall, and one on the side wall. On the back wall was a pair of built-in china closets, which framed a segmental opening that led to a pantry and more storage space, then the kitchen. The closet opening into the kitchen was lit by a thin window on the north wall. The kitchen had windows on the north and west walls, a flue for a stove on the north wall, and another door on the south wall. This door originally opened onto the back porch, but the porch was enclosed in 1935.

On the left wall of the living room were two doors, which led to the front and middle bedrooms. The front bedroom was presumably Paul and Ida's room; with two windows on the front wall and one on each side wall, it was the best ventilated of the three. There was also a door connecting the front and middle bedrooms. The middle bedroom had a half bath at the northeast corner. The third bedroom had a door on the north, which also opened onto the porch. Behind the third bedroom was a bathroom.

When the family moved into this house, they had one child, Peter, named for his paternal grandfather. Over the next decade, three daughters were born in the house: Hedwig, Paula, and Ida. Sometime after the main house was completed, a playhouse was built for the children. Originally sited behind the house, it was later moved to the northeast corner of the property. It was a wood-frame structure with chimneys of reddish brick, which most likely came from the new brick factory at D'Hanis, west of San Antonio. The cast-iron fence around the property, made in nearby Kerrville, was added in 1954. Paula Ingenhuett never married; she lived in the house until her death in 1981. Two years before her passing, Paula wrote the historical documentation for the Recorded Texas Historic Landmark marker, which is attached to the house. The house remains in the family.[15]

Comfort State Bank, now Comfort Heritage Foundation
640 High Street
1907

In the nineteenth century, banking services had been provided by local merchants August Faltin and Peter Joseph Ingenhuett. On April 4, 1907, Vincent J. McAteer, a Kentucky native and editor of the recently founded *Comfort News*, called together several leading citizens of Comfort to discuss the founding of a local bank. The invited citizens viewed the idea favorably; after this things moved with lighting speed. A bank charter was

Figure 7.15. Comfort State Bank, 1907. Photo by Kenneth Hafertepe.

drawn up April 23, and the bank opened in temporary quarters on May 1. This building was ready for occupancy by mid-December of that same year. The owner of the building was Alexander Brinkmann, a Comfort native, who built the structure and then leased it to the bank (fig. 7.15).

The Comfort State Bank was more or less Romanesque in style. The choice of this style was most likely inspired by the Bank of Fredericksburg, built in 1898 to the designs of Alfred Giles. The Bank of Fredericksburg was a much more sophisticated variation on Romanesque themes. (It was not particularly Richardsonian, forsaking any polychromy in its materials in favor of the exclusive use of limestone.) The main commonalities between the Comfort and Fredericksburg banks were the use of limestone, one imposing round arched window, and a tower at the corner. The *San Antonio Express* noted that the bank now had "modern headquarters" while also describing it as "built in the Gothic style." While these terms of praise might be seen as contradictory, the writer pressed on to conclude that it was "one of the handsomest structures in town."

Because the Comfort State Bank sat on a corner lot, the main entrance was at the corner of High Street and Seventh Street. It was marked by a tower, square in plan and with a blind arcade and a hipped roof. Underneath the tower, the wall was angled and contained the double doors. The entrance was framed by columns with polished red granite shafts, probably from the quarries north of Fredericksburg. These columns supported two round arches of limestone. The single window on the High Street facade was also round arched, and on the Seventh Street facade were three rectangular windows. The walls were of local limestone, cut in large and regular blocks. The windowsills were rusticated limestone. The red brick above the limestone walls may have been intended to be covered with plaster. These bricks were possibly from the new factory at D'Hanis, west of San Antonio. Red granite occurred naturally in the Hill Country but was unavailable for use until the 1880s, when industrial-grade saws made it feasible and the selection of the material for the Texas State Capitol in Austin led to the opening of several quarries in the Hill Country.

The large round-arched window lit the president's office, and behind this was the banking room. A counter ran from front to back in the middle of the room, with the vault built against the west wall. When the vault was later removed, the classical cornice was discarded, but in recent years it was rediscovered and returned to the building. At the back of the building was the board room, where decisions were made about proposed loans. The Arts and Crafts side chairs from this room remain in the build-

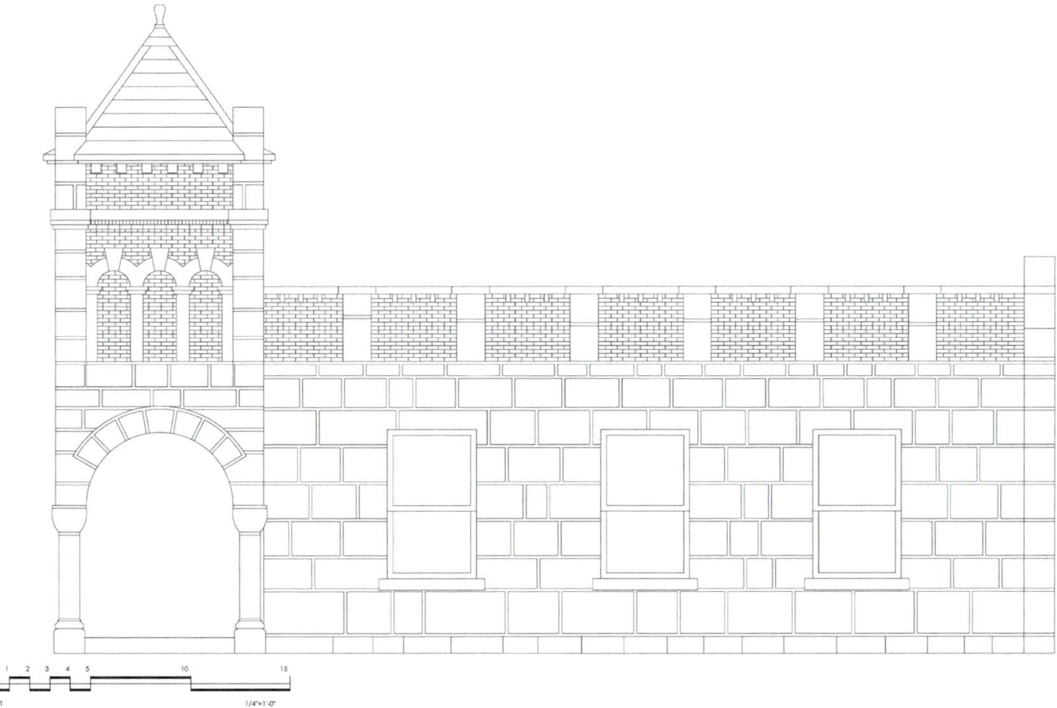

Figure 7.16. Comfort State Bank, north elevation. Measured by Brent R. Fortenberry. Drawing by Hayley M. Field.

ing. A passage on the east wall ran from the main banking room to the back door.

The masonry work has been attributed to Richard Doebbler. No solid evidence has been uncovered to verify this attribution, but Doebbler did grow up in Grapetown, just over the Gillespie County line, and was the son of stonemason Louis Doebbler. The son tried to avoid his stonemason heritage and instead farmed and ranched for many years in Kerr County, but he retired in 1907 and moved to Comfort. In 1910 he and his family were living on Main Street in Comfort, and at age sixty-three he gave his occupation as a contractor in the masonry industry.

Alex Brinkmann sold the building to J. H. and Martha Bierschwale in 1945, when he was seventy-seven years old. Martha Bierschwale outlived her husband and sold it in 1960 to Albert Faltin.

In 1960 the bank built a new headquarters. Albert Faltin then purchased the building and donated it to the Comfort School District, which was one of the few tax-exempt organizations in town. It served as the home of the Comfort Public Library for more than twenty years. Since then it has been home to the Comfort Heritage Foundation and the Chamber of Commerce (fig. 7.16).[16]

Old Post Office, now 814 A Texas Bistro
713 High Street
1908

Peter J. Ingenhuett was postmaster from 1867 to 1891, operating the post office out of his store. When Peter retired, his son Paul took over the store and the post office. This building was erected in 1908, tucked between the Ingenhuett Hotel on the left and the Ingenhuett home on the right. It was the last building in Comfort to have been designed by Alfred Giles—or, to be more precise, the Alfred Giles Co., Architects, as the surviving drawings are signed (figs. 7.17 and 7.18).

The Giles drawings show that the exterior of the building is remarkably intact. The front and back walls had double doors flanked by a window to each side; the side walls were windowless. The parapet on the front of the building concealed the low pitched roof, which ran from side to side but also sloped down to the rear. The principal building material was red brick, probably burned in the newly started factory in D'Hanis, west of Castroville. On the front of the building, the bricks formed four piers, which projected forward to resemble piers consisting of articulated blocks. Giles deployed heavily rusticated limestone as a course at the sill,

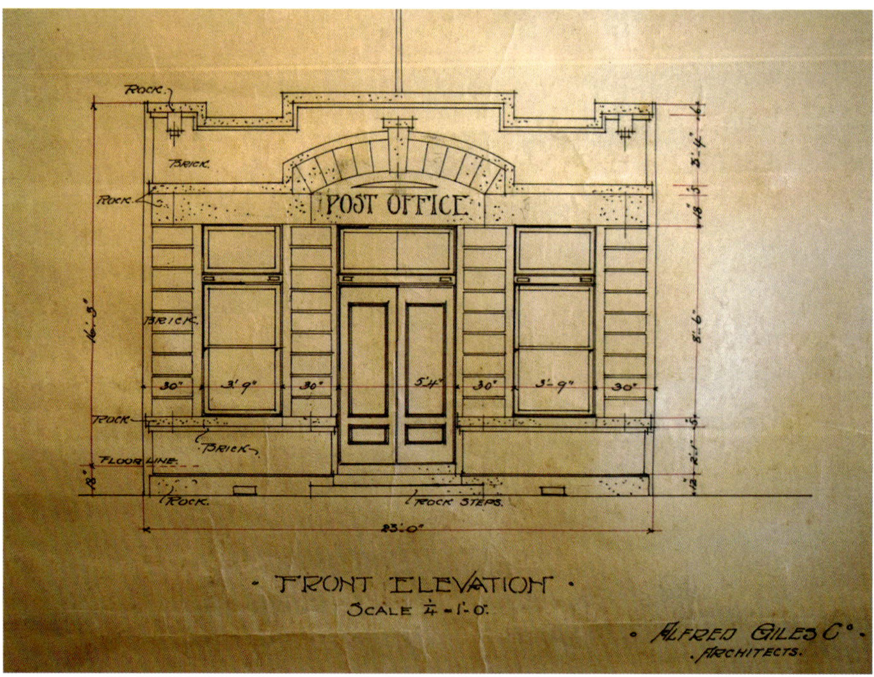

Figure 7.17. Comfort Post Office, front elevation, 1908. By Alfred Giles Co. Courtesy of Roy Perkins III.

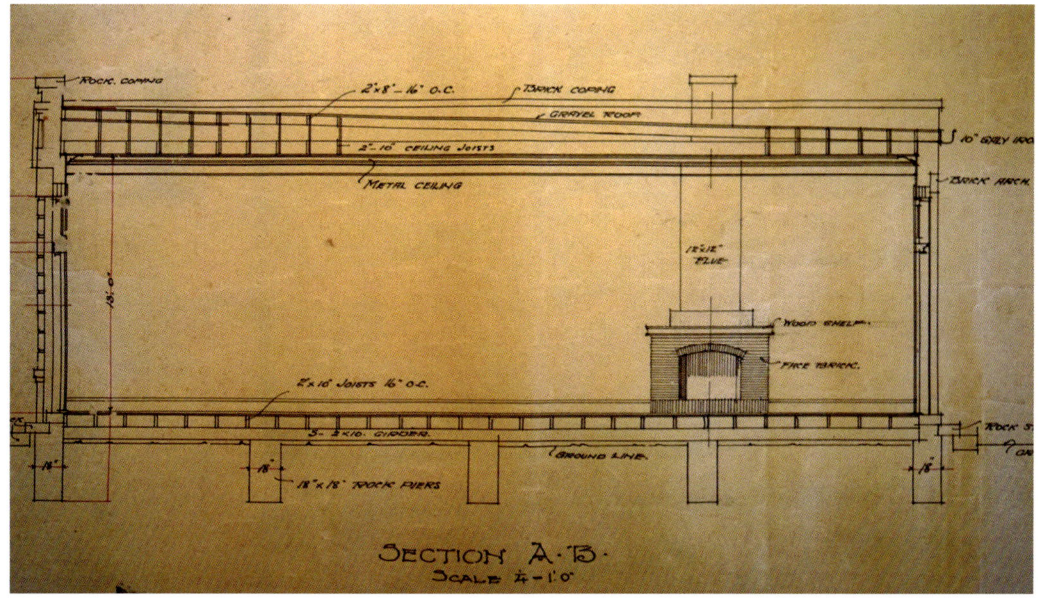

Figure 7.18. Comfort Post Office, Section A.B. By Alfred Giles Co. Courtesy of Roy Perkins III.

Figure 7.19. Comfort Post Office, west elevation. Measured by Brent R. Fortenberry. Drawing by Hayley M. Field.

more prominently at the lintel, and again as coping to outline the parapet. On the side walls the stone coping gave way to brick set in concrete. The Giles drawing called for the words "POST OFFICE" to be carved into the stone above the center transom, but this was left out. However, a rusticated segmental arch framed the entrance and two inner piers.

Giles designed the interior as one open space, but this was certainly subdivided by counters. The front was the public lobby, and on the other side of the counter was the office with the post boxes. The public space was unheated, but there was a fireplace in the office area, which was faced with brick and had a wooden mantel shelf. The segmental opening of the fireplace echoed the segmental arch of the facade. Giles called for a metal ceiling, as used in most Texas commercial buildings of this era.

The building served as the post office until 1952 and since then has had a number of other uses, most recently as a restaurant. The only change to the exterior has been the substitution of single-pane plate-glass windows for the large one-over-one windows of the Giles design, which would have been crucial in the days before air conditioning (fig. 7.19).[17]

Fredericksburg

Friedrich and Maria Kiehne House
405 East Main Street
1850–51, circa 1858, 1930s

This house was the first two-story rock house in Fredericksburg—at a time that almost everyone was living in a log house. It also has the distinction of being the oldest documented rock house in town. It was originally two rooms down and two rooms up, with no central passage—typically German Texan in rejecting the passage. Also typical was the adoption of a front porch—this one the first two-story porch in town. Though the idea of the porch was American, it was inset (under the main roof) in a Creole manner and was heavily framed in a Germanic fashion. (The Victorian trim was certainly added later.) Presumably the east front room, behind the double doors, was the *stube*. The west front room had a single door and a casement window. This room also had a fireplace on the side wall, while the left front room had a flue on the back wall at the southeast corner. The partition between the two front rooms was not rock but *fachwerk* (figs. 7.20–7.22).

Figure 7.20. Map of Fredericksburg sites. Image by Brent R. Fortenberry.

Figure 7.21. Friedrich and Maria Kiehne house, 1850–51, ca. 1858, 1930s. Photo by Kenneth Hafertepe.

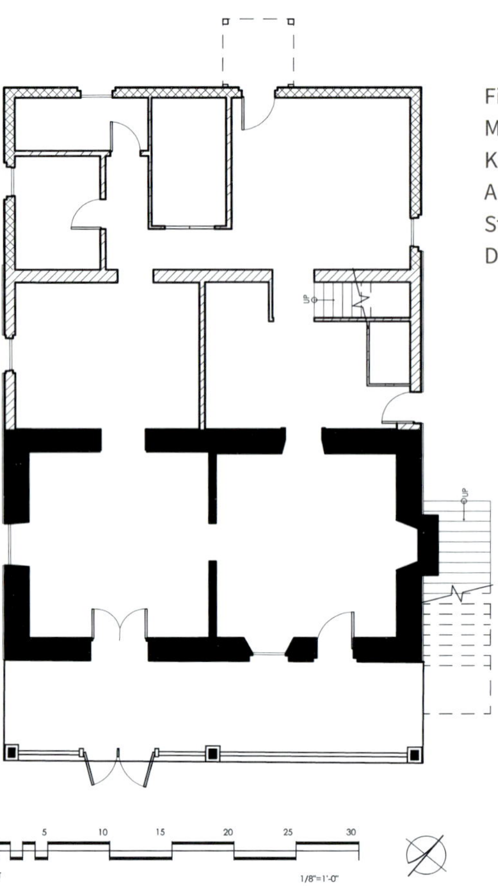

Figure 7.22. Plan of Friedrich and Maria Kiehne house. Measured by Kate Howard, Carter L. Hudgins, Amalia Leifeste, Dana Marks, Sada Stewart, and Christopher Tenny. Drawing by Christopher Tenny.

A most remarkable feature is in the middle of a segmental arch over the double doors: a keystone with the names of Friedrich Kiehne and Maria Johanna Kreinsen and the date 1850. There is no other example in the Hill Country of a keystone or cornerstone with the name of the husband, much less the name of the wife, and with her maiden name. It must be noted that this was Friedrich's second marriage and, given that Maria was the same age, probably her second go-round as well. Her father, Conrad Kreinsen, was also going to be living with them. County property tax records suggest that the house was begun in 1850 but not completed until the next year. Those records also confirm that the Kiehnes added two rooms down and two rooms up around 1858; the rear rooms were not constructed until after 1938. Both the 1936 Historic American Buildings Survey (HABS) photo of the rear elevation and the 1938 update of the 1924 Sanborn map showed a one-story porch stretching across the back of the house.

The original location of the stairs is unclear. There is no evidence of a stair ever having been in either of the two front rooms. A stair may have been on the front porch or against the back wall; indeed, there could have been a back gallery. However, a staircase is present at the southwest corner of one of the rooms that were added around 1858. There was no stair when Richard MacAllister photographed the exterior for HABS, but one was present by the 1980s. This was subsequently removed, and a new external porch was built on the west side. Access to the attic is still through a pull-down staircase on the second-floor gallery.

The house was built for Friedrich Kiehne and his second wife, Maria Johanna Kreinsen. They arrived in Fredericksburg in 1847 and lived for several years in a log house. Friedrich was a *messerschmied* in Germany —a maker of cutlery—but on the Texas frontier his work broadened to include blacksmithing. (He is said to have made the hinges for this house.) Kiehne acquired several town lots in this block early on, which certainly appreciated and thus helped the Kiehnes to be able to afford this house. Kiehne identified himself as a blacksmith in the 1850 census and as a farmer in 1860. In 1850 the household included thirty-eight-year-old Friedrich, thirty-nine-year-old Maria, two sons born in Germany, and two born in Texas. Also living with them was Maria's father, seventy-year-old Conrad Kreinsen, and fourteen-year-old Sophie Burns, presumably a servant girl. In 1860 eldest son Friedrich had begun to farm on his own small spread but was living in town next to his parents. In ten years the value of Friedrich Sr.'s real estate had soared from eight hundred to thirty-six hundred dollars.

Marie died in 1866, and apparently the whole family moved out to their farm in the Palo Alto community north of town. In 1870 thirty-one-year-old Friedrich Jr. was the head of household, and his fifty-eight-year-old father was in semiretirement, though he owned more real estate and more personal property than his son. The elder Friedrich lived to be eighty-seven and died in 1898. That meant that he was able to attend the celebration of the fiftieth anniversary of the founding of Fredericksburg in 1896. He was interviewed by his old friend Julius Splittgerber, who established a lime kiln on the banks of Town Creek, for the history of the town published for the occasion. Splittgerber noted that Kiehne's house was the first stone building, that the stone came from Cross Mountain just northwest of town, and that local limestone had made for good lime.

The Kiehne family worshipped with the Evangelical Protestant congregation that met at the Vereins-Kirche (rather than Zion Lutheran), and the baptismal records of the church shed light on the builders of the Kiehne house. The most likely stonemasons were Johan Joseph Walch and Johannes Ruegner. Walch and Ruegner worked both separately and together, most notably on the Gillespie County Jail of 1852 (demolished). Christian Althaus and Christian Staats are the likely carpenters. Althaus is said to have worked on the Vereins-Kirche, the most prominent building in Fredericksburg before the Kiehne house, though he took up farming by 1860. In that year Staats had begun to specialize in cabinetmaking.

The Kiehne heirs sold the house in 1904, and it then had various owners. The one-story back range was added in the 1930s, which gave the house a modern kitchen. In 1973 Ronald and Maria Herrmann bought the house and launched a campaign of restoration and renovation. Their contractor was William Kargan Perrett, aided by Tyrus Cox, another local contractor who worked on many old buildings. The old floors were removed so that electrical conduits and air-conditioning ducts could be added, and new random-length flooring was installed. (A separate air-conditioning unit for the second floor was installed in the attic.) The double doors between the front and back rooms on the east side were discovered in the attic and returned to their original location. The interior staircase in the back right room may have been added at this time as well. Maria Herrmann also upgraded the kitchen, even adding an early microwave oven.

By 1990 the house had been acquired by Michael Sudderth and his wife, of Dallas, who turned it into a bed and breakfast called the Country Cottage Inn. This was an early adaptation of an old house into a bed and breakfast, a use that is now quite common in Fredericksburg. The house was named a Recorded Texas Historic Landmark in 1975 and is a contributing property to the National Register Historic District.[18]

Adam and Eva Krieger House (aka Krieger-Henke-Staudt House or Staudt Sunday House)

512 West Creek Street

1851, 1855, 1864

The left front room of the Krieger-Henke-Staudt house is the oldest part and is probably the oldest surviving example of *fachwerk* in Fredericksburg. (Close behind are the Walter, Kammlah, and Klingelhoefer houses.) Apparently the rock rooms were added in two campaigns. Adam Krieger was paying taxes on the lot by 1848; the value of $50 suggests that he and Eva were living in a one-room log house, possibly where the right front room now stands. The value rose to $125 in 1851, which probably represents the *fachwerk* room. In 1855 the lot was valued at $250, suggesting

Figure 7.23. Adam and Eva Krieger house, 1851, 1855, 1864. Photo by Kenneth Hafertepe.

the addition of the first rock room. In 1864, as the Civil War dragged on, the property value rose to $500, which probably represents the present four-room house (fig. 7.23).

The initial *fachwerk* room had a centered door with a casement window on each side. There are currently doors on the back (north) and right side (east) walls. Presumably the back door was to the exterior; quite possibly the side door opened into the original log house, which was replaced by the first rock room. A fireplace was on the west side wall. (Such fireplaces were unusual in Fredericksburg, as German Texans had a strong preference for cast-iron stoves.) Originally there was a stair at the northeast corner, which started on the north wall and continued on the east wall. The floor joist below and the beams above ran from front to back, which was typical of German Texan houses. The attic had a wooden floor; the end gable was rock rather than *fachwerk*, and there was a hatch just behind the chimney.

The first rock room added another casement window and a French door. This may well have become the *stube*, if the rock steps and opening in the porch railing documented by HABS in 1934 are original to 1855. This space definitely had a cast-iron stove, as a flue was centered in the east side wall. At the front corner of this wall was a built-in cabinet, and a second cabinet was originally on the northwest corner of the back wall. There was no door on the back wall originally; the ventilation must have been problematic. It was most likely that the exterior walls were first plastered at this point to give some unity to the exterior. When the HABS team arrived in 1934, the *fachwerk* room was still plastered over, though the exterior was in such disrepair that HABS draftsman Anton Heisler marked it as "native stone partially stuccoed." The front porch may well date to 1855; the simple Victorian frieze, created by a pattern of drilled holes, seems a simple invocation of Victorians friezes that were popular in the Hill Country from 1890 to 1910.

If the log room contained the original kitchen and the new room was a *stube* and the old room a *kammer*, it is unclear where the kitchen was before construction of the back rooms. The kitchen of 1864 had a flue and chimney in the east wall, a back door, and three six-over-six sash windows on the back wall. On the east wall was another door, leading into the back right room, which had solid rock walls on the north and south and another sash window on the east. This was used as bedroom for a long time but could have originally been a dairy and/or pantry, given its access from the kitchen. By the 1930s the *fachwerk* room was being used as the living room, the room behind it as the kitchen, and the two east rooms as bedrooms.

The original owners were Adam and Eva Krieger. Adam Krieger was a farmer, and he built a barn on the east side of the lot. Like the nearby Walter barn the ridge ran parallel to the street, but in this case it was set back from the street. (The front wall of the barn lined up with the back wall of the front rooms.) The Kriegers sold the house to Carl and Dorette Henke. Like his new neighbors, various members of the Walter and Dietz families, Carl was a teamster. If a farmer owned a wagon and worked as a teamster, he was more likely to learn English from army personnel in San Antonio and at frontier forts. (Pioneer farmers who farmed but did not own a wagon were more likely to know only German.)

In 1906 Carl Henke and his two surviving children sold the house to the widow Marie Mosel, whose daughter Emma married Louis Dietz, whose family owned the log house across the street. John Mosel had died in 1904, so the household consisted of Marie and her unmarried daughter, Lina. Marie died in 1911, and after Lina bought out her siblings' stake in the house, she became its sole owner. She sometimes worked as a seamstress to bring in extra money.

In 1920 Lina sold the house to Christian Staudt, who was a farmer and rancher near Doss, in far western Gillespie County. In that year Christian and his wife, Anna, were both fifty-one, and they had four children in the house. They used the house as a weekend house, though by this time Lutheran churches had been built in Doss and Harper. Though the house had not been built as a Sunday house, and was much larger than any other Sunday house, the HABS team christened it the Staudt Sunday House. The Staudts in turn sold the house in 1941, and it went through several owners until 1968, when it was purchased by Rodolph and Roberta Smith. (Roberta was the daughter of Fritz and Lillian Stieler of Comfort.)

Rodolph and Roberta restored and renovated the house. The Kriegers and Henkes may have used the first rock room as the *stube*, but the Smiths, as early admirers of old-time *fachwerk*, reprioritized the front rooms. They removed the plaster over the *fachwerk* frame along with twelve layers of paint to expose the wood underneath. In addition, they moved the steps back to the left front room. In 1934 the porch had a wooden railing along the front; however, there was a gate in front of the door to the right front room, and the railing in two of central bays had fallen down. Presumably the Smiths finished the job.

On the interior Rodolph and Roberta reopened the fireplace. The wooden floors had been covered with linoleum, and the wood beneath it was in poor condition, so they removed the floor and placed flagstones in between the floor joists, which were still intact. The original staircase had been removed earlier; the Smiths installed an exterior stair on the east side wall, which provided access to a new heating and air-conditioning unit in the attic. A new door was created between the two east rooms, and the door between the back room and the kitchen was enclosed to create a bathroom. The log house in the backyard was originally in Comfort and was said to have been owned by Edward Steves and Herman Ingenhuett. It was given to the Smiths as a gift and rebuilt it in the backyard of the Krieger house.

The house was documented by HABS in 1934. (The data page was written by local architect Lee C. Kiehne, who was about to start work on the design of the Vereins-Kirche replica.) The house was identified as a contributing property to the Fredericksburg Historic District in the

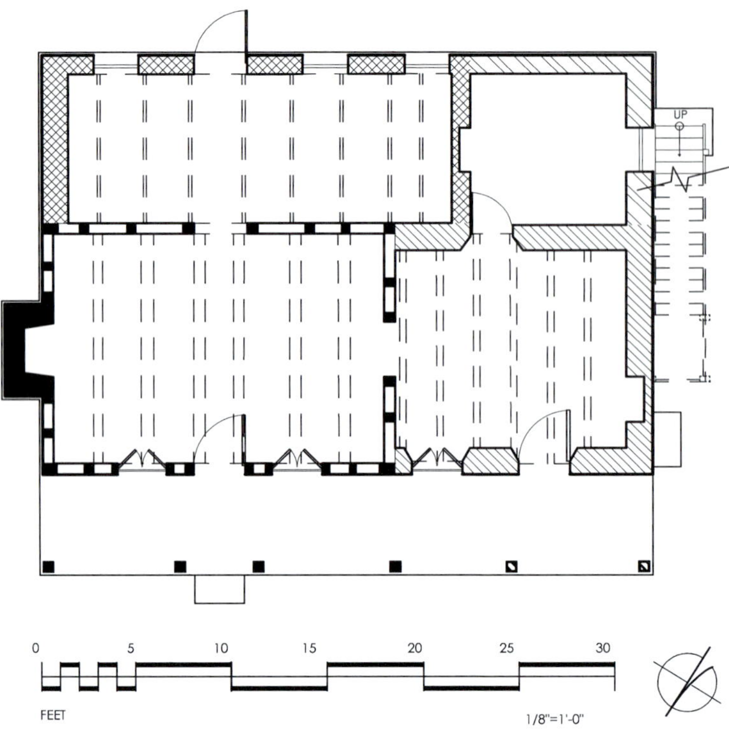

Figure 7.24. Plan of Adam and Eva Krieger house. Measured by Kate Howard, Carter L. Hudgins, Amalia Leifeste, Dana Marks, Sada Stewart, and Christopher Tenny. Drawing by Christopher Tenny.

National Register of Historic Places in 1970. The present owner purchased the house in 1999; it is maintained for the study and enjoyment of future generations (fig. 7.24).[19]

Peter and Anna Margaret Walter House
601 West Creek Street
1853, 1859, 1954

This property was owned by the Walter family for more than one hundred years, from 1847 to 1954. They first erected a small log house, then built a *fachwerk* house in front of it, to which was added a rock lean-to. They acquired most of the town lots on this block, then started farming on them. Though the Walters were a farming family, they also generated income as wagoners—contractors for the US Army, moving supplies from Fort San Antonio to the forts west and northwest of Fredericksburg. In 1850 Peter Walter gave his occupation as wagoner, as did his brother-in-law, Henry Dietz, who lived across Bowie Street. In 1860 Walter identified himself as a farmer, but the disparity between $450 of real estate and $1,080 of personal property indicated that he owned a number of wagons and the oxen to pull them. Peter Walter died in 1865 in a fall from a wagon, but in 1870 two of his sons, Heinrich and Wilhelm, indicated that they were teamsters. Heinrich owned $200 worth of land and $500 worth of personal property, while Wilhelm owned no land but $500 in personal property. Also living in this household was his widowed mother, Anna Margaret, who claimed the $200 for the homestead.

Peter and Anna Margaret Walter arrived in Fredericksburg in 1847. He was forty, she was thirty-seven, and they brought with them five children; one more arrived in 1854. Peter's sister Maria Walter married Henry Gustav Dietz, and they immigrated to Fredericksburg as well, purchasing the lot across Bowie Street. Both couples started with a log house. The Walter log house was set back from the street, while the Dietz house sat at the front of the property. The Dietz house had a front porch, while the Walter log house did not. The Walter log house was just over half the width of the present house. Peter and Anna Margaret's granddaughter, Minna Walter Lang, told the journalist Elise Kowert that the log house had a small fireplace with a raised hearth. This building continued in use as the kitchen even after the construction of the present house (fig. 7.25).

Figure 7.25. Peter and Anna Margaret Walter house, 1853, 1859, 1954. Photo by Kenneth Hafertepe.

The *fachwerk* house was built around 1853. There were two rooms and a front porch. On the left was the door; on the right, a window. There were also small casement windows on both side walls, just forward of a central post. It is unclear whether the *fachwerk* was infilled with rock or sun-dried adobe brick. On the interior a partition wall ran from front to back; beams ran from the side walls to this partition. The roof was a basic common rafter system, typical of early Fredericksburg. The carpenters who built the *fachwerk* portion of the house were likely Jacob Arhelger and Hermann Hitzfeld, who also built the J. J. Klingelhoefer house, where they used adobe bricks as infill. The Walters also built a barn to the west of the house; the long side faced the street and, like the front porch, was at the street line (fig. 7.26).

Figure 7.26. Peter and Anna Margaret Walter House, kitchen and barn. Institute of Texas Cultures, University of Texas at San Antonio, ITC 075–0246 a.

The final phase of construction occurred in 1858–59, with the addition of the rock lean-to. This rectangular space was probably a *kammer*. The rock work was probably done by Fredericksburg stonemason John Peter and his son Georg Peter. The attribution is based on the fact that John Peter's daughter Wilhelmine was married to Heinrich Walter. The rock addition to the *fachwerk* house most likely inspired the family to have both sections plastered to give it a more unified effect. Plasterers were fewer in Fredericksburg than stonemasons; the Walters probably turned to Jacob Neffendorf, whose wife was Katherina Dietz; Jacob and Katherina even named their son after Heinrich Walter. Across the street Heinrich and Maria Dietz also added a rock lean-to to the rear of their log house.

By 1870 Heinrich and his wife, Mina, had established a separate dwelling—perhaps the log kitchen—while Anna Margaret was living with Wilhelm; his wife, Sophie; their only daughter, Minna; and Wilhelm's youngest brother, Louis. Anna Margaret died in 1886, and Wilhelm died in 1920. Sophie lived until 1931, when the house was inherited by Minna Walter Lang. She held on to the property for more than two decades. On June 13, 1954, Minna sold the house to the recently founded Episcopal church for twenty-five hundred dollars.

The church adapted the house for use as a chapel. At some point the house lost its plaster covering, and on the sides the *fachwerk* was covered over with narrow clapboards. When the house was adapted for use as a chapel, shingles were nailed to the clapboards. The interior partition was removed, which, in turn, necessitated removal of the beams that ran from both side walls to the central partition. It served as the place of worship for Episcopalians until the present St. Barnabas Church was dedicated in 1965. In 1983 much work was done on the house, including removal of the shingles from the exterior and installation of an antique wood floor. The beams and walls were stabilized, and the original infill was replaced with larger blocks of stone.

In 1963 the Walter house was one of the first six buildings in Fredericksburg to be awarded a medallion by the State Historical Survey Committee, the forerunner of the Texas Historical Commission. In 1970 it was named a contributing property in the Fredericksburg National Register of Historic Places Historic District.[20]

Heinrich and Auguste Kammlah House
309 West Main Street
1853–54, circa 1858, circa 1867, 1869, circa 1902–10

The Kammlah family arrived in Fredericksburg in 1849, three years after the founding of the town. They owned this lot from 1849 to 1955, when other members of the family sold the house to the Historical Society. The core of early settlement in Fredericksburg was east of the Marktplatz, and most of the early houses in that area were later demolished to make way for commercial construction. The Kammlahs, by arriving a little late, settled on a lot that did not face such intense development pressure, and thereby their house survived into the twenty-first century.

Family tradition suggested that the front rooms of the house were built soon after they purchased the lot, but as cultural geographer Terry Jordan pointed out in the 1960s, most settlers of Fredericksburg quickly built a log house in which they lived for five or even ten years before building a more permanent house of *fachwerk* or rock. Even then the log house would have been used as a kitchen or for some other purpose (fig. 7.27).

Figure 7.27. Heinrich and Auguste Kammlah house, 1853–54, ca. 1858, ca. 1867, 1869, ca. 1902–10. Photo by Kenneth Hafertepe.

Figure 7.28. Heinrich and Auguste Kammlah house, May 29, 1936. Photo by Richard MacAllister for HABS.

The dating of the various rooms is poorly documented. Increases in the property tax valuation of the house suggest a date of 1853–54 for the front rooms. In 1850 Henry was forty-two, and Auguste, forty; they had two sons, eleven-year-old Henry II and seven-year-old William. All were natives of Braunschweig. A daughter, Louise, was born in Fredericksburg circa 1851. Auguste Kammlah died in March 1854, and Henry never re-married. The argument has been made that the two lean-to rooms behind the three front rooms must have been built before Auguste's death, since there would be less of a motive to expand after her death. However, this would be true not only for the lean-to rooms but the second kitchen, the new house, and a connecting lean-to, all of which were built by her husband (fig. 7.28).

The front rooms of the house are constructed using the *fachwerk* technique, with an infill of rock. (In other areas of German settlement where rock was not as available, brick was the preferred material for in-fill.) All other rooms in the house were built with walls entirely of rock. The house was originally covered with wooden shingles; between 1902 and 1910 the main roof and that of the front porch were re-covered with standing-seam metal. The front porch is virtually the only adaptation from Anglo-Texan building techniques; porches were rare in Germany, but German Texans quickly discovered the desirability of a shaded out-door space.

The earliest windows were casements, which opened outward. Start-ing with the "new house" of 1869, double-hung sash began to be used. Casement windows were typical in all of the early houses, and the switch to casements can be seen as a marker of adopting Anglo-Texan building techniques.

Originally, the front section consisted of three rooms, as can be seen in the mortises in the front-to-back ceiling beams, which once received tenons attached to partition walls. As of 1936 there were exterior doors into the central and west rooms; the west door was converted into a window sometime after 1936, perhaps when the house was restored in the 1950s. During the restoration a window in the east side wall was enclosed as well. There is no evidence of a cooking hearth or, for that matter, of flues for cast-iron stoves. Presumably, cooking continued to be done in the log house to the rear.

The most poorly documented developments came next. There are two lean-to rooms, both of rock, supposedly added at the same time. How-ever, the casement windows seem to have been made at different times.

The room on the east has a small fireplace, raised a couple inches off the ground. It has been suggested that the room dates to before 1853, the death year of Auguste Kammlah, but this seems to be wishful thinking. This room has been called the "first kitchen," though the cooking surface would have been very impractical.

The room on the west opens into what has been called the "second kitchen," which has traditionally been dated to 1859, though raised hearths, such as the one that stretches across the entire south wall, seem to have been more popular in the years just after the Civil War. All these rooms were built of rock and had shingled roofs. Presumably, the rock additions inspired the builders to plaster over the entire structure to give a house that was part *fachwerk* and part rock a unified appearance.

When the census taker visited the household in 1860, he found only Heinrich and his two youngest children, sixteen-year-old William and nine-year-old Louise. Heinrich's meager $700 of real estate suggests that only three or four rooms of the current house had been built; his $1,340 of personal property suggests that in addition to being a farmer, as he told the census taker, he had already begun to keep a store. Heinrich Jr. had married Amalia Betz and was working as a wagoner. That had a special meaning in the Hill Country, as Germans contracted with the US Army to haul supplies from San Antonio to the forts that were being established to subdue the Comanches and Lipan Apaches to the west. Heinrich Jr. had no real estate but had $550 in personal property, undoubtedly a large wagon and a team of oxen. He and Amalia had a six-month-old baby boy named August. The close association with the US Army probably motivated Heinrich to join the German Texans who attempted to flee to Mexico in 1862. Many were slain in the Nueces Massacre, but Heinrich managed to return home and to survive the rest of the war. In the years after the war he resumed hauling supplies to US forts, which stretched farther and farther to the west.

In 1869 Heinrich Kammlah Sr. built what he called the "new house." Like the old house, it had three front rooms, but now there was a half story above and a basement below. (Story-and-a-half rock houses were extremely popular after the war, though they usually had one or two front rooms and another room in a rear lean-to.) In this case a lean-to was erected on the north side, nearer the street, with the roof butting against the south wall of the second kitchen. It is unclear whether this was part of the new house or added sometime later. The lean-to has yet another space for cooking on a raised hearth at the east end. This may well be the site of the original log house. These rooms were the first to receive a metal roof, which was present in 1896, though it is unclear if they dated to 1869. The creation of the new house seems to have been spurred by the desire to turn the front rooms into commercial space. Possibly the second front door was added at this time, though the west room might have been an unheated commercial space all along (fig. 7.29).

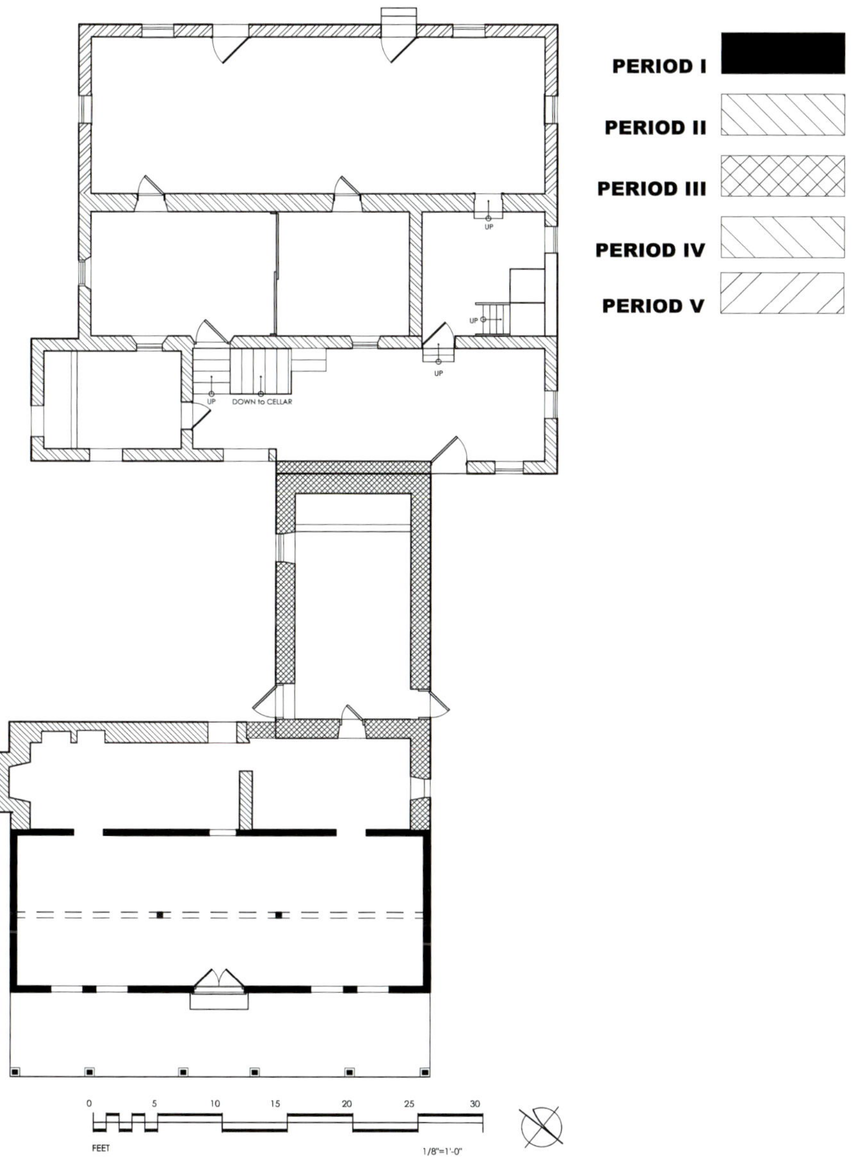

Figure 7.29. Plan of Heinrich and Auguste Kammlah house. Measured by Brent R. Fortenberry. Drawing by Hayley M. Field.

In 1870, Heinrich Sr. was living with his only daughter, nineteen-year-old Louise. The value of his real estate had increased to fifteen hundred dollars, reflecting the new house, but his personal property had dropped to three hundred dollars, suggesting that the transition of the front rooms to commercial use was developing slowly. Heinrich Jr. and Amalia were living a few blocks up the street in a log house Amalia had inherited from her parents, a fact confirmed by their meager three hundred dollars in real estate. Heinrich's occupation was still wagoner, and his wagon and team of oxen had depreciated only a little bit, to five hundred dollars. They now had three daughters—Auguste, Caroline, and Louise—and a son, Henry III.

One theory explaining why a widower with one child at home would build a new house is that in the Hill Country there were no banks, and the proceeds from a successful crop or a successful store could be invested either in more land or in improving the land that one already had. Another theory is that Heinrich was attempting to lure Heinrich Jr. and Amalia to come live with him. That might seem attractive, but Heinrich Jr. may have been reticent about returning to the parental household.

It is unclear when Heinrich Jr. and Amalia moved into the old home. Heinrich Sr. died in 1875, and Heinrich and Amalia moved in sometime before the 1880 census. At that point they were both forty years old, and they now had five children, ranging in age from two to twenty. Heinrich now gave his occupation as farmer—which kept him closer to home—though in 1900 he declared himself a general merchant, which he had probably been since his father's death. In 1898 their son Heinrich had married a girl named Amalia. Both Heinrich III and Amalia attended school only to the fourth grade, suggesting that the family valued work over education. By 1900 Heinrich III and Amalia had two daughters; he gave his occupation as farmer, taking over what his father had done in 1880. The family also had a nineteen-year-old boarder, Carl Metz.

The prospect of a growing family may have inspired a final long shed room, built between 1902 and 1910. This space had a door into each of the three rooms of the new house and a single exterior door on the south side. The household still had two Heinrichs and two Amalias and now four granddaughters. In 1920 eighty-year-old Heinrich Jr., eighty, was proprietor of a general store; his fifty-year-old son, Heinrich III, was a clerk in the store; his eight-year-old son, Heinrich IV, did not yet have an occupation. Amalia (Betz) Kammlah died in 1913, and Heinrich Jr. died in 1923. After the death of Heinrich Jr. his son closed the store.

In 1930 sixty-one-year-old Henry III was running a stock farm, principally sheep and goats. Two of his adult daughters were unmarried: thirty-one-year-old Rosa was a cook in a café, and twenty-nine-year-old Lillie was a helper in a creamery. Ten years later Lillie was a cream tester at the creamery, and Lena was a cook at a hotel. Their younger brother, twenty-eight-year-old Henry V, was a clerk in a package store.

The house was acquired by the Historical Society in 1955 and restored in 1956–57. A key figure in this work was Albert Keidel, a descendant of a prominent pioneer family who had been remodeling old buildings since the 1930s. The focus of the restoration was the front four rooms and the second kitchen. Plaster was removed both inside and out. The exterior of the house was covered in Portland cement, though the interior of the three front rooms remained unplastered to allow visitors to see the *fachwerk* construction. The right front door was converted into a casement window, and the casement window on the east side wall was removed to allow shelving to be installed on the inside of that wall. Keidel also found an old roof to replace the collapsed roof of the second kitchen. A rock wall was built around the house in 1964.

In 1966 the house was made a Recorded Texas Historic Landmark, and it is a contributing property to the National Register Historic District.

Johann Jost and Elisabeth Klingelhoefer House
701 West Main Street
1854–55, circa 1969, circa 1959–61

The Klingelhoefer family has owned this property since their arrival in Fredericksburg in the spring of 1847. Johann acquired six lots in this block, town lots 271 to 276. The family built in lot 271, the corner lot closest to town. Around 1896, a granddaughter from his first marriage, Hulda Saenger Walter, and her husband, Frederick Walter, a grandson of pioneers Peter and Anna Margaret Walter, built a rock house on lot 274, which is now 709 West Main.

This house was inherited by Johann's eldest son, Julius Klingelhoefer, a stonemason. (His younger brother William acquired land just outside town and built his house there.) When Julius died in 1917, the house went to his second wife, Sophie Tatsch Klingelhoefer, a daughter of cabinetmaker John Peter Tatsch and his wife, Maria Elizabeth. Sophie lived to age ninety-two and died in 1949. The house then went to her youngest daughter, Lyne Klingelhoefer Lewis Harper. Lyne lived elsewhere but used the house as her painting studio. She died in 1997, four days short of her hundredth birthday. She left the house to her niece, the current owner.

As was typical of the pioneer settlers, they built a log house to the rear of where they expected to build their permanent house. This temporary house sufficed for some seven years, and even after the construction of the *fachwerk* house it was used as a kitchen. This explains why neither of the original front rooms had a cooking hearth. This first permanent part of the house can be dated to 1854–55 because the valuation of Klingelhoefer property more than doubled between 1853 and 1855. The use of *fachwerk* was traditionally German, but this house included not only a typically American Southern front porch but also a dogtrot, *durchgang* in German. The infill was not stone but sun-dried bricks—essentially, adobe. It seems likely that the builders had noticed the production of such materials in San Antonio. However, adobe required protection against the elements and was always covered with plaster. A small patch of plaster in the northwest corner of the *durchgang* has been removed to show the adobe bricks beneath (figs. 7.30–7.33).

Both doors from the *durchgang* into the front rooms were built forward of center, as were the windows in the side walls. Presumably this was done because the principal beams run from the side walls to the interior walls that frame the *durchgang*. Smaller beams ran from the principal beams to the front and back walls. (These beams were replaced circa 1960 but replicate the placement of the original.) The sash windows on the front and side walls are very early, if not original, and may well be some of the earliest sash windows in Fredericksburg. The walls rise a foot or so above the ceiling, allowing for more head room (if not a half story) in the attic. The roof itself uses a common rafter system, typical for early houses in the Hill Country. While some Hill Country houses have front and back rafters joined by a mortise and tenon, those at the Klingelhoefer house were butted together and nailed.

It is highly likely that carpenters Jacob Arhelger and Hermann Hitzfeld built the Klingelhoefer house. Arhelger was born in Rittershausen, which was three miles from Johann Jost Klingelhoefer's birthplace in Eibelshausen, so they spoke German with the same accent. Hermann Hitzfeld was Klingelhoefer's son-in-law, as he married Elisabeth Klingelhoefer, a daughter from Johann's first marriage, in 1851. When Hermann and Elisabeth's daughter Louise was baptized in 1853, Jacob Arhelger was an official witness. Moreover, when Hermann died in 1857, the probate records indicated that his father-in-law owed him $307.25, which is close to

Figure 7.30. Johan Jost and Elisabeth Klingelhoefer house, 1854–55, ca. 1869, ca. 1959–61. Photo by Kenneth Hafertepe.

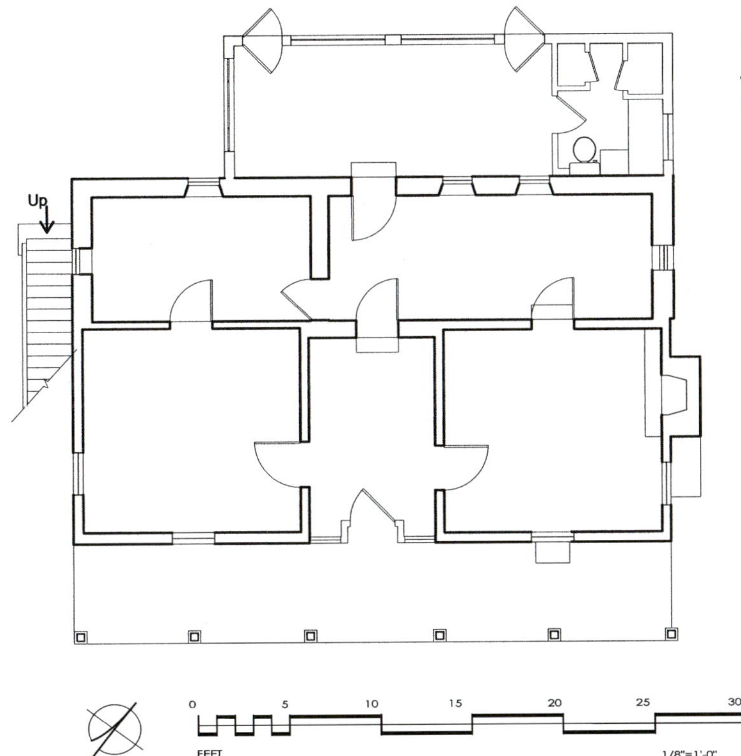

Figure 7.31. Plan of Johan Jost and Elisabeth Klingelhoefer house. By John Klein.

Figure 7.32. Johan Jost and Elisabeth Klingelhoefer house, view from *durchgang* into west front room. Photo by Kenneth Hafertepe.

Figure 7.33. Johan Jost and Elisabeth Klingelhoefer house, adobe brick in enclosed *durchgang*. Photo by Kenneth Hafertepe.

the increase of the value of Klingelhoefer's property in the previous years. Arhelger and Hitzfeld also probably built the Peter Walter house, which did not have a *durchgang* but did have principal beams running from the side walls to the central partition.

The two rock rooms were present by 1870. Between 1860 and 1870 John Klingelhoefer's real estate soared in value from $800 to $2,360. In 1870, John gave his occupation as farmer, and seventeen-year-old son William was listed as a farm laborer. His son Julius, twenty-one, was listed as a stonemason, and he was probably responsible, at least in part, for this addition. There was one large room on the west, a kitchen, and a smaller room on the east, a second bedroom. Family tradition holds that the east front room was originally the *stube* and the west front room a bedroom; perhaps the change in room use came when the second bedroom was placed in the east. It made sense to place the kitchen on the west, because the hatch to a basement under the west front room was now inside the house; the basement would have been useful for cool storage of foodstuffs. Both back rooms had chimneys on the side walls; that for the bedroom is original, and that for kitchen is of extruded brick, made in a factory and imported to Fredericksburg, and would have been much later. The creation of the back rooms partially enclosed the *durchgang*, and it seems likely that a front door was added at this time. (The current front door, however, is second or third generation.) In 1924 there was a single-bay back porch.

Lyne Klingelhoefer Lewis Harper inherited the house after the death of her mother, Sophie, in 1949. About a decade later she renovated the house and added a bathroom and a room for her studio. New flooring was installed in the front rooms, and some of the old floorboards were used to reframe the front entrance. Journalist Elise Kowert reported that the ceiling beams had to be replaced as well, and the fireplace in the west front room was rebuilt at this time.

As the daughter of a cabinetmaker, Sophie owned a number of pieces made by her father, though she preferred the factory-made furniture imported by her brother-in-law, Henry Kuenemann, and sold in his store. The child-sized chairs and tables were used by Sophie when she was a child, and the tables and chair in the west front room are said to have been made by Tatsch. After the death of her unmarried sister, Caroline, John Peter Tatsch's own *schrank* (wardrobe) and a side chair were moved to the house as well. The walnut rocking chair with a rawhide seat has become one of the artifacts most closely associated with the house. This group of furniture has never left the family; it provides remarkable documentation of the skills of a Hill Country cabinetmaker.[21]

John Peter and Maria Elizabeth Tatsch House
210 North Bowie Street
1858–59, 1869–70

More early houses survived at the west end of Fredericksburg because these lots were purchased by later arrivals after all lots in the center of town had been snapped up. This was true in the case of John Peter Tatsch and his wife, Maria Elizabeth. They immigrated from Irmenach in northwestern Germany in 1852 and purchased town lot 12 on October 9, 1854. This lot was twice as deep as that of the current property. The only building on that end of the lot was a board-and-batten barn, which was still present in 1934. The house has been variously dated as built in 1852, 1854, or 1856, but an examination of property tax records suggests that in late 1854 or early 1855 Tatsch built a one-room log house and then built the front two rooms of the current house in 1858 (fig. 7.34).

The rock house had two generously sized rooms. Assuming that upon completion of the rock house the log house became the kitchen, the left room was the *stube* and the right room a *kammer*—a bedroom for the children. In 1858 Peter and Maria had two daughters, Elizabeth and Caroline, and a third, Sophie, was on the way. Two more children, Richard and Wilhelmine, were born in the early 1860s. The family belonged to Zion Lutheran Church, which was three blocks away on Main Street (fig. 7.35).

The house was of local limestone, and the lime for the mortar was produced just a few blocks away by Julius Splittgerber. One of the most striking things about the house is the absence of a front porch, an American feature that was quickly adopted by most German immigrants. The double doors into the *stube* have four raised panels each, a reminder that Peter Tatsch was a cabinetmaker and turner; most of the woodwork on the house is attributed to him. All windows were casements rather than sash, which marked it as an early house. The roof was built with a common rafter system, which was typical of German Texan houses. The roof was originally covered with wooden shingles; between 1924 and 1934 it was replaced with a standing-seam metal roof. Presumably this happened after October 1930, when Walter Tatsch, a nephew, purchased the house from the other heirs.

Figure 7.34. John Peter and Maria Elizabeth Tatsch house, 1858–59, 1869–70. Photo by Kenneth Hafertepe.

Figure 7.35. John Peter and Maria Elizabeth Tatsch house. Institute of Texas Cultures, University of Texas at San Antonio, ITC 075–024.

Inside, the rafters of both rooms ran from front to back, which was typical of German Texan houses. The beams of the *stube* were squarish and stout and seem to be original. Those in the *kammer* are narrower and mill-sawn, presumably later. Other features also reflect Tatsch's craftsmanship, notably the small cabinet on the back wall of the *stube* and the staircase on the south wall of the *kammer*. The latter made good use of

Tatsch's skill as a turner. The *stube* was heated by a cast-iron stove in the southwest corner; the *kammer* had a small fireplace centered on the north wall. The most recent studies of the house have raised the question of whether there were originally windows on the back wall. The shelf in the *kammer* seems likely to have been a window; if there was one in the *stube*, it would push the date of the small cabinet from 1859 to 1870.

The lean-to addition was built circa 1869–70. Originally this was one open space that served as a new kitchen. (At this time the old log kitchen morphed into Tatsch's workshop.) The most notable feature of the new kitchen was the massive chimney stack on the exterior and the raised hearth inside. The chimney stack drew a great deal of attention over the years and even became a symbol of Fredericksburg, even though there was nothing else like it in town. The raised hearth echoed similar features in Germany. It relieved much of the backbreaking lifting of pots from the floor, though most German Texan women wanted a cast-iron stove. (Two other examples of raised hearth can be seen in the Kammlah house at the Pioneer Museum Complex.) The Tatsch hearth also included a separate bake oven with a door on the right side wall.

The oldest Tatsch daughter, Elizabeth, married one of her father's few apprentices, Henry Kuenemann, in 1868. Her father is said to have made them a *schrank* (wardrobe) as a wedding present, which now stands in the kitchen of the Tatsch house. It is one of the best examples of Tatsch's experimentation with the Renaissance Revival style of furniture. The third Tatsch daughter, Sophie, married Julius Klingelhoefer in 1886 and moved into the Klingelhoefer house, an 1854–55 *fachwerk* house with a rock addition. Maria Tatsch died in 1885, but Peter lived until 1907. In his later years his unmarried daughter Caroline cared for him, and she lived in the house until her death in 1929. Within a year the *schrank* and other furniture made by and for John Peter Tatsch moved to the Klingelhoefer house, where it remains to this day.

The Tatsch house was one of the earliest local buildings to be documented by HABS (1934). It was featured in *Pencil Points*, the national architecture journal, which was soon to be rebranded as *Progressive Architecture*. It was one of the first six buildings in Fredericksburg to be named a Recorded Texas Historic Landmark (1963) and is a contributing property in the Fredericksburg Historic District on the National Register of Historic Places (1970).[22]

Figure 7.36. William and Maria Klingelhoefer house, 1883–84, 1887–88.
Photo by Kenneth Hafertepe.

William and Maria Klingelhoefer House
US 87 North at US 290 West
1883–84, 1887–88

This is an excellent example of a German Texan house with two front doors. In addition, it is a story-and-a-half rock house, with the half story being quite tall. The use of two doors seems to be a continued German Texan resistance to having a central passage, which was considered wasted space. Instead, there was an exterior stair at the east end, though at some point a staircase was built at the southwest corner of the left front room, adjoining the wall shared with the *stube* (fig. 7.36).

Apparently the earliest part of the complex was the rock building to the west of the main house, which had one large room above another that is partially underground. Presumably the right front room was the *stube*, or parlor, and the left front room the bedroom. The right front room has a built-in cabinet on the west side wall, like those found in the Krieger and Tatsch houses. At this date the kitchen was in the outbuilding but was moved into the main house with the creation of the lean-to rooms. The current front porch, with its Victorian gingerbread trim, dates to sometime between 1890 and 1910.

It was built on outlot 581, which Johann Jost Klingelhoefer acquired from Jacob Schneider. When he was younger, William worked this outlot as a laborer on the family farm, producing much of the food for the family's table. When his father died in 1886, William inherited the land. Like his brother Julius, William was a stonemason. This was his occupation listed on the US census in 1880, 1900, and 1910, though in 1920, when he was sixty-six, he was listed as a mason in a cement yard. (This would have been the Basse Brothers, who in the early twentieth century made cement blocks that could be used for building. They are known locally as Basse blocks.) William certainly built the walls of this house, and he is thought to have worked on the Bank of Fredericksburg, designed by Alfred Giles, and many of the churches that were rebuilt or enlarged around the turn of the century. His name is one of four on the cornerstone of St. Peter Lutheran Church in Doss (1912–13).

In 1879 William married Maria Eckert, the daughter of farmers Ludwig and Christine Eckert. By 1900 they had eight children: August, Alfred, Alma, Adolph, Albert, Alvin, Arthur, and Armand. Marie died in 1924; and William, in 1937; in 1941 their youngest son, Armand, acquired the property from his siblings. The house remained in the family for decades. It has most recently been used as a bed and breakfast (fig. 7.37).[23]

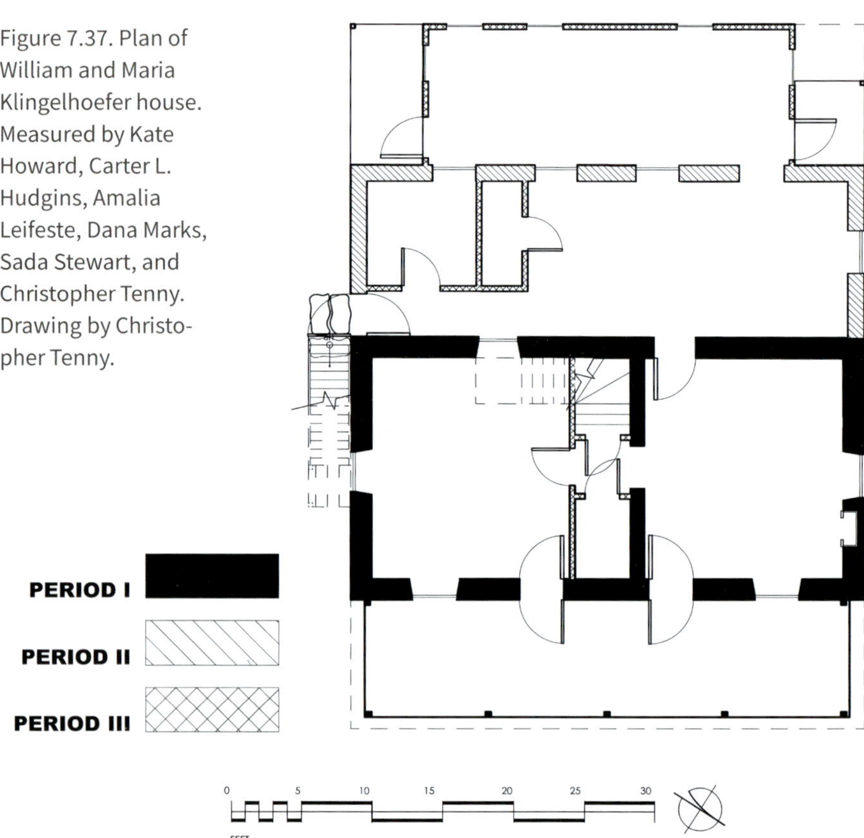

Figure 7.37. Plan of William and Maria Klingelhoefer house. Measured by Kate Howard, Carter L. Hudgins, Amalia Leifeste, Dana Marks, Sada Stewart, and Christopher Tenny. Drawing by Christopher Tenny.

Figure 7.38. William and Lina Bierschwale house, 1888–89. Photo by Kenneth Hafertepe.

William and Lina Bierschwale House
110 North Bowie Street
1888–89

For the Bierschwale family and others in Fredericksburg, this house was noteworthy as one of the earliest houses to be built to two full stories and one of the earliest to have a Victorian floor plan. For English émigré architect Alfred Giles, this was his second building in Fredericksburg, having designed a new Gillespie County Courthouse in 1881–82. (He had previously designed the August Faltin store and residence in Comfort and did much additional work in that community.) Giles had made his Texas reputation designing mansions in the King William District and numerous buildings, including officers' quarters, for the new Fort Sam Houston in San Antonio. Indeed, Giles specified that the masonry for the Bierschwale house should be "first class rustic rubble work (similar to Officer's Quarters at Fort San Antonio) of rock from the best local quarries well laid in mortar" (fig. 7.38).

William was the son of German immigrants Heinrich and Margarete (Treibs) Bierschwale. Heinrich was a native of Hannover; and Margarete, of Prussia. Heinrich was both a farmer and a schoolteacher, first in Cherry Spring in northwest Gillespie County and then in Hilda in southeast Mason County. However, Heinrich was elected clerk of the district court for Gillespie County in 1870, and the family moved to Fredericksburg. As a teenager William watched the construction, in 1872–73, of a story-and-a-half rock house that still stands at 209 West Austin Street. By 1880 William was living in Comfort in the household of his oldest sister, Johanna, and her husband, John A. Nichols, a native of Tennessee. Both Nichols and William were listed as farmers in the 1880 census; perhaps William was living with them to sharpen his English-speaking skills, a language rarely heard in Fredericksburg.

In 1884 William married Lina Jung, the eldest daughter of a farming couple, Jacob and Anna Jung. Lina had five sisters and three brothers. William and Lina bought the two town lots on which the present house sits in 1886. In 1888 they hired Alfred Giles to design their house. He submitted specifications and ink-on-linen drawings in September of that year. There were four drawings: foundation and first-floor plans; second-story and roof plans; the front elevation and both side elevations; and the rear elevation and a section through the house. In 1888 Fredericksburg builders would have seen this level of specificity only on the

Figure 7.39. William and Lina Bierchswale house. Plan by Alfred Giles.

Gillespie County Courthouse, also by Giles. However, 1888 also saw the design of Holy Ghost Lutheran Church by James Wahrenberger of San Antonio, an Austin native who had studied in Germany. And in the early twentieth century Leo M. J. Dielmann and Ed Stein would also produce detailed drawings (fig. 7.39).

The house was the most fully developed Victorian house in Fredericksburg. The walls were built of tried-and-true Hill Country limestone, with vermiculated quoins at the corners. At the lower right corner of the projecting left bay is a date stone, reading 1889. The house continues to have a standing-seam metal roof; this covering was supported by common rafters that meet at a ridge board. This was also the roof system that Giles used on the Faltin store and residence in Comfort.

The left bay projected forward, with a narrower "office room" in front that shared a chimney stack with a wider sitting room behind. The extra width of the sitting room allowed for windows placed at both front angles. Double French doors led from the gallery into a somewhat cramped stair hall, while a side door on the gallery provided direct access into the office room. Though the hall was cramped, it was unusual to have such a space at all in Fredericksburg, where most houses had either one front room or two rooms, often with direct access onto the front porch.

From the hall a door to the left led into the sitting room, to the right into the dining room, and on the back wall onto a back gallery (now partially enclosed to allow for a powder room). The dining room had a fireplace on the north side wall. Like passages, fireplaces tended to be rare in Fredericksburg, as most German Texans much preferred cast-iron stoves. The door on the back wall of the dining room led into a one-story ell. A small passage provided access to the kitchen at the rear; to the right was a storeroom, which was later removed to create a larger, more modern kitchen.

Upstairs were three bedrooms. When the house was built, the Bierschwales had two sons and another was on the way. By 1900 they had two daughters and five sons; two more daughters soon followed. The daughters slept over the office room, William and Lina slept over the sitting room (minus space for a narrow upper hall), and the boys slept over the hall and dining room, though they probably spilled out onto the sleeping porch on a regular basis. The two-story gallery was, in fact, the only major change that William and Lina made to the Giles drawings, preferring this to a one-story gallery that would wrap around on the north side.

By October 1924 the house had several small rooms added to the rear, including one that the Sanborn mapmaker marked as having a water tower on the second story. One large outbuilding was at the rear of the lot. It consisted of three small rooms, perhaps added incrementally; an attached barn for animals; and a garage for an automobile.

In 1898 William succeeded his father as district and county clerk, but he later founded Citizens Bank, one of the earliest banks in Fredericksburg. By 1910 eldest sons Ernest and Max had become clerks at the bank, son Walter was working as a cowboy, while Alfred was a laborer on the farm that produced the family's food. Ten years later Max had risen to cashier at the bank, and his unmarried sister, Concordia, known as Cordie, was a bookkeeper. Their brothers Alfred and Henry were living at home but managing a ranch. In 1930 the house held only William, Lina, and Cordie.

William died in 1932 at age seventy-four, and in 1940 only Lina, seventy-seven, and Cordie, thirty-nine, remained. Lina died in 1944; Cordie continued to live in the house until her death in 1987. Both the Bierschwale and Jung families were Methodist; however, at some point William and Lina converted to Catholicism. They and most of their children are buried in St. Mary's Catholic Cemetery.

The house survives in a state remarkably close to its original form. However, several outbuildings visible in the yard were moved to the house in the 1990s, when an attempt was made to convert the house into a bed-and-breakfast property. The house is now a private residence.[24]

August and Alwina Weber Sunday House
325 West Main Street
1904, moved 1972

Sunday houses were owned by people who ranched and/or farmed outside town. They were simple one- or two-room structures, usually built near the church that the owners could attend on a regular basis, hence the term "Sunday house." Families would also shop and socialize but still be back on the ranch late Sunday night or early Monday morning (figs. 7.40 and 7.41).

The original owners of this Sunday house were both born in Gillespie County before the Civil War. August grew up on the farm, while Alwina grew up in Fredericksburg, where her father, Conrad Carl Wehmeyer, had a bakery. The Webers farmed in the neighborhood of the Pedernales com-

Figure 7.40. August and Alwina Weber Sunday House, 1904, moved 1972. Photo by Kenneth Hafertepe.

Figure 7.41. August and Alwina Weber Sunday House. Photo by Kenneth Hafertepe.

munity, about ten miles southwest of Fredericksburg. Daughter Bertha was born in 1890, and son Adelbert, in 1898. Alwina's father died in 1898, and her mother, Louise (Klingelhoefer) Weber, in 1903. Alwina inherited an empty lot at the west end of town in the new West End subdivision. Here she and her husband built a Sunday house in 1904. As the Webers were Lutherans and attended Zion Lutheran Church, a lot on the west end was close to their church.

In 1926 Adelbert married Valeska Moellering, and she joined the family in their farmhouse near the Pedernales. Valeska studied at the University of Texas at Austin and earned a bachelor of science and master of education from Southwest Texas State University in San Marcos. She was a schoolteacher at the rural Pedernales School from 1924 to 1926 and again from 1928 to 1945. Both August and Alwina Weber died in 1929, just a few weeks apart, having used their Sunday house for nearly twenty-five years. In 1930 the household consisted of Adelbert and Valeska, and older sister Berta, still unmarried at thirty-nine. Around 1950 Adelbert and Valeska moved to New Braunfels, and she continued to teach there. Bertha died in 1968, and Adelbert, in 1969, which left Valeska the sole owner of the Sunday house.

In 1971 she offered the Gillespie County Historical Society the house and the lot on which it was built; the board preferred to move it to the Pioneer Museum Complex, where it would be seen by more visitors. The foundation was prepared in September by volunteers, including local contractor Tyrus Cox and August Faltin III of Comfort, and the house was moved to its new location in December. Valeska also donated furniture for the house and occasionally served as a volunteer docent in the 1970s and 1980s. She died in 2004 at age 104.

In recent years the term "Sunday house" has been corrupted to refer to any small or old house, which is antithetical to the origin of the term. Sunday houses were never meant to be used for full-time living, although some owners may have enlarged their houses when their oldest son was ready to take over the ranch. Sunday houses were never found before 1880, even though the Comanches and Apaches had been pushed far to the west after the end of the Civil War. The era of Sunday houses ended in the 1920s with the introduction of automobiles and trucks, which allowed families to quickly drive into town and still be back at the ranch by bedtime.

Figure 7.42. Friedrich and Christine Sauer house, ca. 1869. Photo by Kenneth Hafertepe.

Stonewall

Sauer-Beckmann Living History Farm
Lyndon B. Johnson State Park
1860s–1910s

On this well-restored and well-curated farmstead one can examine the evolution of German Texan housing from the 1860s to the 1910s, and also several original outbuildings. In a history covering more than one hundred years it was owned by only two families, both engaged in farming and both worshipping at Trinity Lutheran Church just a few hundred yards away.

Johann Friedrich Sauer and Christine Strackbein, both natives of Nassau in Germany, married in Fredericksburg in 1865 and started their family there. In 1869 they and their three children moved to this site in what was then known as the Pedernales community. By 1880 they were living here with nine children, and one more would arrive in 1881. The family farmed here and, later, in the Doss community in far western Gillespie County.

The house began with a single room with a porch. The porch was adapted from Southern US culture, but alternating logs with mortared rocks was a Hill Country innovation. The logs were joined with a V notch, which was very popular with Anglo-Southerners and also with their enslaved African American carpenters. As typical in smaller German Texan houses, the ceiling joists ran from the front wall to the back wall without interruption. There was a front door and a back door and one window on the west wall (figs. 7.42 and 7.43).

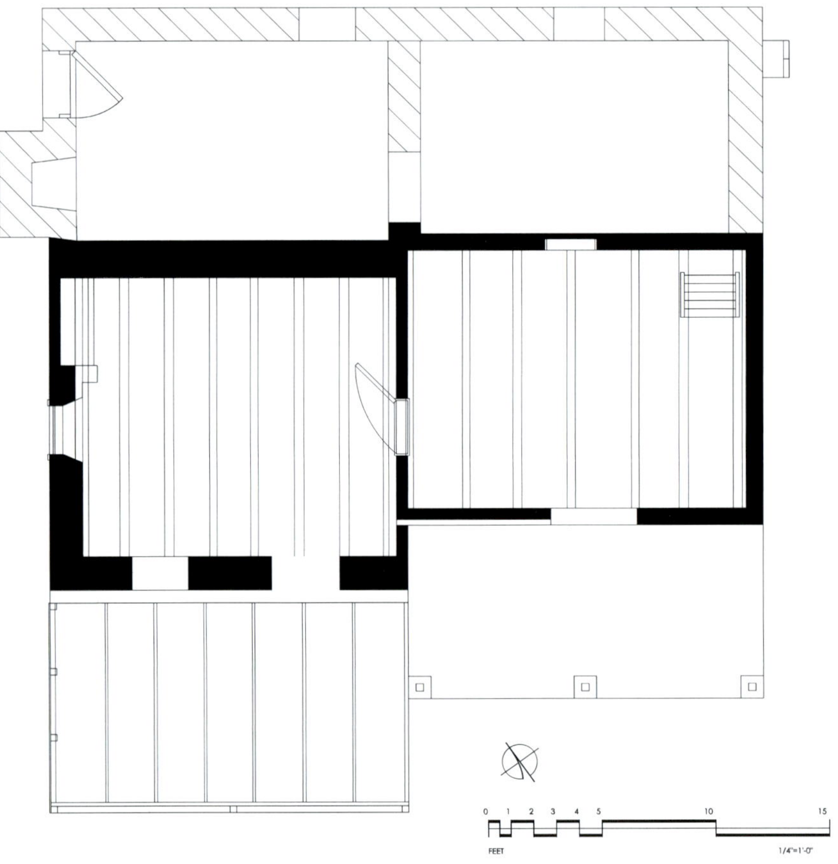

Figure 7.43. Plan of Friedrich and Christine Sauer house.
Measured by Brent R. Fortenberry.

This single room was followed by a lean-to room made of rock to the north, with a cellar beneath. Next came a rock front room to the west, which had its own front porch, and then a lean-to room behind this. The northwest room is clearly the last, as the stones used in the walls were both larger and more regular. Possibly the two earlier rock rooms were built by Christine Sauer's cousin Christian Strackbein, who was a stonemason. In addition to his own two-room house at 414 West Austin Street in Fredericksburg (1872–74), Christian probably built the house of Martin and Elizabeth Dittmar at Cherry Spring. The Sauer rock front room had a second front door, a six-over-six sash window, and another window on the west side. The earliest German houses had casement windows, but after the Civil War double-hung sash windows began to ap-

Figure 7.44. Emil and Emma Beckmann house. Photo by Kenneth Hafertepe.

pear. Curiously, the two back rooms, though built well after the war, have one small casement window apiece, which did not provide much light. The original window on the log-and-rock room was retained (rather than turned into a door), presumably to aid in lighting and ventilation. Even a decade or more after the Civil War German Texans did not add a central passage to their house, preferring to use the front porch as a circulation space (figs. 7.44 and 7.45).

The Sauer family also built a large frame barn and two rock outbuildings. The one in front was a tank house, which most likely served as a laundry; above the enclosed space was a large wooden cistern to catch

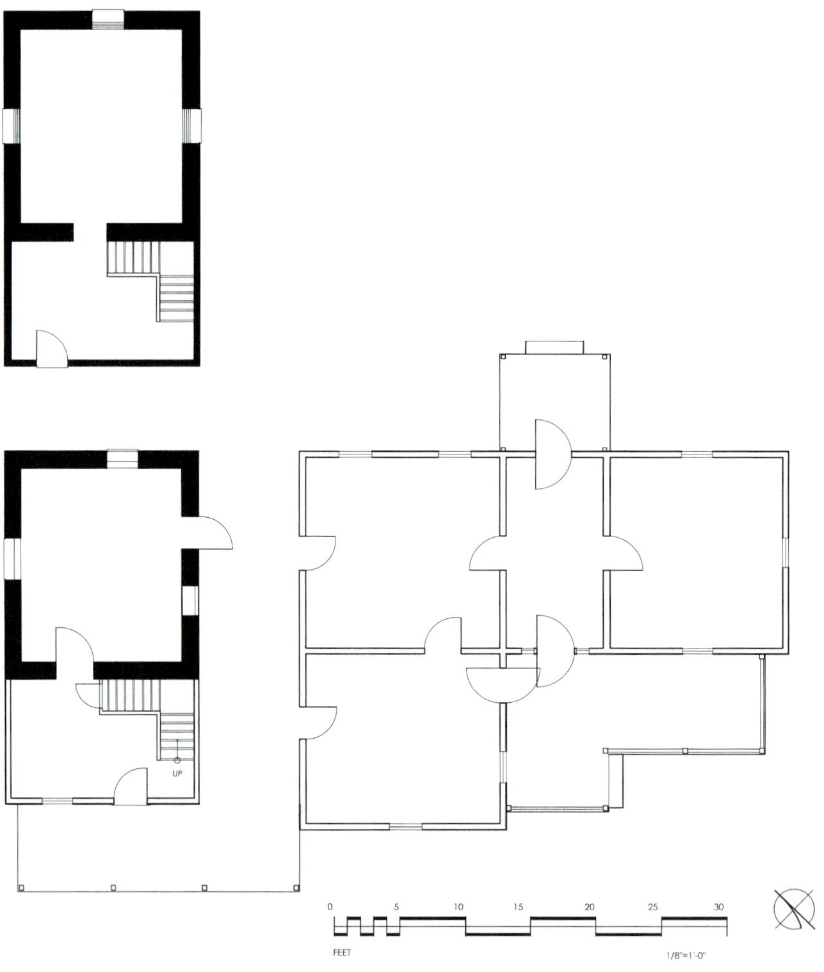

Figure 7.45. Plan of Emil and Emma Beckmann house. Drawing by Hayley M. Field after Texas Parks and Wildlife Department park drawings.

whatever precious rainwater came their way. To the northeast of the house was a one-and-a-half-story outbuilding, which has traditionally been thought to have been used as a smokehouse, though a room with that function on the ground floor would have made the upper floor useless.

In 1900 Friedrich and Christine Sauer sold the house and 205 acres to Hermann Beckmann. The Sauers moved to Doss, where their sons had been farming since 1887. Hermann and his wife, Mary, were both fifty-seven and natives of Germany. Like the Sauers, they had ten children. They had previously farmed in the Luckenbach area southwest of Stonewall. In the year that they purchased the farm, their oldest sons were twenty-seven-year-old Otto and eighteen-year-old Emil. In 1907 Emil married Emma Mayer, who had also grown up on a nearby farm. The next year Emil bought the farm from his father, with the proviso that his older brother Otto could continue to live on the property until 1910.

The first Beckmann addition was the story-and-a-half rock building east of the earlier house. The ground-floor room seems to have become a combination dining room and kitchen. Next came a frame addition to the front, which contained a staircase to the upper floor and a new kitchen, allowing the back room to have the more specialized function of dining room. Around 1915 Emil and Emma built a new frame house with three rooms and a passage. It had an L-shaped plan with a porch on the right (east) side. The porch had two doors, one into the central passage and the other into Emil and Emma's bedroom. The passage had a door onto a small back porch, as well as doors into the parlor and into the second bedroom.

The parlor had windows on the front, back, and east sides, providing ample ventilation. A cast-iron stove heated the room in winter. Emil and Emma covered the walls of this room and others with wallpaper, which had been highly unusual in the Hill Country for the first several decades of settlement. The back bedroom, occupied by their children, Ruben, Edna, and Elgin, had three doors—from the hall to the east, from their parents' room on the south, and from a covered passage on the west; there were two windows on the north wall. The covered passage, essentially a dogtrot, provided a sheltered connection to the kitchen. At some point Emil and Emma enclosed the south end of the porch to create a bathroom, which had a tub, toilet, and lavatory.

Emil Beckmann died in 1951, three days shy of his seventy-first birthday. Emma lived another ten years, dying in 1961 at age seventy-three. They are buried side by side in Trinity Lutheran Cemetery, next to the church where they had worshipped for decades. After Lyndon B. Johnson became president, the State of Texas began to purchase additional land near the LBJ ranch to develop a state park. Edna Beckmann Hightower, daughter of Edna and Emil, sold the farm to the State of Texas in 1966. The nearby Danz, Behrens, and Hodges farms were also purchased around that time.

In 1969 the Texas Parks and Wildlife Department hired Brooks, Barr, Graeber and White of Austin to design a new visitors center and to restore the Sauer-Beckmann property. Texas Parks and Wildlife long predated the Texas Historical Commission and had charge of any number of historic sites, including the San Jacinto Battlefield and adjacent Monument and the Varner-Hogg Plantation in West Columbia. Architect Max Brooks was a longtime friend of Johnson, and his firm had done work for Johnson at the ranch, usually under the direction of junior partner J. Roy White.

Their work included repairing and refinishing floors throughout, installing new flooring in the rock kitchen/dining room to match the existing floor, and removing sheetrock from the walls and ceilings of the parlor and Emil and Emma's bedroom. Later the bathroom was removed and the dogtrot reopened. On the earlier house, some thought was given to replacing the original log room, but this was not done. However, the chimney on the west wall had to be rebuilt; an exterior staircase, also on the west wall, was removed; and the stone walls in the cellar were repointed. The Sauer-Beckmann Living History Farm opened in 1975 (fig. 7.46).[25]

Figure 7.46. Aerial view of Sauer-Beckmann Living History Farm.
Photo by Brent R. Fortenberry.

Luckenbach Dance Hall and General Store

412 Luckenbach Town Loop

1910, 1930 (new dance hall)

The Texas dance hall is a vernacular form that evolved out of meeting halls for various social organizations, many of them associated with immigrants from central Europe to Texas. The organizations included *gartenvereins*, *gesangvereins*, *schutzenvereins*, and *turnvereins*—garden clubs, singing clubs, shooting clubs, and exercise clubs—as well as religious groups and agricultural societies. Often it is difficult to date the structures, which sometimes promote the year in which an organization was founded. Moreover, the buildings often evolve so much over the decades that it is difficult to get a sense of their original appearance.

However, dance halls tend to be octagonal, circular, square, or squarish rectangular in floor plan, because in most of the dances that were popular dancers moved around the room in a counterclockwise direction. The quality of the wooden floor was another critical element for the comfort of the dancers. And for the comfort of everyone, the halls often featured large windows to allow as much air circulation as possible. In the simplest form of dance hall, the band would stand on one side or corner of the room; as halls became larger and more elaborate, a separate stage area might be built out from one wall.

Dance halls were built in areas where the population was largely Catholic and/or Lutheran. Areas where Methodists or Baptists predominated rarely built dance halls, because those religions frowned on drinking, dancing, and gambling. However, dance halls were also useful for the closing exercises of the school year, which often concluded with a rodeo, a play or concert, and a dance.

For its first thirty years, Luckenbach was known as South Grape Creek. However, the area was settled by three Luckenbach brothers—Albert Jacob, William, and August—and their wives—Justina, Catharine, and Henriette. (August was one of the German Texan men who were killed along the Nueces River while attempting to get to Mexico during the Civil War.) Carl Albert Luckenbach, a son of Jacob and Justina, married Wilhelmina Sophie "Minna" Engel, a native of New Braunfels. Two of her brothers also moved to Luckenbach, and it was the Engels family who built a house, a general store, and a dance hall. A general store and dance hall were built around 1910; the current dance hall was built around 1930 (figs. 7.47 and 7.48).

Figure 7.47. Luckenbach Dance Hall. Photo by Kenneth Hafertepe.

Figure 7.48. Interior of Luckenbach Dance Hall. Photo by Kenneth Hafertepe.

In spite of its recent renown in story and song—or perhaps because of it—the Luckenbach Dance Hall has survived with a high degree of integrity. It is a rectangular structure with a pitched roof, longer from north to south. In the center of the north end was the stage, framed by two small rooms. The room on the left was reserved for the band to change and to take breaks; the room on the right was reserved for mothers with young children. When dances began, pallets were laid on the floor, and all young children were left in the care of one mother. Over the course of the evening, the mothers took turns watching the children while the others danced. The dance hall was also used for closing ceremonies of the Luckenbach School, which always included a barbecue.

In 1971 Benno Engel sold the dance hall and store—which was the better part of the town—to John Russell "Hondo" Crouch and his partners, Kathy Morgan and Guich Koock. A native of the town of Hondo—west of San Antonio and Castroville—Crouch attended the University of Texas, where he was an All-American swimmer. In 1945 he married Helen Ruth "Shatzie" Stieler, daughter of Adolph Stieler, the self-proclaimed "Goat King of the World," and settled into a life of ranching near Comfort. Hondo dubbed himself mayor of Luckenbach, or sometimes its clown prince. He dreamed up many crazy celebrations, including a Non-Buy Centennial in 1976, satirizing the commercialization of the bicentennial of the Declaration of Independence. He died of a heart attack in September 1976.

Hondo had become good friends with the singer-songwriter Ronald Crosby, better known as Jerry Jeff Walker, whose brand of folk-country-rock fit into the formats of very few commercial stations. Jerry Jeff moved to Austin, which had become a haven for the jazz-tinged country of Willie Nelson and other varieties of nonconformist music. In August 1973 Jerry Jeff recorded an album in the Luckenbach Dance Hall, titled *Viva Terlingua*. The recording sessions culminated with a live concert on Saturday, August 18. The album featured many Jerry Jeff originals but also songs by Guy Clark, Michael Martin Murphy, Ray Wylie Hubbard, and Gary P. Nunn. The latter's "London Homesick Blues" became the theme song of the PBS series *Austin City Limits* when it premiered in 1976.

In 1977 Memphis music producer Chips Moman and session keyboard player Bobby Emmons, who had both worked with Elvis Presley to record the songs "Suspicious Minds" and "In the Ghetto," heard about this eccentric place called Luckenbach, Texas, and decided to write a song about it. The song, "Luckenbach, Texas (Back to the Basics of Love)," was a lament about the pressures that stressful modern life was putting on the singer's marriage. Neither writer had actually been to Luckenbach, but the place was imagined to be an antidote to modern life. It also name-checked Willie Nelson, Waylon Jennings, Mickey Newbury, and Jerry Jeff Walker and mentioned the songs "Blue Eyes Crying in the Rain," which had recently been recorded by Willie, and, indirectly, "Desperados Waiting for a Train," a Guy Clark song that Jerry Jeff had recorded at Luckenbach. Moman and Emmons pitched the song to Waylon Jennings because he was mentioned in the song. Willie Nelson was also recruited to sing the final verse. The song reached Number 1 on the Billboard Hit Country Singles and Number 25 on the Billboard Hot 100. Ironically, Jennings disliked the song, which seemed to him to be typical "Countrypolitan" easy listening from Nashville, but he learned to love it when the royalty checks started rolling in.

The Luckenbach logo is familiar on T-shirts and bumper stickers in Texas. The town motto is that "Everybody's Somebody in Luckenbach." It has evolved from a local dance hall to an iconic Texas venue, and playing there has become a lifetime goal for many Texas musicians.[26]

Notes

1. Terry G. Jordan, "Hill Country," *Handbook of Texas Online*, accessed September 27, 2019, http://www.tshaonline.org/handbook/online/articles/ryh02. Jordan was author of one of the most important studies of German Texans: *German Seed in Texas Soil: Immigrant Farmers in Nineteenth-Century Texas* (Austin: University of Texas Press, 1966).

2. Rudolph L. Biesele, *The History of the German Settlements in Texas, 1831–1861* (1930; repr., Austin: Von Boeckmann-Jones, 1964).

3. Kenneth Hafertepe, *The Material Culture of German Texans* (College Station: Texas A&M University Press, 2016), 44–73.

4. Hafertepe, 74–110.

5. Hafertepe, 111–70.

6. Hafertepe, 11–43.

7. Hafertepe, 171–206.

8. Kenneth Hafertepe, *A Guide to the Historic Buildings of Fredericksburg and Gillespie County* (College Station: Texas A&M University Press, 2015), 70–71, 242–43.

9. Hafertepe, 9, 65–67, 131–32, 210–11, 241–42, 261–62, 264–65.

10. Hafertepe, *Material Culture of German Texans*, 373–91.

11. John Henry Brown, *Indian Wars and Pioneers of Texas* (Austin: L. E. Daniell, 1880) 524, accessed via *The Portal to Texas History*, https://texashistory.unt.edu/ark:/67531/metapth6725/?q=Indian%20Wars%20and%20Pioneers; Alfred Giles drawings of the Faltin store, dated 1878 and 1879, and blueprint for the addition, dated 1907, Alexander Architecture Archive, General Libraries, University of Texas at Austin; documentation of the Goldbeck-Faltin house, Historic American Buildings

Survey, https://www.loc.gov/pictures/collection/hh/; Drury Blakeley Alexander and Todd Webb, *Texas Homes of the Nineteenth Century* (Austin: University of Texas Press for the Amon Carter Museum of Western Art, 1966), 240, plate 44; Mary Carolyn Hollers Jutson, *Alfred Giles: An English Architect in Texas and Mexico* (San Antonio: Trinity University Press, 1972), 102–3; Willard B. Robinson, *Texas Public Buildings of the Nineteenth Century* (Austin: Published for the Amon Carter Museum of Western Art by the University of Texas Press, 1974), 90–91; and August Faltin III, conversation with Kenneth Hafertepe and Clifton Ellis, 2003.

12. Jutson, *Alfred Giles*, 104–5; J. E. Grinstead, *South-West Texas: From the Mountains to the Sea* (Kerrville: J. E. Grinstead, 1904); United States Census for Comfort, Texas, 1860 to 1940; and historic marker application, "Ingenhuett-Faust Hotel," 1895, Texas Historical Commission files, accessed via *The Portal to Texas History*, https://texashistory.unt.edu/ark:/67531/metapth491610/?q=Ingenhuett-Faust%20Hotel.

13. Historic marker application, "Ingenhuett-Karger Saloon," 2009, Texas Historical Commission files, accessed via *The Portal to Texas History*, https://texashistory.unt.edu/ark:/67531/metapth491830/?q=Ingenhuett-Karger%20Saloon.

14. V. J. McAteer, "Comfort Museum and Historical Society," *Comfort News*, April 27, 1933, 1; and historic marker application, "The Gass Schmiede," 1986, Texas Historical Commission files, accessed via *The Portal to Texas History*, https://texashistory.unt.edu/ark:/67531/metapth491575/?q=Gass-Schmiede.

15. Jutson, *Alfred Giles*, 28; historic marker application, "Paul Ingenhuett Home," 1979, Texas Historical Commission files, accessed via *The Portal to Texas History*, https://texashistory.unt.edu/ark:/67531/metapth491796/?q=Paul%20Ingenhuett%20Home.

16. *Comfort News*, April 12 and 19, 1907; *San Antonio Express*, December 22, 1907, 8; historic marker application, "1907 Comfort State Bank Building," 1988, Texas Historical Commission files, accessed via *The Portal to Texas History*, https://texashistory.unt.edu/ark:/67531/metapth491757/?q=1907%20Comfort%20State%20Bank; and Hafertepe, *Historic Buildings of Fredericksburg*, 41–42.

17. Alfred Giles, drawings for a post office, in private collection, Comfort, Texas; and historic marker application, "Comfort Post Office," 1985, Texas Historical Commission files, accessed via *The Portal to Texas History*, https://texashistory.unt.edu/ark:/67531/metapth491492/?q=comfort%20post%20office.

18. Hafertepe, *Historic Buildings of Fredericksburg*, 67–69; Hafertepe, *Material Culture of German Texans*, 118–22; Kowert, *Old Homes*, viii, 41–43; *Pioneers in God's Hills: A History of Fredericksburg and Gillespie County* (Austin: Von Boeckmann-Jones, 1960), 92–93; Sanborn Map: 1896, sheet 2; 1902, sheet 2; 1910, sheet 1; 1915, sheet 1; 1924, sheet 2; and 1924/1938 sheet 2; United States Census, 1850 to 1870; and Gillespie County Property Tax Records, 1849–65.

19. Hafertepe, *Historic Buildings of Fredericksburg*, 171–73; Hafertepe, *Material Culture of German Texans*, 30–31, 95–98; Kowert, *Old Homes*, 154–56; "Staudt Sunday House, 512 West Creek Street, Fredericksburg, Gillespie County, TX," Historic American Buildings Survey; see also Gillespie County Property Tax Records, 1848–65; United States Census, 1850 to 1870; and Sanborn Map, October 1924, sheet 6.

20. Hafertepe, *Historic Buildings of Fredericksburg*, 174–75; Hafertepe, *Material Culture of German Texans*, 60, 96, 98–100; Kowert, *Old Homes*, 92–94; Alexander and Webb, *Texas Homes of the Nineteenth Century*, 240, plate 40; Gillespie County Property Tax Records, 1848–65; United States Census, 1850 to 1880; and Sanborn Map, October 1924, sheet 6.

21. Hafertepe, *Historic Buildings of Fredericksburg*, 114–16; Hafertepe, *Material Culture of German Texans*, 21–23, 100–102, 238–46; Kowert, *Old Homes*, 38–39;

Gillespie County Property Tax Records, 1848–65; United States Census, 1850 to 1940; and Sanborn Map, 1924, sheet 6 (inset at lower right).

22. Hafertepe, *Historic Buildings of Fredericksburg*, 206–9; and Hafertepe, *Material Culture of German Texans*, 25–26, 121–27, 238–43, 439–40. See also "John Peter Tatsch House," Historic American Buildings Survey; *Pencil Points*, April 1931; Alexander and Webb, *Texas Homes of the Nineteenth Century*, 239, plate 37; and Kowert, *Old Homes*, 5–6. For primary evidence, see Gillespie County Tax Records; United States Census, 1860–1930; and Sanborn Map, 1924, sheet 7.

23. Hafertepe, *Historic Buildings of Fredericksburg*, 186–87, 41–42 (Bank), 270 (St. Peter); Hafertepe, *Material Culture of German Texans*, 28, 31–33, 123; Kowert, *Old Homes*, 131–32; and United States Census, 1860 to 1930.

24. Hafertepe, *Historic Buildings of Fredericksburg*, 213–14; and Hafertepe, *Material Culture of German Texans*, 33–35, 41–43, 176–82, 189–91. Two useful earlier discussions are Jutson, *Alfred Giles*, 38–39; and Elise Kowert, *Old Homes and Buildings of Fredericksburg* (Fredericksburg: Fredericksburg Publishing, 1977), 116–18. For a biography of Bierschwale, see *Pioneers in God's Hills*, 1:3–4. For further information on the family, see United States Census, 1900–1940; and for more information on the house, see the Gillespie County Tax Records, Gillespie County Clerk, Fredericksburg, Texas, and the Sanborn Map, 1924, sheet 6, Briscoe Center for American History, University of Texas at Austin.

25. Hafertepe, *Material Culture of German Texans*, 68–71, 204–6, 311–13; Hafertepe, *Historic Buildings of Fredericksburg*, 201–2 (Strackbein-Roeder), 304–11 (Sauer-Beckmann and nearby properties); Marian L. Martinello, *The Search for Emma's Story* (Fort Worth: Texas Christian University Press, 1987); and Brooks, Barr, Graeber and White, Sauer Homestead Restoration Drawings, Texas Parks and Wildlife Department files, Austin.

26. Hafertepe, *Historic Buildings of Fredericksburg*, 290–95; Ora Ann Knopp, interview by Kenneth Hafertepe, April 21, 2014; Glen E. Lich and Brandy Schnautz, "Luckenbach, TX," *Handbook of Texas Online*, accessed September 24, 2019, http://www.tshaonline.org/handbook/online/articles/hnl48; Becky Crouch Patterson, *Hondo, My Father* (Austin: Shoal Creek Publishers, 1979); Jan Reid, *The Improbable Rise of Redneck Rock* (Austin: Heidelberg Publishers, 1974), 93–118; Jerry Jeff Walker, *Viva Terlingua* (MCA Records, 1973), album cover and liner notes; and J. Roy White and Joe B. Frantz, *Limestone and Log: A Hill Country Sketchbook* (Austin: Encino Press, 1968), 58–59.

Vernacular Buildings East of San Antonio

Kenneth Hafertepe and
Brent R. Fortenberry

Seguin and Gonzales sit in the Guadalupe River valley east and southeast of San Antonio. The river rises on western Kerr County (west of San Antonio) and flows through the German settlement of New Braunfels as well as Seguin, Gonzales, and Victoria for some 230 miles on its way to San Antonio Bay, just off the Gulf of Mexico. Alonso De León named the river in 1698 for Nuestra Señora de Guadalupe, the icon of Roman Catholicism in Central America (fig. 8.1).

Under the Constitution of 1824 Texas was merged with the provinces of Nuevo León and Coahuila; when Nuevo León was separated, the state became known as Coahuila y Tejas. This constitution followed the federal model, and a state constitution was approved in 1827. The area north of the Rio Grande was thinly settled until the 1820s, when the Mexican government instituted a policy of encouraging colonists from the United States. The organizers of this system were called empresarios; most notable was Stephen F. Austin. Martín De León founded Victoria in 1824, and on April 15, 1825, the Mexican government approved the petition of empresario Green C. DeWitt to establish a colony. DeWitt had already sent James Kerr to survey the land around what would become Gonzales in January. However, the Mexican government refused to recognize Kerr as surveyor, leading to the appointment of Byrd Lockhart to resurvey the town site in 1831. The town of Gonzales was name for Rafael Gonzales, the governor of Coahuila y Tejas from 1824 to 1826. The name was the only Hispanic thing about the town, which was settled entirely by colonists from the United States.

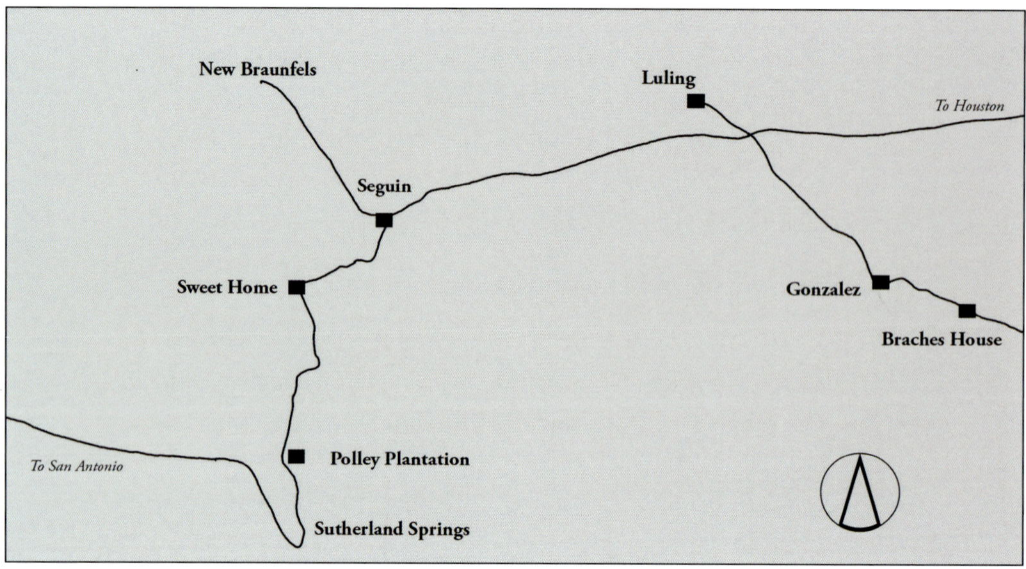

Figure 8.1. Map of the vernacular landscapes east of San Antonio. Image by Brent R. Fortenberry.

By 1831, there were 531 people living in the area, and the Mexican government sent a six-pound cannon for their protection. In 1833 Antonio López de Santa Anna was elected president of Mexico; although he had campaigned as a liberal, he quickly emerged as an autocrat bent on centralizing power in Mexico City. In Texas, meetings where residents clamored for independence from Mexico began that year, which the new government considered to be treasonous. Finally, in September 1835 troops were sent to retrieve the cannon. A confrontation with the colonists on October 2 became the first armed encounter of the Texas Revolution. The defiant cry of "Come and Take It" became one of the catchphrases of the revolution. (It has in recent years become a brand for the promotion of history-based tourism for the city of Gonzales, but on a much broader level it has become a popular rallying cry for those opposed to what they see as big government and the danger of gun control.)

After the Battle of Gonzales the conflict shifted to San Antonio. In December 1835 the Texians won a decisive victory in the Siege of Bexar, but in March 1836 the Texians inside the Alamo were all killed by General Santa Anna after a thirteen-day siege. The scene shifted back to Gonzales ever so briefly a few days later. General Sam Houston was leading his troops in a strategic retreat to the east and stopped late at night on Peach Creek at a live oak tree in front of the McClure house. After resting his troops for a couple of hours, he gave orders to torch Gonzales so that the goods and munitions there would not fall into the hands of Santa Anna. Additionally, he ordered all settlers to flee to the east. This they did, in what quickly became known as the "Runaway Scrape." The refugees did not return to their homes until after the victory of Sam Houston over Santa Anna at San Jacinto on April 21, 1836.

Though Seguin was founded ten years after Gonzales, the torching of Gonzales erased that difference. Ironically, Seguin has preserved more of its early buildings than Gonzales, which has much more of a Victorian character. In 1838 immigrants from the United States, including some former Texas Rangers, settled along the river at Walnut Springs, and the town was given that name for a short while. The next year former ranger Benjamin McCulloch laid out the town and named it for Juan N. Seguín, a Tejano from San Antonio and one of the founding fathers of the Republic of Texas. Even after Texas joined the United States in 1846, the area remained lightly populated.

The city plans of both Seguin and Gonzales are different from those of most towns in Texas. Instead of the typical Texas placement of the courthouse in the center of the town square, Seguin followed the lead of San Antonio, which had courthouse and church facing an open square, in a more traditional European fashion (fig. 8.2). The arrangement at Gonzales might seem more typical, with the courthouse sited in the middle of a central square, but this was elaborated by four additional squares. In addition to the center square were Jail, Church, Military, and Park Squares.

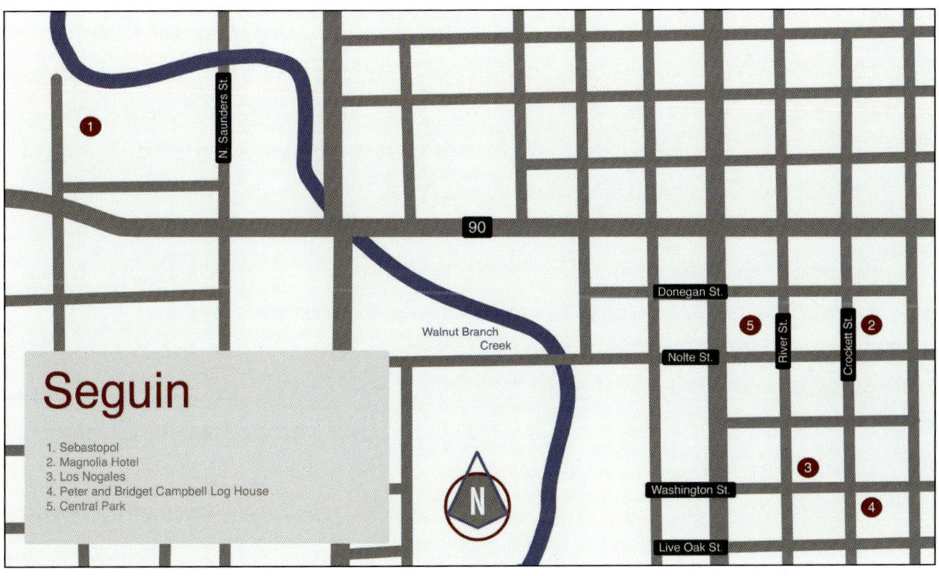

Figure 8.2. Map of Seguin. Image by Brent R. Fortenberry.

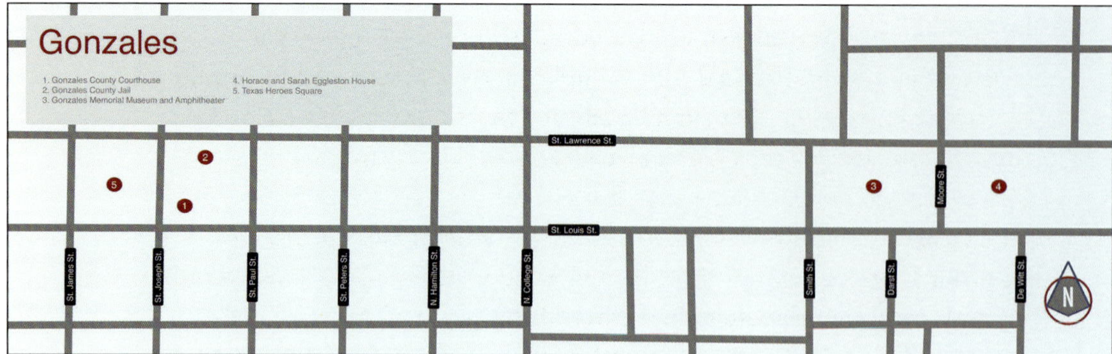

Figure 8.3. Map of Gonzales. Image by Brent R. Fortenberry.

These names evolved over time, but two churches still face the courthouse from Church Square (fig. 8.3).

After statehood the area grew rapidly. In 1850 Guadalupe County had 1,171 white residents and 335 enslaved African Americans; by 1860 there were 3,689 whites and 1,748 enslaved blacks. There were 202 slaveholders in the county in 1860: 20 percent owned one slave; 28 percent, between two and four; 23 percent, between five and nine; and 27 percent, between ten and forty. Only three slaveholders had more than forty slaves.

In 1860 carpenters in Gonzales were predominantly from the Upland South: five from Tennessee and one each from Kentucky and Missouri. Another four were from the Coastal South: two from North Carolina; one each from Virginia and Maryland. One carpenter came from Alabama, the only representative of the Deep South.

Seguin had a much stronger German presence. In 1850 there were five carpenters: one from Kentucky, one from South Carolina, and three from Prussia. Ten years later the carpenters from Kentucky and South Carolina were joined by one from Virginia, but there were now two from Prussia and one each from Nassau and Hesse.

There were only two stonemasons, both German, in Gonzales and Guadalupe Counties in 1860. In Gonzales County a mason from Hesse-Darmsradt lived in Gonzales and a mason from Prussia lived in Belmont, about halfway to Seguin. In Guadalupe County there were masons from Hesse and Switzerland but only one brickmason in each county in 1860: a mason from Nova Scotia in Gonzales and one from Tennessee in Seguin.

Germans also took a prominent role in the production of furniture at the time of the 1860 census. In Seguin there were four cabinetmakers, one each from Prussia, Hesse, Saxony, and North Carolina. Apparently enough

furniture was being made to allow another German—from Nassau—to
pursue the more specialized trade of upholsterer. In the town of Gonzales
the only cabinetmaker was from Baden, and in Belmont there was a cabinetmaker from Tennessee and a chairmaker from South Carolina.

Frederick Law Olmsted visited both Seguin and Gonzales in early 1854
and clearly preferred the former. Seguin, he opined, was "the prettiest
town in Texas," at least of those he had visited. He noted that the town
"stands on elevated ground, in a grove of shaggy-lined oaks, which have
been left untouched, in their natural number and position, the streets
straying through them in convenient directions, not always at right
angles. How wonderful, that so cheap and rich an ornamentation should
not be so common." He was not so enthusiastic about Gonzales, which
he estimated had a thousand inhabitants. "It is a centre of distribution
for hardware and whisky for a rich district, and is probably destined to a
steady increase until the soil of the district is exhausted. It has at present
nothing to distinguish it from other towns. There is the usual square of
dead bare land, surrounded by a collection of stores, shops, drinking and
gambling-rooms, a court-house, and a public-house, or two, with the
nearly vacant streets mapped behind."

After the war some former slaves lived in Seguin—an office of the
Freedmen's Bureau opened in 1866—while others sharecropped in
the surrounding countryside. Some formerly enslaved people founded
the rural communities of Capote and Sweet Home. Formerly enslaved
Hyrum Wilson and his brothers founded H. Wilson & Company pottery,
which produced stoneware jars, jugs, and more specialized ware used
across Central Texas. The Wilson Pottery is now acknowledged as the
earliest business in Texas owned and operated by African Americans.

Seguin was a stop on the Galveston, Harrisburg and San Antonio
Railway, which began in Galveston and reached Seguin in 1876 and San
Antonio the next year. When this railroad bypassed Gonzales in 1881, the
Gonzales Branch Railroad Company was formed to build twelve miles of
track and tie in with the main railroad at Harwood.

In the 1880s and 1890s both Seguin and Gonzales participated in the
statewide improvement of public buildings. In 1883–84 Alfred Giles of San
Antonio (see chapters 5 and 7) designed a new Guadalupe County Courthouse for Seguin. This building had hipped roofs that looked almost like
mansards and second-story windows with segmental tops. Ironically, the
principal entrance faced north toward Court Street rather than to the open
square, though there was a one-story porch on the south that allowed

views. Gonzales turned to professional architects for both a new jail and courthouse, although not without a struggle. Apparently the county commissioners were populists and distrusted professional men such as architects, preferring instead a practical builder. In spite of such qualms, Eugene T. Heiner of Houston provided the design for the jail, and J. Riely Gordon of San Antonio the design for the courthouse, though Gordon's name was left off the cornerstone.

In 1910 the two remaining open squares in Gonzales received monuments that emphasized different parts of Texas history. In Texas Heroes Square (formerly Park Square), a bronze and granite monument memorialized the Texas Revolution, including the inevitable phrase "Come and Take It." The sculptor was an Italian immigrant, Pompeo Coppini, who became the leading sculptor in Texas in the early twentieth century. Both the statue and bas relief on the plaque beneath it were cast in New York City at the Roman Bronze Works. North of Central Square, the former Jail Square was renamed Confederate Square. The monument that gave the square its name was by Frank Teich, a German immigrant who produced gravestones and monuments first from his marble yard in San Antonio, then from Llano, north of Fredericksburg, which was close to his source of Texas red granite. Ironically, Coppini's first job in Texas was as a stone carver for Teich, but he quickly realized that Teich was a businessman, not an artist, and left to pursue his own path. Gonzales is the only city where they produced competing monuments.

Seguin seems to have been more deliberate in its desire to become a regional center for business and recreation. In 1916, on the very eve of American entrance into World War I, two hotels were built in town, both designed by San Antonio architects. The Aumont Hotel at 301 Austin Street was designed by Atlee B. Ayres, while the Plaza Hotel was designed by Leo M. J. Dielmann. Born of German-immigrant parents, Dielmann traveled to Germany to study building technology. He was also a prolific designer of Catholic churches, including the new St. Mary's in Fredericksburg (see chapter 7) and the St. James Catholic Church in Seguin. In a town where a large number of concrete buildings had dotted the antebellum landscape, the Plaza Hotel brought concrete back in the form of the latest technology. The frame, floors, and roof were all reinforced concrete; partition walls were built of twelve-inch brick. The hotel fronted on the east side of the public square or park—hence its name. The lobby could be reached either from South River Street or East Market Street.

Both Seguin and Gonzales have buildings that demonstrate the desire of Franklin D. Roosevelt to simultaneously end the Great Depression and keep the state of Texas in the Democratic fold. In Seguin the present Guadalupe County Courthouse was built in 1936 with assistance from the Public Works Administration. In Gonzales the local museum dedicated to the town's role in the Texas Revolution was built with New Deal funds, which not only helped rebuild Dallas's Fair Park for the 1936 Texas Centennial but also funded a variety of museums across the state, from the Gulf Coast to the Panhandle.

Seguin

Magnolia House (hotel)
203 South Crockett Street
Late 1840s

Although write-ups of this house in the popular press are filled with certitude, the early years of this complex are sketchy. The presence of a two-room log house has been hypothesized as being on the site as early as 1844; apparently this date was settled on to allow the construction of additions of limecrete to be made by John Park in 1846, the first year he came to town. This was necessary because local antiquarian Willie Mae

Figure 8.4. Magnolia Hotel, north elevation, late 1840s. Photo by Brent R. Fortenberry.

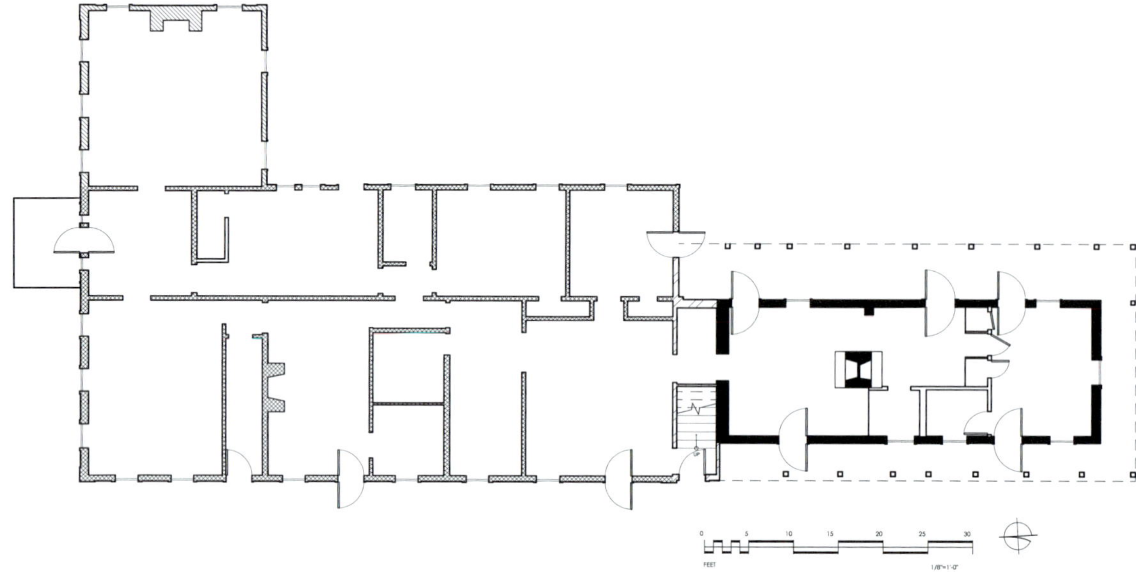

Figure 8.5. Magnolia Hotel, plan of ground floor. Measured by Kate Howard, Carter Hudgins, Amalia Leifeste, Dana Marks, Sada Stewart, and Christopher Tenny. Drawing by Kate Howard.

Weinert had concluded that when Susan Calvert married Captain John Coffee Hays, a noted Texas Ranger, on April 27, 1847, it was in the southernmost concrete room. It is unclear why she concluded that, given that the limecrete rooms were essentially an ell to the log house, and even more so after the construction of the large two-story frame hotel. Even the date of the large frame building is uncertain. It may have been constructed in the late 1840s or early 1850s (figs. 8.4 and 8.5).

What is known is that in 1850 Jeremiah S. Calvert, a native of Culpeper, Virginia, was a tavernkeeper. He and his wife, Priscilla (Smithers) Calvert, had five children and perhaps one domestic servant. They had five boarders, all unmarried men in their twenties and thirties; their occupations included clerk, tinner, and tanner. Thus, the building operated as a tavern but also as a boarding house and perhaps also let short-term rooms as well. The present frame building may well date to before 1850, as Calvert claimed to own five thousand dollars of property on the 1850 census. A substantial part of that property consisted of ten enslaved African Americans, though five of them were twelve or under and thus not considered as valuable as they would be in their adult years.

The hotel was known as the Magnolia House by the early 1850s, when it was owned by William M. Carpenter and William P. Read. Carpenter was the proprietor, while Read was the minister of the Methodist Church. (The Calverts remained in the area but had begun farming.) The complex was built on thirteen town lots on blocks 26 and 32; the hotel proper was on block 26.

A livery was built on block 32, the next block to the north, though it fronted on Court Street (the opposite end of the block from the hotel). The livery had a limecrete core and sheds on the east and west sides. The 1854 description claimed that the roof of the livery was covered in zinc, but by 1885 it was covered with shingles. Inside were numerous stalls, five mangers, two corn cribs, and a granary above in a loft; a well with a pump was just at the stable door. There was also a large fenced-in yard where the horses could move about. The owners considered it "one of the finest in the state."

The house, at least in the eyes of the owners trying to sell it, was "very handsome and imposing in appearance . . . very substantially built, and finished off in the modern and fashionable style." Though the Greek Revival style was long out of fashion on the East Coast, the style reached the apogee of its popularity in Texas in the 1850s. The main building featured "large, airy rooms" and was "built with an eye for comfort" and convenience. The owners also noted that it was specifically designed as a hotel with a "very large, fine, dry cellar underneath," which was well ventilated. (The bars in the outer openings were thus for ventilation and not to make it usable as a fortress or jail.)

Detached from the main building was a large kitchen and washhouse, one story and built of limecrete (though the owners referred to it as concrete stone). Other outbuildings included a smokehouse, a storeroom, and two log houses for servants. The owners pointed out that the logs of these houses were hewn, an upgrade from logs left in the round.

As has already been noted, Frederick Law Olmsted characterized Seguin as "the prettiest town in Texas" after his visit in February 1854. He further noted that "the hotel is large and good," which suggests that he and his brother, John Hull Olmstead, had stayed there.

By 1860 the hotel was owned by Thomas D. Johnston and his wife, Katherine (Calvert) Johnston, who was the daughter of Jeremiah and Priscilla Calvert. Thomas was a native of North Carolina, while Katherine, who went by Kitty, had been born in Alabama while her family resided there. Apparently they owned the hotel but did not run it for many years. In 1860 they were farming. In that year they owned eleven enslaved workers; presumably most of them worked on the farm, but perhaps a few were detailed to the hotel. In 1870 they were living in San Antonio, where Thomas was a banker. (Katherine's father, Jeremiah, had passed away, but her mother, Priscilla, was living with them in San Antonio.)

By 1880 the family was back in Seguin and living at the hotel. Thomas was retired, but Kitty was still keeping house. Their eldest son, Rollin, was the hotel keeper, while younger brothers Jerry and Willie were in charge of the livery and the farm, respectively. Priscilla Calvert, now eighty-four, was still living with them. Also in the household were four black and three mulatto servants. Annie Clack, thirty-six, was the cook, while her sons, nineteen-year-old Louis and seventeen-year-old Jeff, were a laborer and a "dining room servant," respectively. Amanda Coly, eighty-six, was working as a chambermaid, while her three grandsons were laborers. (Presumably these two family units were living in the log houses, an eerie echo of enslaved housing from before the Civil War.)

Although census records at this time recorded anyone staying in a hotel, this record shows no guests but only three longer-term boarders: William Stafford, a native of England, was a farmer; William Neal, from Georgia, was a lawyer; and David Bunty, a native of Ireland, was a hostler, which suggests that he may have been working for Jerry at the livery.

In 1885 the first Sanborn map of Seguin showed the main building as being entirely wood frame, missing the concrete walls of the south rooms. To the east of these rooms was the one-story, two-room kitchen, marked in blue, which could have been stone but was actually concrete. The south rooms and the kitchen had shingle roofs, while the two-story unit to the north had a metal roof. Between the kitchen and the main house was the cistern. The three public rooms of the hotel were on the west side facing Crockett Street: the office, parlor, and dining room. The best historic photo of the building shows a two-story gallery shading the Crockett Street elevation; however, this was removed by 1885, perhaps because the building was erected on the property line and the gallery extended into the street. By 1891 the kitchen had been replaced by a new two-story frame kitchen with an external stair on the south side. The main house was still marked as frame.

The Sanborn maps of 1902 and 1906 noted that Magnolia House was "not running" as a hotel; by 1912 it had been downgraded to a boarding house. Ironically, the 1912 map was the first Sanborn map to pick up that the south rooms were not frame but concrete. However, in 1924 the Sanborn mapper speculated that the rooms might be "adobe."

On April 29, 1936, Arthur W. Stewart came to photograph the house for the Historic American Buildings Survey (HABS). (Alas, no drawings were made.) He took four photographs, all of the exterior. The last photo was of the south rooms, which he labeled "West Elevation of Adobe House." The single data page by Homer Lansberry stated that the south rooms, "constructed of an early type of concrete," were built in 1846. He hypothesized that Read added much of the rest of the complex at a later date.

In 1937 Edgar and Inez Lannom purchased the property and converted it into an eight-room apartment house, with seven apartments in the two-story frame building and one in the concrete ell. Edgar died in 1950, but Inez Lannom was interviewed in 1981—she was then a widow and living in one of the apartments. She recalled that when they bought the place, each of the rooms had only an iron bed, a chair, and a washstand.

In 2012 Preservation Texas put the building on its list of the most endangered places in Texas. In March 2013 it was purchased by Jim and Erin Ghedi of Austin, who have slowly rehabilitated the property and have opened it as an Airbnb property.[1]

Los Nogales
415 South River Street
Circa 1850 and after

Los Nogales (*nogales* is the Spanish word for walnuts) is a one-story adobe structure sitting on the southern edge of Seguin city center. Central inward-swinging, board-and-batten doors are flanked by six-over-six sash windows for a symmetrical, three-bay facade. The gable roof is clad with replacement shingles from the restoration of the building. The history of this little house is wrapped in obscurity, but it seems to have been built in 1849 or early 1850. Arthur Swift sold lots 7 and 8 of block 12 to Justus Gombert for thirty-five dollars in May 1848. In December 1849 Gombert sold the lots to Joseph Zorn for three hundred dollars, which suggests that Gombert had improved the property, either with the front room of the present house or a temporary log house. Zorn, a native of France who had been living in Louisiana, had moved into the present house within six months. By the time the census taker arrived in mid-1850, Zorn valued his property at seventeen hundred dollars. Given that Zorn was a merchant, more than half of that figure would be the stock-in-trade of his store, but even six hundred dollars in real property would represent a

Figure 8.6. Los Nogales, west facade. Photo by Brent R. Fortenberry.

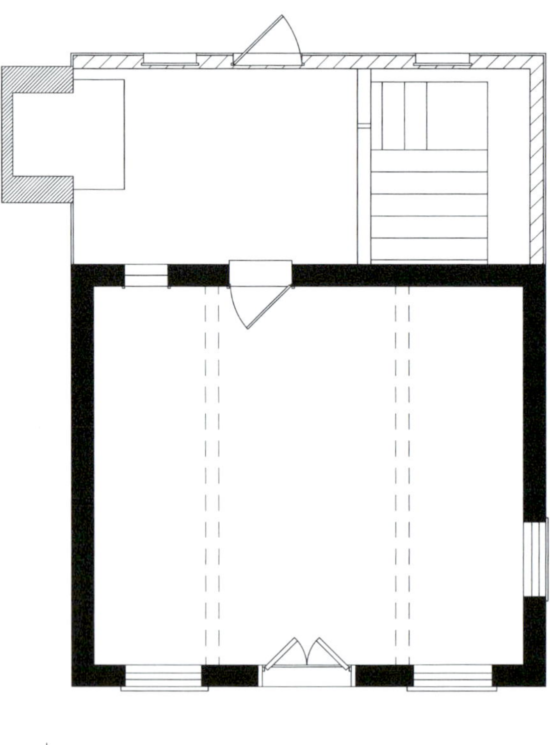

Figure 8.7. Plan of Los Nogales. Measured by Brent R. Fortenberry. Drawing by Hayley M. Field.

doubling of its value in less than a year. Zorn was a widower, living with his sixteen-year-old son, Louis, and fifteen-year-old daughter, Josephine. In 1854 he married a widow, Therese Kreusser (figs. 8.6 and 8.7).

The core space is sixteen feet, two inches wide and fourteen feet, four inches deep, lit by the two front windows, and a single six-over-six sash window on the south side wall. Interestingly, there is no evidence for a window on the north end. On the rear wall a small sash window has been filled in to create a recessed set of shelves, and a somewhat centered door provides access to the rear shed addition.

Above in the core, the gable roof is supported by a common rafter roof with tie beams. The timber appears to be pine. It is unclear if these are original or date to a restoration. The timbers are roughly hewn on the bottom faces, looking roughly worked, and are butted and nailed at the ridge. Similarly, the collars are butted and nailed to the common rafters. The wall plate is of similar preparation and seems too clean to date to the nineteenth century. Two roughly worked tie beams run front to back in the space, with only modern nails on the bottom faces, giving no indication of now-lost partitions.

The adobe walls have a thin layer of plaster that, due to lack of maintenance, is starting to deteriorate, revealing the distressed adobe. A light gray color might indicate a gray finish on the adobe; a red finish below the chair-rail level infers some color in the otherwise white space; microscopy would provide concrete evidence of interior finishes.

The general store seems to have been a success: Zorn's net worth increased from seventeen hundred dollars in 1850 to fifty-five hundred dollars in 1860. At the time of the 1860 census Theresa was living with Joseph and their son Joseph Jr., who was now working alongside his father in the store. Sometime after the Civil War Joseph Sr. left the house to his children, said good-bye to Therese, and moved to Hermann, Missouri. The younger Joseph would serve as mayor of Seguin for twenty years and in 1874 purchased the house known as Sebastopol.

The elder Zorn sold the house to Thomas Hollamon in 1859, but it is not clear who lived there during his ownership. Hollamon went bankrupt in 1870, and the property was purchased for $650 by Ben E. McCulloch, the nephew of Benjamin McCulloch, veteran of the Texas Revolution and the Mexican-American War and Confederate brigadier general who died at the Battle of Pea Ridge in 1862. McCulloch sold it later that year, and in 1875 it was purchased by Jerry G. Walker, who built a two-story Victorian house fronting on Washington Street at the other end of the block. Walker used the little house for storage.

Because it was four blocks south of the courthouse, Los Nogales did not appear on a Sanborn map until 1906. In that year the front room was marked as being of stone, and frame rooms were located to the east and another to the north (since removed). All rooms had a metal roof.

Arthur W. Stewart took two photographs for HABS on May 13, 1936. The first shows that the frame room on the north side was a lean-to room, which was subsequently removed. For the data page Homer H. Lansberry interviewed Willie Mae Weinert; she dated the house to 1854 and emphasized the brief ownership of Ben E. McCulloch; either she or Lansberry conflated the younger McCulloch with his much more famous uncle.

Exterior plaster evidence in the building implies that the rear space with stairs leading to the cellar was original and everything to the north was added. Indeed, the attached chimney and firebox were attached directly to the exterior surface of the building. The exposed adobe on the right rear space shows internal framing inside the adobe.

The house was purchased in 1952 by the Seguin Conservation Society; by 1960 it was being referred to as "Los Nogales Museum." This was a concession that the early history of the house was quite murky. However, the house was awarded one of the earliest Texas Historical Landmark markers—number 13—in April 1962. Marker number 1, for the Eggleston log house, was in nearby Gonzales.[2]

Sebastopol (LeGette-Zorn House)
704 Zorn Street
Circa 1855–56, restored 1988

Sebastopol is one of the most remarkable houses in Texas. It was one of the first Texas structures documented by HABS in 1934, was made a Recorded Texas Historic Landmark in 1964, and was placed on the National Register of Historic Places in 1970. From 1976 to 2011 it was a historic house museum operated by the Texas Parks and Wildlife Department (TPWD); in 2011 ownership was transferred to the City of Seguin, which continues to operate it as a museum. It is quite striking because of its limecrete construction, but it is unusually austere in ornamentation and distinctive in its floor plan.

The date of construction has been given as early as 1851, but a date of 1855–56 seems more likely. It was built for a widow from South Carolina, Catherine Maria (Young) Legette. Born in Wilmington, North Carolina, in 1810, she married Ebenezer LeGette of Marion, South Carolina, in 1830. In 1850 they were living in rural Marion County; Ebenezer, fifty years old, was apparently retired and claimed no property, but his younger brothers David and Ashley were both farming nearby. Ebenezer and Catherine had seven children, and two more arrived in the early 1850s. However, Ebenezer died around 1852, and Catherine decided to take her children and join her brother Joshua in Texas.

Joshua W. Young, a year younger than Catherine, was farming in Texas by 1847. He and his wife, Jane, came to Texas after stays in Alabama and Mississippi, and they had children at each stop. In 1850 they had five children. In that year they were also the owners of twenty-one slaves, a substantial number for Guadalupe County. From 1847 to 1865 they owned anywhere from sixteen to twenty-five enslaved workers.

For Joshua, the peak years in terms of number of slaves owned and of total value were 1856, 1857, and 1858, soon after his sister and her children arrived from South Carolina. These were also years of economic expansion in Texas, and in Austin monumental Greek Revival mansions such as the Governor's Mansion and the Neill-Cochran house were being built. However, the economy soon went into recession, which, along with the completion of his sister's house, would explain the drop in Joshua Young's slaveholding from twenty-five to sixteen.

In 1860 Catherine was forty-five and settled in the house with seven of her children, ranging in age from eight-year-old Mary to twenty-one-year-old Henry. Catherine informed the census taker that her real estate, mainly the house, was worth two thousand dollars and that she owned one thousand dollars' worth of personal property. Most striking was that the family was not farming and she owned no slaves. Eldest sons Henry and Jessie were clerks, suggesting that their mother had a mercantile future in mind for them.

The house was compact—it had no passages at all—and only two spaces for entertaining—the parlor (twenty-one by twenty-two feet) on the principal floor and the dining room on the ground floor. On three sides the parlor opened onto the wraparound porch lit by two windows on the left and right walls and two on the front facade with a central doorway. Two doors flanking the central fireplace in the north wall led into one of

Figure 8.8. Sebastopol, primary elevation, 1855–56, restored 1988. Photo by Kenneth Hafertepe.

three bedrooms. One quirk of the plan is that there was not originally an internal staircase; whether the group was only family or included friends from Seguin, they had to walk down the central staircase and around to the back wall of the house, which was the only door into the back set of three rooms. The later internal staircase connects the right (east) section of the porch to the dining room below. The large center dining room had a large fireplace on the back wall. The kitchen was in the west room; the function of the room on the opposite side is unclear. The single chimney stack served the parlor, central rear upper chamber, and the kitchen below. Perhaps there was the expectation of a live-in cook, whether free or enslaved. However, in the 1860 and 1870 censuses there was no hired cook living with the family (figs. 8.8 and 8.9).

Fourteen-foot-high ceilings on the main floor and ten-foot-high ceilings on the lower floor collected the rising hot air in these spaces and are a testament to the comfort-oriented design of the house. The roof is an anomaly. The principal span runs front to back (south to north); a hipped roof supported by a principal rafter roof covers the parlor and central chamber in the rear. The porch and flanking rear chambers are covered by an inward-sloping shed that supports a tall continuous parapet around the building, wood-framed above the porch, and limecrete

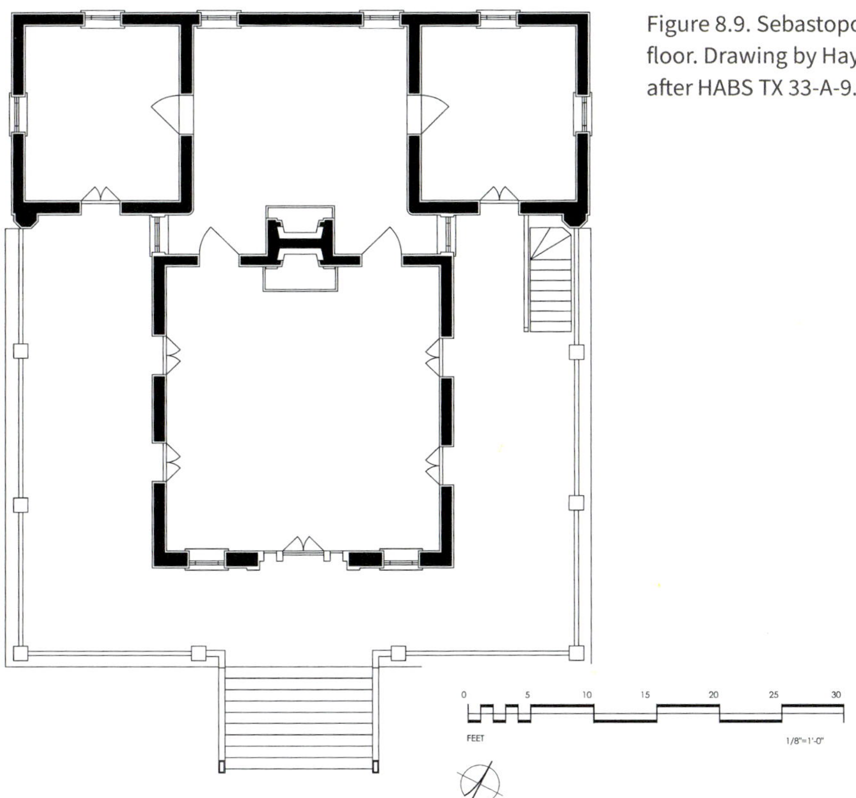

Figure 8.9. Sebastopol, plan of upper floor. Drawing by Hayley M. Field after HABS TX 33-A-9.

around the rear flanking rooms, an ideal design for water catchment. The framing has been hidden by modern HVAC systems, but visible connections suggest that the roof used typical English-influenced joinery. During the twentieth century when TPWD owned the property, archaeologists excavated the area under the parlor, revealing much of the original floor framing, including a large pine summer beam running front to back. Interesting also is that an open storage area under the front porch is fenestrated with diamond-set bars, indicating some level of high-value storage.

Ten years later Catherine and the remainder of her family were still in the house. She was sixty; Henry, now a bookkeeper, was thirty; and daughters Jane and Mary were eighteen and seventeen, respectively. Clearly, an empty nest was on the horizon. One other person was living in the household: Harry Young, fifty-nine, an African American Methodist Episcopal minister. Harry's last name and his birth in North Carolina suggest that he had been a slave to Joshua Young. Now that he was free, he was devoting his life to spiritual matters. On June 24, 1874, Catherine Legette sold the house to Joseph Zorn and his wife, Catherine Antoinette

Zorn, known as Nettie. Catherine then moved to Wilson County to live with her daughter Julia and her husband, Edward Rex Tarver, a Confederate veteran and lawyer.

Joseph Zorn had come to Seguin with his father, also Joseph Zorn, around 1850. In that year the senior Zorn was forty-two and the younger one, ten. They lived in the house now known as Los Nogales from 1850 to 1859 and began to acquire real estate as they established themselves as merchants. By 1860 both the senior and younger Zorn were identified as merchants in the census. The younger Zorn married Catherine Antoinette Watkins around 1871.Their first child, Therese, was named for Joe's stepmother, and their first son was named for the senior Joseph. They had two children when they moved into Sebastopol and had three more children by 1880. The household also came to include Nettie's mother, Mary Watkins, and her younger sister, Letty. In addition, a ten-year-old mulatto, Willie Williamson, lived with the family and worked as a servant. The Zorn family was not particularly wealthy—they did not own slaves before the war—but Joseph Zorn distinguished himself in public service to his community. In 1880 Zorn was the postmaster of Seguin and served as mayor of the town for twenty years, from 1890 to 1910.

The house was documented by HABS in 1936, with six drawings, five photographs, and two data pages. Bartlett Cocke spoke with Nettie Zorn, the widow of Joseph Zorn Jr., who reported that she and her husband acquired the house on June 24, 1874. (Nettie was born in 1850 and was a young child when the house was built, and her family did not own the house at that time, so she was not a firsthand observer.) She also mentioned that the house was built during the Crimean War, which led to the name Sebastopol. The Siege of Sebastopol—now spelled Sevastopol—lasted nearly a year, from October 1854 to September 1855. Perhaps some wag observed the large tank for collecting water on the roof and referred to it as a Sebastopol.

Nettie explained to the HABS workers that Richard Park of Seguin had come up with the formula for limecrete; this, as we know from scientific analysis, is not the case. She also attributed the woodwork in the house—doors, mantels, trim—to a Henry Erkel. The inclusion of this name has led to the designation of Erkel as architect of the house, at least on Wikipedia. However, there was no Henry Erkel in Texas in 1850 or 1860. The eighty-four-year-old Nettie was remembering something about the construction of a house that her parents did not own for nearly another two decades, but there may be a kernel of truth in her recollection. One of the most prosperous carpenters in Seguin in 1860 was George W. Eikel, a native of Nassau in Germany. In 1860 he had acquired two thousand dollars in real estate and one thousand dollars in personal property; only Virginian Peyton Medlin was more successful. The shouldered architraves and other Greek Revival trim could have been done by an Anglo or a German carpenter, but the six-panel door with raised and beveled panels is more characteristic of German Texan work.

Both Nettie and her eldest daughter, Therese Zorn Tegener, died in 1937, and the house and furniture were inherited by the Zorns' youngest son, Calvert Watkins Zorn. When Calvert died in 1952, Hazel Dean Tegener, the surviving child of Frederick and Therese Tegener, inherited the house and the furniture that the Zorn family used in Sebastopol. Hazel sold the house to the Seguin Conservation Society in 1961 but held on to the furnishings. In 1976, not long after the house was sold to TPWD, the department purchased some forty pieces of furniture—said to be three rooms' worth—from Hazel. This included the bed in which her grandmother, Nettie, had given birth to her six children. This furniture remains on display in the house.

In recent years the museum has added a display of Wilson pottery. Reverend John M. Wilson, a native of North Carolina, came to Seguin around 1857 with his family and twenty enslaved workers. He soon opened the Guadalupe Pottery, which manufactured utilitarian stoneware. Among his slaves were Hyrum, Wallace, and James Wilson, who learned to become potters. After the end of the war, they opened their own pottery, calling it H. Wilson & Company. Although they were initially trained in the tradition of Edgefield stoneware from South Carolina, which utilized an ash glaze, they shifted to an alkaline glaze (also known as salt glaze), which gave their wares a cleaner appearance. The pottery was in business from 1869 until Hyrum's death in 1884. It was the earliest Texas business owned by African Americans. In addition to the wares shown at Sebastopol, their work can be found in the Bayou Bend Collection of the Museum of Fine Arts Houston and the Smithsonian's National Museum of American History.[3]

Figure 8.10. Campbell log house, 1860.

Peter and Bridget Campbell Log House
211 East Live Oak Street
Circa 1860

This log house was originally on a farm five miles south of Seguin; it was moved into town in 1979 as a memorial of pioneer times. The log construction and the floor plan with two rooms separated by a dogtrot make it a classic Texas starter house. The carpenters used a double notch to join the walls, which was very rare in Texas and, indeed, the United States. The logs were hewn rather than left in the round, giving them a more finished appearance. Jordan pointed out that double notches were essentially a saddle notch with a squared-out saddle. (Saddle notches were used in 14.5 percent of houses in his survey; $N = 78$.) Two of the four double notches he observed were found in D'Hanis in Medina County, settled by immigrants from Alsace and Germany (fig. 8.10).

The historical marker in front of the house states that John Campbell "possibly" built the first room of this house "about 1850." Although Campbell told the census taker in 1850 that he was a carpenter, he was living in the household of Colonel Andrew Neill, a lawyer and veteran of the Battle of San Jacinto. Campbell did not report that he owned any real estate. He is said to have gone back to his native Ireland and convinced several relatives to come to Texas.

What is certain is that John Campbell's brother, Peter; his wife, Bridget McLaughlin; and their three children moved from Inver, County Donegal, Ireland, to Texas between 1851 and 1854. Peter Campbell was a farmer, and by 1870 he and Bridget had eight children and had amassed $3,000 in real estate and $1,350 in personal property. By this time, they also had two servants living with them, both natives of Germany, one a farmhand and the other a maid or cook. They were members of St. James Catholic Church in Seguin. Peter died in 1888, and Bridget, in 1902. The house remained in the family until 1957.[4]

South of Seguin

Whitehall (Polley Mansion)
Sutherland Springs
Circa 1853–57

Whitehall was the mansion of the Polley Plantation, which was developed between 1847 and 1861. Joseph Henry Polley was a native of Upstate New York, while Mary Augusta Bailey Polley was born in Tennessee, in the Upland South. The house and the property have undergone many changes, but the house is still standing (figs. 8.11 and 8.12).

Joseph H. Polley was a native of Whitehall in Washington County, New York. As a very young man he had fought in the War of 1812, then settled in Missouri, where he met Moses Austin and his son Stephen, the future colonizers of Texas. Polley first came to Texas with Moses Austin in 1820 and, after the death of Moses, returned with Stephen the following year, thus earning a substantial land grant.

Mary was the daughter of James Britton Bailey, born in North Carolina in the middle of the American Revolution. Bailey lived in Kentucky and Tennessee before moving to the Spanish state of Texas in 1818. Apparently, Bailey considered Stephen F. Austin a Johnny-come-lately when he arrived in Texas in 1820, but Bailey grudgingly became an Austin colonist soon thereafter. Joseph H. Polley and Mary Augusta Bailey married in a civil ceremony in 1823, in a Protestant ceremony in 1826, and then in a Catholic ceremony in 1831. The Polleys were thus part of what was known as Austin's "Old Three Hundred"—the Texas version of the First Families of Virginia.

Figure 8.11. Whitehall Plantation, western facade of main house. Photo by Kenneth Hafertepe.

Figure 8.12. Whitehall Plantation, plan of main house ground floor. Drawing by Hayley M. Field after HABS TX 3-26).

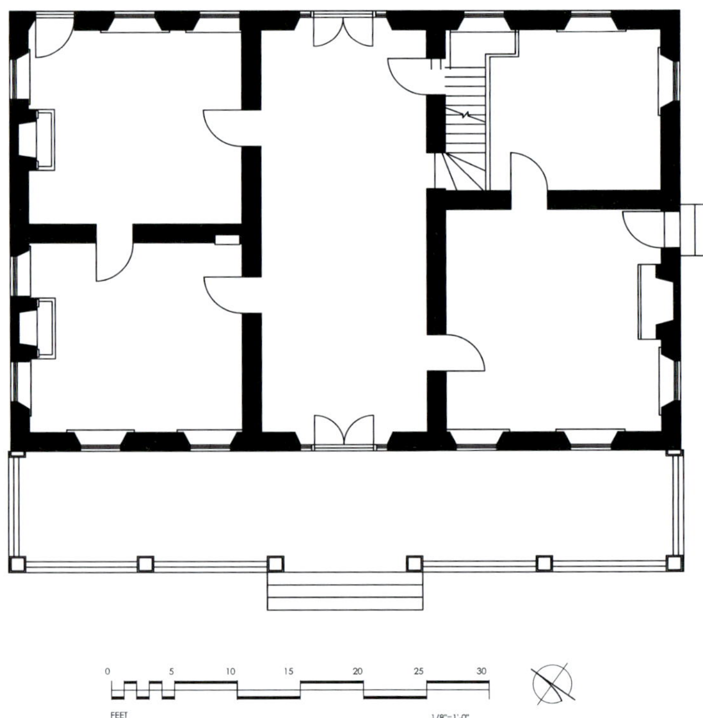

Initially the couple lived near Mary's father at Bailey's Prairie in Brazoria County. From 1826 to 1828 they lived in San Felipe de Austin, the administrative headquarters of the Austin colony. They returned to Brazoria and concentrated on their plantation, focused first on cotton but then on stock raising. In 1847, after Texas had joined the United States, Polley acquired land from his soon-to-be son-in-law John James, a surveyor who married the Polleys' second-eldest daughter, Emeline Elizabeth Polley.

In 1850 the Polleys were well-off but not fabulously wealthy. Joseph Polley told the census taker that his occupation was farmer and that he owned some $20,000 in property. Ten years later his wealth had escalated to $70,000 in real estate and another $65,351 in personal property. A considerable amount of the latter would have consisted of the value of their nineteen enslaved workers, eight of whom were older than twenty-one.

For perhaps a decade the family lived in what they called a "stake house"—a house with vertical logs thrust into the ground. Such a system certainly had echoes of the *poteau en terre*—post in ground—construction that Polley may have seen in St. Genevieve while living in Missouri. However, Joseph and Mary certainly planned for something grander and more permanent. Joseph's brother Jonathan came for a visit in 1849, and planning for the house seems to have begun in earnest at this point.

The sandstone that formed the walls was quarried nearby, probably by some of the family's enslaved workers. The framing for the floors and the roof came from farther away, the sawmill of Edward Quirin Kriegner on Curry Creek, just north of Boerne in the Hill Country west of San Antonio. Even more remarkable is the fact that the doors, windows, and blinds were made in New York, shipped to Lavaca on the Texas coast, and then carted to the construction site. Jonathan coordinated the work with Alex Coats in New York. Letters back and forth between Texas and New York documented that the doors and windows cost $133. Jonathan further noted that the blinds were to be painted "Paris green," a color popular in New York and New Orleans in the 1850s. The key years of construction seem to have been 1853 to 1857.

Whitehall boasts a classic symmetrical shape, five bays wide with a central door; the house faces west. The center-passage plan provides circulation for four principal lower rooms. The two front parlors are both heated, and the south front room is slightly deeper than the east. The heated dining room in the northeast corner has a service entrance for

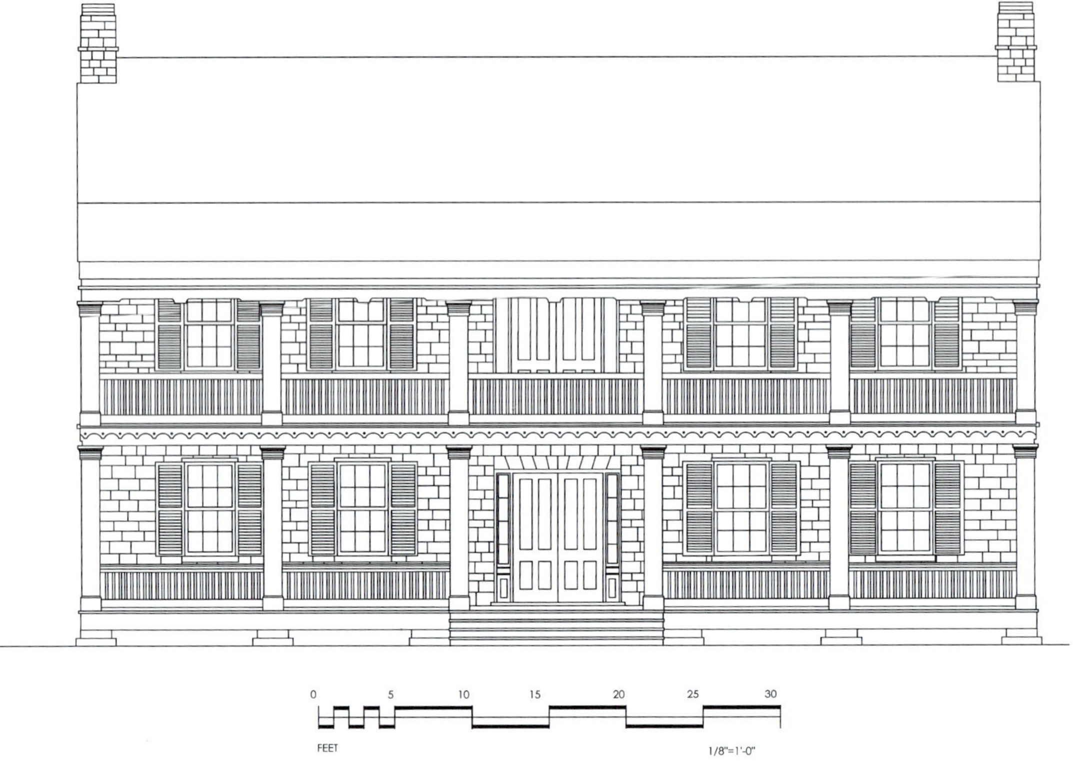

Figure 8.13. Whitehall Plantation, western elevation of main house. Drawing by Hayley M. Field after HABS TX 3-26.

ease of movement between the kitchen dependency and the main block. The dining room and kitchen were connected by a walkway covered with an arbor, where family and visitors might eat when the weather made the house uncomfortable. An unheated bedchamber at the southeast now provides service storage. The stairs are encased in a space between the passage and the southeast rooms. Upstairs, the plan mirrors the lower level with four bedchambers. However, only the southwest and northeast chambers were heated (fig. 8.13).

The typical common rafter pine roof is butted and nailed at the ridge. Many of the common rafters are sash-sawn on all four faces, while later replacements are circular-sawn. The common rafters (three by five inches) have a continuous, set-in purlin roughly four and a half feet above the joists. Rising knee wall posts are tenoned and pegged in the purlins with similarly sized down braces for support. This purlin support appears to be original, as all of the surviving first-period timber is sash-sawn. Slight evidence for lath and plaster remains, suggesting that the attic space was occupied by the domestic servants. Original collars have been removed, and later replacements are side-butted and nailed to the central set of common rafters. Tall and narrow joists are set directly into the stone walls of the building below.

A surviving kitchen outbuilding sits to the north and east of the main building. The V-notch log construction is contemporary with the main house and a regular construction technique in this subregion of Central Texas, especially for outbuildings. The stone chimney in need of conservation work is now strapped into place to prevent it from collapsing (figs. 8.14 and 8.15). The owners indicated that a recent archaeological survey of the property by the Texas Historical Commission found evidence for a row of slave dwellings to the northeast of the property. The slave schedule of the 1860 census indicates that the nineteen slaves lived in five houses. Four to five people per house was typical for slave quarters in Texas.

The eldest son, Joseph Benjamin Polley, served in the Civil War as a quartermaster sergeant for Hood's Texas Brigade, one of the most noted regiments from Texas. He lost his right foot because of an injury sus-

Figure 8.14. Whitehall Plantation, elevation of kitchen quarter. Photo by Brent R. Fortenberry.

Figure 8.15. Whitehall Plantation, V-notching detail of kitchen quarter.
Photo by Brent R. Fortenberry.

tained in battle. (He later became very involved in Confederate veterans' organizations and wrote a history of Hood's Texas Brigade.)

After his return from the war he married Mattie LeGette, who had grown up in Sebastopol in nearby Seguin. His father died in 1869, and in 1870 his sixty-year-old mother was head of the household. In spite of financial setbacks arising from the loss of the war, she still owned twenty-five thousand dollars in real estate and fifty thousand dollars in personal property. Eldest son Joseph gave his occupation as farmer and lawyer, and he claimed an additional fifteen thousand dollars in personal property. Most of their personal property would have been livestock, and, in fact, the household included two stock hands, Peter and Victor Garcia, both natives of Mexico. In 1876 he and his family moved to Floresville, which became his permanent residence for the rest of his life.

In 1880 Mary was seventy-one, and she was living with her two unmarried children; Joseph and his family were nearby. Mary died in 1888, after which Joseph inherited the house. In addition to maintaining the house, he began to write columns about family history for the local newspaper, adding a rich layer of details to the bare boncs of history.

The San Antonio office of HABS documented the house in 1936, which included nine photographs and eight drawings.[5]

East of Gonzales

Charles and Sarah Braches House
Late 1840s or 1850s

This remarkable property tells the story of the land and a family that stretches from Texas as a northern province of the republic of Mexico to a free-standing republic, then to a state in the United States of America, then into the Confederacy, and finally back into the Union. All this time the property was held by one family and, in fact, by one extraordinary woman: Sarah Ashby McClure Braches (1811–94).

Sarah Ashby was born in Shelbyville, Kentucky. She married Bartlett McClure in Spencer County, Kentucky, in 1829. Her father, John Miller Ashby, and her husband, Bart, decided to immigrate to Texas, where large tracts of land were being offered in the Green DeWitt colony. Bart and Sarah settled on this land on the east side of Peach Creek in 1831. At that time they had a young son, Alexander, born in Kentucky. A second son,

John, born on this place in 1832, and a daughter, Martha, born the next year, both died in infancy.

In the autumn of 1835 the Texas Revolution began in earnest just a few miles west in the town of Gonzales. Though the events of late 1835 seemed auspicious, those of March 1836 took a shocking turn for the worse; both the execution of all prisoners at Goliad and the killing of all men without quarter at the Alamo sent the Texians reeling. Sam Houston ordered his troops into hurried retreat, and they stopped their frantic retreat for a few hours' rest near the oak tree on this property. Here Houston decided to torch the town of Gonzales and order a general retreat of all colonists.

This became known in Texas history as the "Runaway Scrape," as soldiers and civilians alike headed east in fear of the Mexican army. Bart and Sarah McClure were part of this exodus, though Sarah was pregnant at the time. In the course of the evacuation six-year-old Alexander McClure contracted a fever and died; as this was not tragedy enough for the young family, Sarah gave birth prematurely to a son, Jonah, who soon died. Not until April 21, 1836, did Houston turn and surprise the Mexican army at San Jacinto, winning the day and capturing Santa Anna in the process. After that, Bart and Sarah could feel safe returning to their property.

They resumed their lives, now as citizens of an independent republic. In 1837 Bart McClure became chief justice of Gonzales County—what today would be known as county judge, the chief executive for the county. Bart and Sarah had another son, Joel D., in 1839. However, Bart died in April 1841. She then married Charles Braches, a native of Germany, on March 2, 1842—Texas Independence Day.

Charles and Sarah began to make a family of their own, but four of their five children died in infancy or early childhood. When the census taker finally made it to Peach Creek in November 1850, he found seven people: thirty-seven-year-old Charles and thirty-nine-year-old Sarah; their children, three year-old Mary and one-year-old Henry; Sarah's son from her first marriage, eleven-year-old Joel; and Sarah's brother and sister, twenty-four-year-old William and twenty-two-year-old Francis, both born in Kentucky. The next year Francis married Roderic von Gelhorn, a native of Prussia, and moved away.

In 1850 Charles and Sarah were essentially running a ranch. They owned nearly seventy-three hundred acres, but only fifty were in cultivation. They estimated that the land was worth $1,000, but the livestock—horses, asses, mules, oxen, sheep, swine, milk cows, and other cattle—were worth $4,870. They gave the total value of their estate as $12,890, which would include the house in which they lived and whatever slaves they owned. (It is unclear whether this house was built by 1850, and the family has not been found on the 1850 slave schedule of the census.)

The next decade was economically good for Charles and Sarah. By 1860 they estimated the value of their real estate at $12,740 and their personal property at $26,190. The latter consisted in part in the fifteen enslaved workers that they owned: nine males, age eight months to twenty-six years; and six females, age eight months to forty years, housed in three slave buildings. The household also included Charles and Sarah's fourteen-year-old daughter, Mary, and Sarah's twenty-one-year-old son, Joel, also a stock raiser who already owned ten thousand dollars in real estate and six thousand dollars in personal property. (The latter included the value of seven enslaved servants, all living in one house.)

The Civil War was a cataclysmic event for Texas, as it was for all states that joined the Confederacy. This was true for Charles and Sarah, as Sarah saw her only surviving son, Joel McClure, go off to war. He did survive but was wounded by a gunshot to the groin. He died in 1870, having never fully recovered. In spite of having lost the ownership of their enslaved servants, Charles and Sarah did relatively well in the aftermath of the war. In 1870 they valued their real estate at $12,000, close to their 1860 figure, though their personal estate dropped to $10,980.

Living near Charles and Sarah was another couple with a similar last name: Madison and Sarah Brachas. He was forty-seven, she was thirty-seven, and they were both black. They were not listed as farmers but as renting, which seems to be the local code for sharecropping. They had five children, and Madison's seventy-seven-year-old mother, Emily, lived with them.

In 1880 Charles, at age sixty-seven, and Sarah, at age sixty-nine, were still living in the house. The only other members of the household were six African Americans, five of whom were listed as servants. (The six-year-old girl was not given an occupation.) Clearly, Charles and Sarah were the sole occupants of the big house, while their servants lived in what had once been the slave quarter. Sarah Ashby McClure Braches outlived two husbands, as Charles passed away on July 7, 1889. Sarah outlived her second, younger husband by more than five years, as she died on October 17, 1894.

The Braches house is a two-story Greek Revival structure with significant Creole elements. In front a double gallery extends across the width

Figure 8.16. Aerial view of Charles and Sarah Braches house site, ca. 1850. Image by Brent R. Fortenberry.

Figure 8.17. Charles and Sarah Braches house, east elevation. Photo by Kenneth Hafertepe.

of the house and is set underneath the main roof (figs. 8.16 and 8.17). Such an inset roof is most common in Louisiana and is found on many one-story houses. The most monumental example of an inset porch on a two-story house is the David Weeks house, now known as Shadows-on-the-Teche, in New Iberia. In Texas examples are more rare, but include the Schuddemagen house in Round Top and the Kiehne house in Fredericksburg (see Chapter Seven). The Braches house is building with a central passage, a larger parlor to the left and a lesser chamber to the right. In the rear, a petite galerie is flanked by two "cabinets," presumably service rooms. Such an arrangement is also present on the somewhat more formal Robertson house in Salado and the Jeremiah Dashiell house in La Villita in San Antonio. (The Robertson house has a very formal central passage, while the Dashiell house does not.) Such a feature suggests the influence of Creole floor plans from Louisiana, though the central passage is a striking statement of Anglo ascendancy.

In the central passage the stairs begin their ascent at the rear—that is, closer to the petite galerie than to the principal galerie. Such an arrangement is relatively rare in Texas; one notable example is Liendo, the plantation of Leonard and Courtney Groce in Hempstead. A much older example of this feature is the Josiah Quincy house in Massachusetts (1770), for which there is also no good explanation. Perhaps the best rationale for the plan of the Braches house is that the two upper rooms were the province of the family, not guests, and that such spaces would also require cleaning. A staircase pointing toward the rear would be closer to service areas, including an outdoor area for doing the laundry, a task that was certainly performed by enslaved workers.

The plan is mirrored on the upper floor with a central passage that has a larger unheated bedchamber to the left and a smaller heated chamber to the right. A petite galerie with flanking cabinets is also present on the upper floor. A canted wall on the right partition of the upper floor is an interesting plan feature. Presumably, the angle permits the middle right window to light the passage when the doors are closed, a convenience in the winter months.

The building has a relatively simple finish with notable applied moldings on the two-panel, exterior doors. Originally the walls were plastered: much of the split lath and framing are now exposed on the upper floor. Through the upper set of stairs in the attic, an exposed common rafter roof is joined with a ridge board. Circular-sawn member preparation implies that this roof is a later replacement for its midcentury predecessor (fig. 8.18). Struts devoid of lath nails or ghosts indicate that this was not a habitable space, at least during its second period, despite the double windows on both end walls.

Fletcher and Jane Johnson bought the house in the mid-1980s and began to renovate and restore it in 1995. The restoration of the house created a bifurcated state of preservation. Much of the work concentrated on

Figure 8.18. Charles and Sarah Braches house, common rafter roof system. Photo by Brent R. Fortenberry.

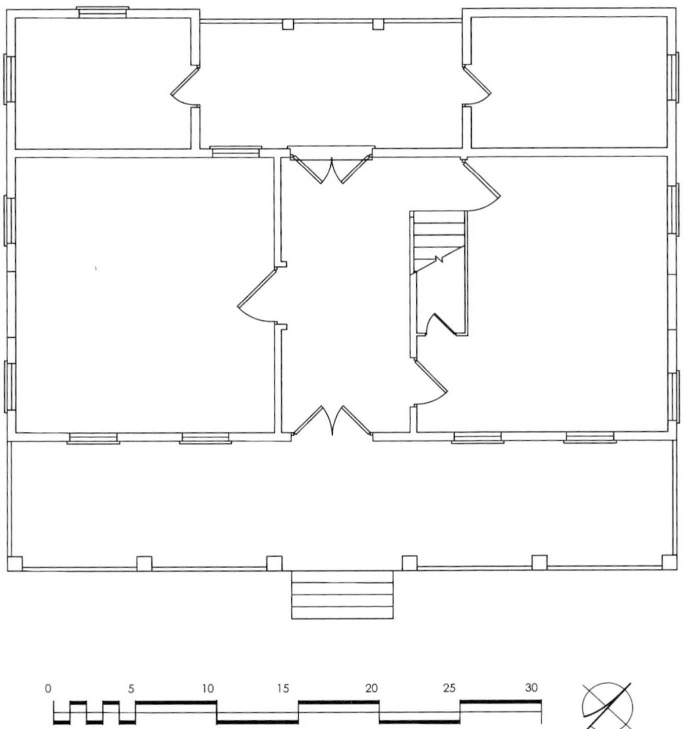

Figure 8.19. Charles and Sarah Braches house, plan of ground floor. Measured by Brent R. Fortenberry. Drawing by Hayley M. Field.

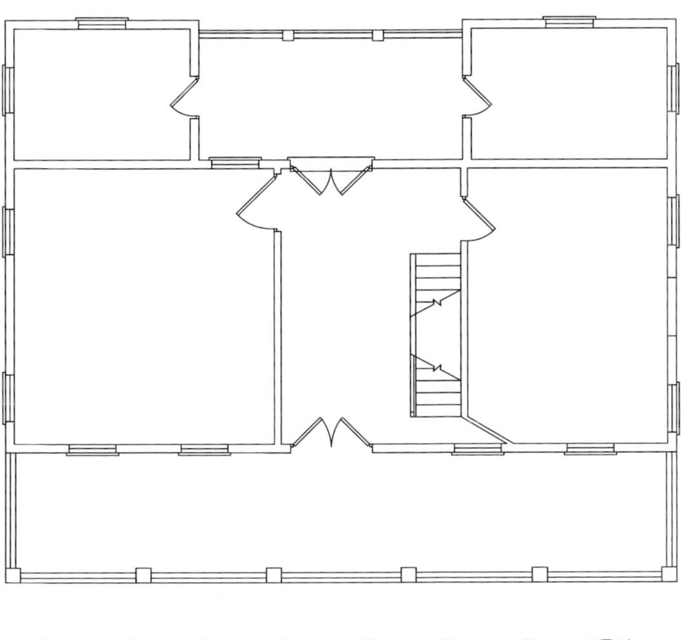

Figure 8.20. Charles and Sarah Braches house, plan of upper floor. Measured by Brent R. Fortenberry. Drawing by Hayley M. Field.

the lower floor, repairing plaster and replacing window frames. Indeed, only the back left window on the north end wall is original; the remaining sash muntins (that is, the strips of wood separating and supporting individual window panes) are obviously twentieth-century replacements. The front-porch floorboards and many of the exterior clapboards are twentieth-century replacements as well. During this period of restoration it seems that the chimney stacks on the left and right ends of the building were taken down, likely because of high maintenance costs and safety; indeed, all the brick masonry was removed from the house, including the brick hearths associated with each firebox (fig. 8.19). Upstairs much of the original plaster, finish, and framing survives in an unadulterated (and unrepaired) state; the only major change that took place was the removal of the brick masonry in the hearths. Details of the restoration are chronicled in the photographs in the right room on the lower floor (fig. 8.20).

McClure-Braches Cemetery, some hundred yards north of the house, is a cultural landscape in its own right. There are at least fourteen burials, including Sarah and her two husbands and nine of her children. There are gravestones for seven of the children. Although some of the children died in the 1830s and others in the 1850s, all of the family stones appear to date from after the Civil War (fig. 8.21).

Figure 8.21. Mc-Clure Braches Cemetery. Photo by Kenneth Hafertepe.

The most prominent early family stone is for Sarah's son Joel McClure, who died in 1870 of a wound received during the Civil War. He rests under a white marble obelisk. Most of the other markers are smaller but also of marble, which was typical of work produced in early Texas marble yards. The stones of Sarah and her two husbands are granite, which did not come into common usage until the 1890s. Bart McClure and Charles Braches rest under stones of Texas red granite, while Sarah herself is under a gray granite marker, which would have to have been imported from the eastern United States.

Perhaps the oldest stone is the ledger stone of James D. Owen (1811–43). His relation to the McClures is not known, but like Sarah he was a native of Shelby County, Kentucky. He came to Texas in 1836, just in time to join the Texian army on March 6. After San Jacinto he was granted 640 acres in DeWitt County as well as an additional 320 acres elsewhere. His white marble ledger stone is signed by H. Blakesley of New Orleans. In addition, a 1936 Texas Centennial marker of red granite was placed beside his grave where a headstone would usually stand.[6]

Gonzales

Horace and Sarah Eggleston House

228 St. George Street

Circa 1848

This is the oldest building in Gonzales and was moved to this location only in the 1950s. Horace Eggleston was born in East Bloomfield, Ontario County, New York, in 1800. He married in 1819, but that marriage ended in divorce and he went to Texas for a new start. There he met Sarah Ann Ponton, who was born in Missouri in 1820 and came to Texas with her parents in 1829. Her father, William Ponton, was from Amherst County, Virginia, and her mother, Isabella, was a native of Pennsylvania. Horace and Sarah married in May 1835.

Though the town of Gonzales dates to 1825, the town was burned on March 13, 1836, by orders of General Sam Houston in the aftermath of the catastrophic conclusion to the siege of the Alamo. Horace Eggleston was already a merchant in Gonzales at that time. His dwelling house, store, and furniture, worth some two thousand dollars, were lost, along with three thousand dollars in merchandise in the store and seventeen head of cattle valued at sixty-eight dollars.

After the revolution, Horace demanded restitution from the government of the Republic of Texas. He seems to have been paid out of the account for veterans of the Battle of San Jacinto, which led to the assumption that he had participated in that triumphant conclusion to the war, though he is not on the earliest lists of soldiers in that battle. He did, however, command a company when the Mexican army attempted to retake Texas in 1842.

It is unclear where Horace and Sarah lived for the next ten years; this cabin was built sometime between 1845 and 1848. It was originally located on West St. Michael Street south of the center of town and about three blocks from the Guadalupe River. The house originally faced west toward the river rather than north toward town.

Initially it had two rooms separated by an open passage (a dogtrot), with a front porch. At a later date, a lean-to was added across the back. As was typical with Texas log houses, the doors were not on the front of the house but opened onto the dogtrot. The rooms were fairly spacious, as there were two windows, six panes over six, on the front wall of both rooms. There were no windows on the back or side walls. The logs of the house were hewn to give them a more regular appearance and were joined at the corners by half-dovetail notches. Cultural geographer Terry G. Jordan noted that the half-dovetail was the most typical joint on log houses in Texas: it was used in 187 of the 537 houses he surveyed (35 percent). Next in frequency were the square notch, V notch, and saddle notch; he observed only one house with a full dovetail. Half-dovetails were also used on 10 percent of log outbuildings (fig. 8.22).

In 1850 Horace Eggleston was fifty and gave no occupation to the census taker. The rest of the household included thirty-year-old Sarah; four children between the ages of one and thirteen; and Sarah's mother, sixty-eight-year-old Isabella Ponton. He estimated his property to be worth five thousand dollars, which included not only this house and the real estate on which it sat but also five enslaved African Americans. The two females were forty-eight and twenty; the three males were twenty-three, twenty-two, and thirteen. Horace died in 1855, and by 1860 Sarah had remarried.

Her new husband was Benjamin Franklin Minter, a farmer who was a native of Kentucky. In 1860 they were living with Sarah's sons John, William, and Isaac Newton Eggleston. It is unclear if they continued to occupy this house. The family owned six thousand dollars in real estate and six thousand dollars in personal property. Some of that personal

Figure 8.22. Horace and Sarah Eggleston house, south elevation, ca. 1868. Photo by Kenneth Hafertepe.

property consisted of enslaved African Americans. Minter owned five slaves, and three of them may have come to the marriage with Sarah. (The two youngest had been born since the 1850 census.) Sarah passed away in February 1880.

By the early twentieth century, the little house was part of a complex of private barns. However, around 1901 former congressman James F. Miller bought the property and built an imposing two-story brick Colonial Revival house at the eastern end of the block. In 1912 the log house had become an outbuilding of this mansion and was being used as a shed, but by 1922 the building was once again being used as a dwelling.

In 1954 E. E. Smith and his wife gave the building to the City of Seguin, which decided to move the house to its present location. While the original floor plan was preserved, the lack of a loft or any rafters gives the two rooms the appearance of a cathedral ceiling, even though a household of eight (excluding the five enslaved workers) would certainly have wanted to use that space.[7]

Gonzales County Jail
414 East St. Lawrence Street
1885–87

Plans were announced for a new jail for Gonzales County in May 1885. The building had already been designed by Eugene T. Heiner, the leading architect in Houston, and plans and specifications could be seen at the courthouse in Gonzales or the architect's office in Houston. Heiner was born in New York City in 1852, was apprenticed to a Chicago architect just after the Civil War, and was in Texas by 1877. Over the next twenty-three years he designed seventeen Texas county courthouses and nineteen county jails. The earlier buildings were in the French Second Empire style, while the later ones were in the Richardsonian Romanesque. According to the *Houston Post*, Heiner was "regarded as a pioneer of improved and modern jail architecture."

The contract to build the Gonzales Jail went to Henry Kane. Born in Peru, Clinton County, New York, to Irish-immigrant parents, Kane was in Texas by the late 1870s. At the time of the 1880 US census he was living in Palestine, Texas, and gave his occupation as carpenter, but over the next decade he moved into contracting. Heiner and Kane worked together on a number of buildings, including the Austin County Courthouse in Bellville, also built in 1886. On that building Kane was managing a number of subcontractors, including separate contracts for tin and galvanized iron, plumbing, brickwork, plastering and cementing, and general ironwork.

The brick building was expected to cost $20,175; the interior iron and steel work, $15,850. The architect's fee of $1,812 brought the anticipated total cost to $37,837. (The historical marker on the building states that the cost was $21,660.20, but this clearly omitted most of the interior.)

Figure 8.23. Gonzales County Jail, north facade, 1885–87. Photo by Kenneth Hafertepe.

The jail in Gonzales was built of brick with a cruciform plan, three stories tall and with a five-story tower marking the entrance. Both the main roof and the roof on the tower sloped inward as they rose, which, if not a proper mansard roof, was similar. The tawny-colored brick was used for segmental arches on the first floor and for flat arches above (fig. 8.23).

Inside Heiner used modern technology similar to that in his concurrent jails in Fort Worth and Wichita Falls. In the latter building the floor of the second story was framed with eight-inch iron I-beams, thirty inches apart, into which were set twenty-six-gauge corrugated-iron arches, which were then filled with concrete and finished with Portland cement. A similar arrangement is visible in the rooms in the northwest corner of the Gonzales jail. Heiner's jails typically provided separate areas for females, juveniles, and those with mental disabilities, in addition to ordinary criminals.

The jail cells were made by Snead and Company of Louisville, Kentucky. Charles Scott Snead and Udolpho Snead developed bars in a lattice pattern, as well as a locking device for jails, which had been patented on August 4, 1885. One of the doors in the jail has a patent date of August 4, 1886, which means it must have been installed that autumn.

Construction on the building was ongoing in September 1886, when Henry Kane advertised in the *Galveston Daily News* that he wanted good bricklayers for the jail and would pay fifty cents per hour. The ad must have worked, because the county commissioners accepted the building on January 28, 1887.

The most notable subsequent change to the building was the removal of the mansard roof. The building was named a Recorded Texas Historic Landmark in 1966 and now houses the Gonzales Chamber of Commerce and the Old Jail Museum.[8]

Gonzales County Courthouse
414 North St. Joseph Street
1894–96, restoration 1997

A fire on December 3, 1894, destroyed the old Gonzales County Courthouse. This sandstone structure sat in the middle of Center Square. At the time the Commissioners Court was dominated by Populists, who had a deep-seated suspicion of professional men, including architects. In February 1894, they put such suspicions on hold and called for plans for a "first-class, fireproof courthouse" that could be built for sixty-five thousand dollars. Plans were to be submitted by their next meeting on March 26.

In spite of such a short time frame, eleven architects submitted plans, including Eugene T. Heiner of Houston, who had designed the Gonzales County jail less than a decade earlier; James Wahrenberger of San Antonio; A. O. Watson of Austin; W. C. Dodson of Waco; and E. E. Myers, a Detroit architect who had designed the Texas State Capitol. Noticeably missing were three preeminent Victorian architects in Texas: Nicholas J. Clayton of Galveston and Alfred Giles and J. Riely Gordon, both of San Antonio. Perhaps these three had heard that trouble was brewing and declined to participate. And, indeed, the prize went to the most obscure architect of the competitors, T. S. Hodges of Lockhart.

One month later, the County Commissioners changed their minds and requested proposals from contractors to be submitted by June. They thus sided with practical builders over professional designers. Eight contractors answered the call, including Henry Kane, who had built Heiner's jail of the previous decade; Martin, Byrnes and Johnston of Victoria, who had established a track record of building courthouses and jails; and Davey & Schott of Kerrville, who worked extensively in that Hill Country town and in Comfort, where they built Peter J. Ingenhuett's store and perhaps other structures as well. (See chapter 7 for more on this firm.)

The prize went, however, to Otto P. Kroeger of San Antonio. Kroeger had built the Bexar County Courthouse on Main Plaza in San Antonio and the Ellis County Courthouse in Waxahachie. The San Antonio courthouse was begun in 1892 but was not completed until 1897, while the Waxahachie courthouse was built 1894–97. Both of these buildings were designed by J. Riely Gordon. Though Kroeger's name appeared on the cornerstone, a Gordon rendering of the building still exists. He later claimed authorship of the building in a promotional brochure, and it is consistent with the Gordon designs for courthouses in Ellis and Wise Counties.

The inner walls were built with local brick known as southwestern white brick, manufactured three miles from town. The exterior facing, however, was of red hydraulic-pressed brick. (Other Gordon courthouses were sheathed in stone, a more expensive material.) The rock trim was gray sandstone from Warrensburg, Missouri, while columns and steps were red granite from Llano in the Hill Country. This granite had also been used on the Texas State Capitol and was a locally distinctive material. The roof was slate, with copper guttering and terra-cotta at the cornice

Figure 8.24. Gonzales County Courthouse. Photo by Kenneth Hafertepe.

level. At a later date the slate roof was removed and replaced with red tile (fig. 8.24).

Like Gordon's other courthouses of the 1890s, the one in Gonzales has its roots in the Romanesque Revival, particularly in the work of Henry Hobson Richardson. Although the low budget for the Gonzales project meant that stone would be used sparingly, Gordon still successfully created a rich polychromy through use of a variety of materials. Also Richardsonian is the complicated massing of the building, which draws from Richardson's Trinity Church in Boston but also, perhaps, from Richardson's own sources in the Provençal region of France.

While the polychromy and the picturesque character of the building situated it within the Richardsonian fold, Gordon developed his own distinctive plans for his courthouses. While earliest ones, such as the Fayette County Courthouse in La Grange (1890–91), featured a large unroofed light court in the center, courthouses like the one in Gonzales had a central tower, beneath which was a cast-iron staircase surrounded on all four sides by an arcade that served as the primary circulation space. Entrance into the building was from four porches, one at each re-entrant corner of the cross-shaped core. The Commissioners Court was at the east end

Figure 8.25. Gonzales County Courthouse, early 1900s. Courtesy of University of Texas Architecture Library.

of the first floor, and above this was the main courtroom on the second floor. This courtroom had a balcony accessed from the third-floor hall. Various county offices were placed in the north, west, and south wings of the building (fig. 8.25).

A practical advantage of the central staircase was that it acted as a ventilation shaft, drawing hot air up and then out through louvers in the tower. The *Gonzales Inquirer* noted that the "tower serves the quadruple purpose of light shaft, air shaft, main stair shaft and base of the main tower." The newspaper also claimed that "the design of the building is of the Spanish-Venetian type and thus emphasizes the historical relations of our quaint and heroic town."

The building is a Recorded Texas Historic Landmark and is on the National Register of Historic Places. However, the building fell on hard times in the late twentieth century, and talk had even begun about demolishing the courthouse and replacing it with a new one. Especially troubling was the extreme structural distress of the central tower and accompanying roof damage from lightning strikes, water infiltration from clogged gutters, and open joints at the balconies.

In the 1990s Volz and Associates of Austin restored the building, addressing these issues as well as restoring windows, doors, and hardware; reproducing historic finishes; and addressing accessibility issues. The project was funded locally, with some assistance from federal funds under the Intermodal Transportation System Efficiency Act. This was done prior to the creation of the Texas Courthouse Preservation Program, which was initiated by Governor George W. Bush and Lieutenant Governor Bob Bullock. In 1999 the Gonzales County Courthouse was given an Award of Excellence in Historic Architecture by the Texas Historical Commission.[9]

Gonzales Memorial Museum and Amphitheatre
414 Smith Street
1936–37

Although it may be hard to grasp today, Texas was a critical part of the New Deal coalition, and this museum complex is a reflection of the Franklin D. Roosevelt administration's determination to keep Texas in the Democratic fold. Further, this complex is one example of a large number of federally funded buildings erected for the celebration of the Texas Centennial—that is, the centennial of the successful revolution for Texas independence from Mexico.

The New Deal was a key funder for the Texas Centennial Exposition in 1936 at Fair Park in Dallas. However, the fact that so much money was flowing to Dallas displeased other areas of the state. As a result, funds were provided for historical projects in areas across Texas. The New Deal paid for the reconstruction of Mission San José in San Antonio; for a museum building at the Alamo; and for a museum dedicated to Texas Pioneers, Trail Drivers, and Rangers, built next to the Witte Museum on the north side of San Antonio. (Perhaps it does not need to be said that San Antonio's congressman, Maury Maverick, was a vocal supporter of FDR and the New Deal.)

In addition, museums were built in Austin, Canyon, Corpus Christi, El Paso, Huntsville, and Lubbock. Centennial markers became the first historical marker program in Texas. State parks were built across Texas by the young men of the Civilian Conservation Corps, including Palmetto State Park near Gonzales. Sites related to the Texas Revolution include the San Jacinto Monument at the spot of the conclusive battle of the revolution, and this site, in the town where the first shots of the revolution were fired.

Such New Deal projects were also a boon to architects whose practices were devastated by the Great Depression. The architects were Raymond Phelps and George Dahl Dewees, both San Antonio natives who worked as draftsmen for Henry T. Phelps. Raymond, Henry's younger brother, began working as a draftsman at age eighteen and worked there for nearly a decade. Dahl Dewees, two years older than Raymond Phelps, worked as a draftsman for several San Antonio architects, including Carl von Seutter and Atlee B. Ayres, before joining the Phelps office in 1914. Raymond thus worked on the Atascosa County Courthouse in Jourdanton (1912) and the Mills County Courthouse in Goldthwaite (1913). After Dewees joined the office, the firm designed courthouses in Blanco County (Johnson City, 1916) and Brown County (Brownwood, 1917). Atascosa was in the Mission style, but the other three were variants of Beaux-Arts classicism. The firm of Phelps & Dewees was formed in 1919.

The Gonzales project consisted of the museum property, with a reflecting pool and a monument to the Gonzales men who died at the Alamo on the east, and a semicircular amphitheater on the west. This complex was built on part of a 150-acre section of municipal parkland due east of the central square, which had been deeded to the state in 1913. In 1936–37 the Commission of Control for Texas Centennial Celebrations allocated $30,000, while the Public Works Administration chipped in some $24,545, which, with some local donations, allowed the total cost of the project to be set at $64,045.

The initial plans for the complex, dated September 24, 1936, list Phelps & Dewees as architects but also credit George Willis as consulting architect. Willis had worked in Chicago before establishing his own practice in San Antonio; he had previously worked with Phelps & Dewees on the expansion of the 1892–95 Bexar County Courthouse in 1928. These initial drawings show the museum and amphitheater essentially as built, but without the reflecting pool. In its place was an oval water feature marked "future reflecting pool." Revised blueprints, dated November 3, 1936, show the reflecting pool as built; apparently some additional funding allowed all parts of the project to be done at the same time. However, Willis's name had been removed.

The main building utilized Texas shellstone, which was trimmed with Cordova cream limestone as well as some cast concrete at the cornice.

The exterior was quite boxy, with ornament focused either on the cornice or the steps leading to the entrance. The reflecting pool (now, alas, rarely filled) allowed the pattern of stones carved with festoons to be echoed in the water below (fig. 8.26). Between the reflecting pool and the museum proper was a memorial to the thirty-two Gonzales men and boys who fought their way into the Alamo on March 1 and were among those who fell in the cause of Texas independence on March 6. Raoul Josset, a French-immigrant sculptor, provided the bronze sculptural panel, while Page & Southerland of Austin designed the base of Texas red granite. Josset designed a number of other sculptures to honor the heroes of the Texas Revolution, and Louis C. Page Jr. did some work for HABS, specifically at the French Legation and Simms-Vance house in Austin.

Figure 8.26. Gonzales Memorial Museum, west facade, 1936–37. Photo by Brent R. Fortenberry.

From the memorial, steps led to an open passage in the middle of the building, which led to a museum room to each side and also to the amphitheater ahead. The large museum rooms had windows on the east wall but none on the west because organizers anticipated that the west walls of the two principal rooms would be the site of important murals.

In this case the award went to a Texas artist, James Buchanan Winn Jr. A native Texan, "Buck" Winn studied art at Washington University in St. Louis; among his teachers was Oscar E. Berninghaus, already renowned as a founding member of the Taos Society of Artists. Winn then studied at the Académie Julian in Paris—Americans who studied there included Cecilia Beaux, Ernest Blumenschein, and Thomas Hart Benton—then settled in Dallas in 1929. For the 1936 Centennial Exposition Winn worked with Eugene Savage on the historical murals in the Hall of State and on his own designed the Great Seal of Texas for that building and other features of the fair.

Two years later Winn was commissioned to paint the two murals in this building. The one in the north room focused on the geopolitical aspects of the Texas Revolution, featuring Stephen F. Austin and Sam Houston and, of course, the "Come and Take It" cannon that precipitated the first battle of the revolution. The mural in the south room was of a more personal nature, though it proclaimed Gonzales as "The Lexington of Texas." On the left was Matthew Caldwell, sometimes called the "Paul Revere of Texas," while on the right was a generic "Pioneer Mother." (Both man and woman clutch matching rifles.) In the middle was the Sam Houston Oak, at the McClure-Braches house a few miles east of town, where, in the aftermath of the Alamo in March 1836, Sam Houston decided to torch Gonzales and retreat in the face of the pursuing Mexican army.

The murals and, indeed, the entire complex, suggest at once Texas as All-American—Gonzales as Lexington, Matthew Caldwell as Paul Revere—but also Texas as exceptional, an independent nation before becoming a state and ferocious in its defense of liberty, at least for white males.

Phelps & Dewees was awarded another New Deal project, this one in San Antonio: the Texas Pioneers, Trail Drivers, and Rangers Museum in Brackenridge Park, which was designed in collaboration with the San Antonio firm of Ayres & Ayres. Henry T. Phelps also received a New Deal commission for the design of a museum building for the Alamo. For many years this building has served as the Alamo gift shop. Phelps attempted to create a building that was sympathetic with the chapel and *convento* of the old mission and may have been too successful, as visitors often think that it is an original building rather than a 1936 revival.[10]

Notes

1. United States Census, 1850–1900, HeritageQuest Online, https://www.ancestry heritage
quest.com/HQA; Sanborn Maps: 1885, sheet 1; 1891, sheet 2; 1896, sheet 2; 1902, sheet 4; 1906, sheet 4; 1912, sheet 9; 1916, sheet 11; and 1924, sheet 5, digitized by the University of Texas at Austin Libraries at https://legacy.lib.utexas.edu/maps/sanborn/ texas.html; Frederick Law Olmsted, *A Journey through Texas; or, A Saddle-Trip on the Southwestern Frontier* (1857; repr., Austin: University of Texas Press, 1978), 231; "Magnolia Hotel," Historic American Buildings Survey, Library of Congress, https:// www.loc.gov/pictures/collection/hh/item/tx0386/; and Willard Robinson, "Texas Public Buildings of the Nineteenth Century," *Seguin Gazette-Enterprise*, February 12, 1981, 15.

2. Sanborn Maps: 1902, sheet 4; 1906, sheet 4; 1912, sheet 9; 1916, sheet 11; and 1924, sheet 5; "Ben McCulloch House," Historic American Buildings Survey, Library of Congress, https://www.loc.gov/pictures/collection/hh/item/tx0469/; "Seguin Plans 122nd Birthday Celebration," *Seguin Gazette-Enterprise*, June 15, 1960, 4; "Los Nogales Museum," *Seguin Gazette-Enterprise*, July 27, 1960, 1; "Conservation Society Marks Tenth Anniversary," *Seguin Gazette-Enterprise*, February 14, 1962, 3; and "Historical Medallion Unveiled," *Seguin Gazette-Enterprise*, April 11, 1962, 8.

3. "Colonel Joshua Young House," Historic American Buildings Survey, Library of Congress, https://www.loc.gov/pictures/collection/hh/item/tx0387/; Drury Blakeley Alexander, *Texas Homes of the Nineteenth Century* (Austin: University of Texas Press for the Amon Carter Museum of Western Art, 1966), 244, plate 73; Sandra R. Sauer, Art Black, and Cynthia Brandimarte, *Sebastopol: Sebastopol State Historic Park (41GU9). Seguin, Texas: Archeological Excavations, 1978–1988*, Texas Parks and Wildlife Department, Reports of Investigations, Number 111 (May 1998); and Gerald Moorhead, ed., *Buildings of Texas: Central, South, and Gulf Coast* (Charlottesville: University of Virginia Press, 2013), 189.

4. United States Census, 1850 to 1900; and Terry G. Jordan, *Texas Log Buildings: A Folk Architecture* (Austin: University of Texas Press, 1982), 51, 53, 71–73.

5. Alexander, *Texas Homes of the Nineteenth Century*, 238, plate 28; Moorhead, *Buildings of Texas*, 199; Jordan, *Texas Log Buildings*, 10–11; John Michael Vlach, *Back of the Big House: The Architecture of Plantation Slavery* (Chapel Hill: University of North Carolina Press, 1993), 50; John Michael Vlach, "Slave Quarters as Bi-cultural Expression," in *Black and White: Cultural Interaction in the Antebellum South*, ed. Ted Ownby (Jackson: University Press of Mississippi, 1993), 89–90 (the Polley kitchen is illustrated in fig. 1); Richard B. McCaslin, *Sutherland Springs, Texas: Saratoga on the Cibolo* (Denton: University of North Texas Press, 2017), 34–42; and Melinda Creech, "The Material Culture of the Polley Mansion, Whitehall: Vernacular Architecture, Decorative Arts, and Domestic Arts" (master's thesis, Baylor University, 2018).

6. United States Census, 1850–1880, HeritageQuest Online, https://www.ancestry heritage

quest.com/HQA; John Henry Brown, *Indian Wars and Pioneers of Texas* (Austin: L. E. Daniel, 189[?]); Gonzales County Historical Commission, *The History of Gonzales County, Texas* (Dallas: Curtis Media, 1986), [page for Sarah Ann]; and Rob Ford, "If Walls Could Talk . . ." *Gonzales Inquirer*, May 4, 2012.

7. United States Census, 1850–1880; Sanborn Maps: 1912, sheet 11; and 1922, sheet 2; Alexander, *Texas Homes of the Nineteenth Century*; and Jordan, *Texas Log Buildings*, 54–58, 186.

8. Sanborn Map: 1891, sheet 1; Willard B. Robinson, *Texas Public Buildings of the Nineteenth Century* (Austin: University of Texas Press, 1974), 98–99; and Moorhead, *Buildings of Texas*, 191.

9. "Gonzales County Temple of Justice, a Beautiful and Imposing Building," *Gonzales Inquirer*, April 23, 1896, as transcribed by Murray Montgomery Jr. and preserved by Chris Meister; Robinson, *Texas Public Buildings*, 203–4, plate 155; Willard B. Robinson, *The People's Architecture: Texas Courthouses, Jails, and Municipal Buildings* (Austin: Texas State Historical Association, 1983), 171–74; "Gonzales County Courthouse," Volz & Associates, Inc., 2018, http://volzassociates.com/projects/gonzales-county-court house/; Chris Meister, *James Riely Gordon: His Courthouses and Other Public Architecture* (Lubbock: Texas Tech University Press, 2011), 117–19, 285; Moorhead, *Buildings of Texas*, 190–91; and Chris Meister, email message to Kenneth Hafertepe, July 12, 2019.

10. Gonzales Memorial Museum and Amphitheatre, Blueprints and Drawings Collection, Archives and Information Services Division, Texas State Library and Archives Commission (Boxes 821–42 and 821–43 contain two sets of prints by Phelps & Dewees dated September 24 and November 3, 1936, and July 2, 1937); *Monuments Erected by the State of Texas to Commemorate the Centenary of Texas Independence* (Austin: Commission of Control for Texas Centennial Celebrations, 1938); Robinson, *The People's Architecture*, 283; James Wright Steely, *Parks for Texas: Enduring Landscapes of the New Deal* (Austin: University of Texas Press, 1999), 209; and Dorothy S. Schmidt, "Winn, James Buchanan, Jr.," *Handbook of Texas Online*, accessed July 20, 2019, http://www.tshaonline.org/handbook/online/articles/fwi86.

Lewis F. Fisher, an independent scholar of San Antonio, is also the author of *Saving San Antonio: The Preservation of a Heritage.*

Lewis S. Fisher is a San Antonio preservation architect and independent scholar.

Brent R. Fortenberry is Director of Preservation Studies and Christovich Associate Professor of Historic Preservation at Tulane University. He is also the coeditor of *Modern Materials: Contemporary and Historical Archaeology in Theory.*

Sarah Z. Gould presently serves as interim executive director of Mexican American Civil Rights Institute in San Antonio.

Kenneth Hafertepe, chair of the Department of Museum Studies at Baylor University, is also the author of *The Material Culture of German Texans, Historic Homes of Waco, Texas,* and other works.

Maria Pfeiffer, a fourth-generation San Antonian, is a self-employed professional historian, historical researcher, and consultant.

Paul Ringenbach is an independent scholar and architectural historian living in San Antonio.